Predict and Surveil

Data, Discretion, and the Future of Policing

SARAH BRAYNE

OXFORD
UNIVERSITY PRESS

OXFORD
UNIVERSITY PRESS

Oxford University Press is a department of the University of Oxford. It furthers
the University's objective of excellence in research, scholarship, and education
by publishing worldwide. Oxford is a registered trade mark of Oxford University
Press in the UK and certain other countries.

Published in the United States of America by Oxford University Press
198 Madison Avenue, New York, NY 10016, United States of America.

Library of Congress Cataloging-in-Publication Data
Names: Brayne, Sarah, author.
Title: Predict and Surveil: Data, Discretion, and the Future of Policing / Sarah Brayne.
Description: New York, NY : Oxford University Press, [2021] |
Includes bibliographical references and index. |
Identifiers: LCCN 2020014315 (print) | LCCN 2020014316 (ebook) |
ISBN 9780190684099 (hardback) | ISBN 9780190684112 (epub) | ISBN 9780190684129
Subjects: LCSH: Police—California—Los Angeles—Data processing. |
Crime analysis—California—Los Angeles—Data processing. | Crime forecasting—
California—Los Angeles—Statistical methods. | Criminal behavior, Prediction of—
California—Los Angeles—Statistical methods.
Classification: LCC HV7936.A8 B73 2021 (print) | LCC HV7936.A8 (ebook) |
DDC 363.2/32—dc23
LC record available at https://lccn.loc.gov/2020014315
LC ebook record available at https://lccn.loc.gov/2020014316

9 8 7 6 5 4 3 2

Printed by Sheridan Books, Inc., United States of America

CONTENTS

ACKNOWLEDGMENTS

This book, and this research, were fundamentally shaped by Devah Pager. Devah was by my side from this project's inception. Her mentorship motivated, encouraged, and challenged me. It still does—although she passed away in 2018, she will always be my role model. There were countless moments as I was finishing this book when I wished I could ask her to read a passage or share her reaction. Instead, I am left to imagine what she would say. I am fortunate that a gracious community of researchers have offered to read this work "through Devah's eyes," yet the final draft would surely have benefitted from one more pass from my brilliant advisor. This book is dedicated to her.

Turning to that gracious community, I must thank many who have given feedback on this book—whether tiny fragments or the whole—over years and drafts. At Princeton, the inimitable Paul DiMaggio carefully thought through this project with me during its early phases, then lent his peerless attention to detail, right down to line edits, as I produced drafts. I'll never cease to wonder at his capacity to know something about everything. Kim Lane Scheppele was pivotal in formulating my research questions, and Janet Vertesi taught me much about the complex interrelation of technology and society. I am also grateful for the generosity and wisdom of Maria Abascal, Mitch Duneier, Elaine Enriquez, Edward Felten, Matthew Incantalupo, Rourke O'Brien, Karen Levy, David Pedulla, Scott Lynch, David Reinecke, Matthew Salganik, and Robert Wuthnow.

My postdoc at the Social Media Collective at Microsoft Research New England was transformative. Nancy Baym, danah boyd, Christian Borgs, Jennifer Chayes, Kate Crawford, Kevin Driscoll, Tarleton Gillespie, Mary Gray, Shannon McGregor, and Lana Swartz strengthened my work and opened my mind. I benefitted enormously from the warm and energetic intellectual environment, stimulating conversations, and precious gift of *time*.

My colleagues at the University of Texas at Austin—including but not limited to Amelia Acker, Minou Arjomand, Javier Auyero, Shannon Cavanagh, Diane Coffey, Rob Crosnoe, Jennifer Glass, Becky Pettit, Ken Hou Lin, Yasmiyn Irizarry, Abena Mackall, Chandra Muller, Kelly Raley, Mary Rose, Harel Shapira, Deb Umberson, and Christine Williams—welcomed me, influenced me, and showed me where to find the good tacos. Among the fantastic students at UT, I especially thank Riad Azar, Lindsay Bing, and Faith Deckard for their assistance with this manuscript.

I would not be where I am today without my mentors at the University of British Columbia—Neil Guppy, Wendy Roth, and Dan Zuberi—who sparked my sociological imagination and encouraged me to apply to graduate school in the first place.

For inspiration, feedback, and many other kinds of support along the way, I thank Kristin Barragan, Danielle Citron, Liz Chiarello, Angèle Christin, Andrew Ferguson, Barry Friedman, Sarah Lageson, Jeffrey Lane, John Laub, Ron Levi, Meredith McInnis, John Monahan, Katherine Newman, Laura Beth Nielsen, Andrew Papachristos, Samantha Pollard, Florencia Torche, Robert Sampson, Andrew Selbst, Michael Sierra-Arévalo, Ric Simmons, Christopher Slobogin, Chris Uggen, Bruce Western, and Katie Young. Special thanks to Issa Kohler-Hausmann and Forrest Stuart, who are absolutely brilliant scholars, friends, and ghouls.

James Cook, my editor at Oxford, had faith in this project from the very beginning and adeptly shepherded me through the publication process. Letta Page is a wizard who injected new life into this book through her edits. She is truly a master of her craft. David Hallangen created illustrations and offered comic relief. I also thank the anonymous reviewers of this book, as well as those that edited and reviewed related papers in the *American Sociological Review* and *Social Problems*.

I am grateful for having presented parts of this project and received helpful feedback from my peers at the following institutions and conferences: AI Now Institute, American Sociological Association, Brown University, Data & Society Research Institute, Duke University, George Mason University, Harvard University, Law and Society Association, MacArthur Foundation, Massachusetts Institute of Technology, Microsoft Research, New America Foundation, New York University, North Carolina State University, Northwestern University, the Ohio State University, Privacy Law Scholars Conference, Rutgers University, Stanford University, University of British Columbia, University of California at Davis, University of Chicago, University of Colorado Boulder, University of Massachusetts Amherst, University of Michigan, University of Pennsylvania, University of Texas at Austin, University of Toronto, University of Virginia, University of Washington, Vera Institute of Justice, and Yale University.

I received generous funding for various stages of this project from the Social Sciences and Humanities Research Council of Canada, Horowitz Foundation for Social Policy, Center for Information Technology Policy, NICHD (P2CHD042849), and the UT Austin College of Liberal Arts and Office of the Vice President for Research.

I thank the Los Angeles Police Department for providing research access. This project would not have been possible without individuals in the department opening their doors and allowing me to learn about *doing* police work. Although I cannot name them here, a few key individuals were integral in my fieldwork, and to them I am incredibly grateful. I also thank individuals within the Los Angeles County Sheriff's Department, the Center for Policing Equity, PredPol, and Palantir Technologies for helping with this research.

I feel endlessly privileged to have learned from and worked alongside my dedicated students in New Jersey and Texas prisons. Each has helped me understand a small part of the lived experience of criminal justice involvement.

Above all, I'd like to thank my family. My parents, Robin and Shirley, are stalwart supporters who never wavered, even when I veered off the path. Thank you for always encouraging me and catching me when I stumbled. Your steadfast love empowered me in ways I hope to empower my daughter, born as I finished this book. She is the light and joy that I never knew I was missing. Finally, to Steve: your support, partnership, love, and sense of humor bring light into my life. Thank you.

ALPR	Automatic License Plate Reader
ASD	Air Support Division
AVL	Automatic Vehicle Locator
CalGang	California Gang Database
CII	California Information and Identification number (identifier used on rap sheet)
CSLI	Cell Site Location Information
DICV	Digital in-car video
FI	Field Interview Card
JRIC	Joint Regional Intelligence Center (fusion center)
LAPD	Los Angeles Police Department
LASD	Los Angeles County Sheriff's Department
Operation LASER	Los Angeles Strategic Extraction and Restoration program (predictive policing program)
RACR	Real-Time Crime Analysis Center
SAR	Suspicious Activity Report
TEAMS II	Training Evaluation and Management System II (early intervention system)

Predict and Surveil

| Introduction

Policing Our Digital Traces

"SO, WE HAD THIS body dump." Sergeant Michaels was sitting across the table from me, reclined in a gray office chair. The homicide case had started with the discovery of a dead body in a remote location near a tourist attraction in Los Angeles County. An automatic license plate reader installed at the location provided the first clues. After determining when the body might have been dumped, then searching readings captured within that time frame, police had narrowed their focus to just three plates: "One plate from Utah, probably not, New Mexico, probably not, Compton, probably yes." The sergeant ran the plate from Compton, took the name and home address of the registrant, and then ran that information through a law enforcement database called CalGang. The car's owner was affiliated with a gang—which just so happened to be at war with the victim's gang. That information was enough to establish probable cause for a search warrant, which in turn allowed the police to go to the suspect's home, find and search the car for trace evidence, and arrest the suspect. A case that might have taken months of "shoe leather" policing was closed within 48 hours.

We all leave hundreds of digital traces—clues, should it come to that—every day. When we use our cell phone, run an Internet search, or buy something with a credit card, we leave a digital trace. Take a moment to think of all the digital traces you left today. I have already used maps and location services on my cell phone, scanned my parking pass to access a secured garage, read news articles online, scrolled through social media applications, and sent and received e-mails—and it is not even noon. Later, I will buy lunch with my credit card, go to the doctor (who will enter information into my electronic medical record), call and text friends and family, use my smartphone to order a ride share for dinner, and send money to a friend. To participate in modern life is to unwittingly scatter millions of digital traces and data points in our wake.[1]

From finance to politics, insurance, sports, medicine, and marketing, savvy professionals leverage these vast troves of digital data. Law enforcement is no exception. Even if we have never had any direct contact with the police, our trace data can incriminate or exonerate us, whether through showing that we're friends with a suspect on Facebook or that we were physically nowhere near a given crime scene. Policing the digital traces of everyday life is now a routine, if inconsistent, element of contemporary law enforcement, because we have collectively provided unprecedented opportunities for surveillance. In addition to using data in the course of investigations, the police increasingly rely on big data and automated systems to decide who, when, and where to police. To varying degrees, we are all subjects of digital surveillance.

The intersection of big data and the overgrown US criminal justice system motivates my work in this book. As many have documented, the scope of criminal justice surveillance—from policing to incarceration—has expanded rapidly over the past half century.[2] The penal population began rising in 1972. A 500 percent rise translates to 2.2 million people in prison or jail and over 7.1 million people—just over 3 percent of all adult US residents—under direct criminal justice supervision (on probation, in jail or prison, or on parole) as of 2017.[3] And a third of this country's adult population—*over 70 million Americans*—has a record on file with criminal justice agencies.[4] That is important because, although the rise of "mass incarceration" receives the most attention, no one is incarcerated without first having contact with the police. Police contact is the feeder mechanism into the broader criminal justice system, whether or not you are ever arrested, charged, or convicted. Almost 54 million individuals had face-to-face police contact in 2015 alone.[5] Such contacts are both the result and site of production for even more churning data.

Despite its take-up, big data is an ambiguous term that means different things to different people. The most commonly cited technical definition is the "three Vs"—volume, velocity, and variety.[6] Big data represents large amounts of information (volume), high-frequency observations and fast data processing (velocity), and comes from a wide range of institutional sensors and involves merging previously separate data sources (variety). In colloquial terms, "big data" roughly corresponds to large amounts of data that are crunched by computers with large computing capacity, and analyzed to find associations people might not otherwise find. Throughout the book, I adopt a definition that incorporates both the technical and popular conceptions. At its core, I argue big data is a *data environment* made possible by the mass digitization of information[7] and associated with the use of advanced analytics, including network analysis and machine learning algorithms. Much like big data, the term "algorithm" has both a technical and a nontechnical meaning. An algorithm is technically a formally specified set of instructions used to analyze data and automate decisions.[8] People often analogize algorithms to a recipe. Today, however, people tend to use the term "algorithm" to connote a more general process by which computers make automated, predictive decisions about a dataset.

Fingerprints provide a concrete example of these concepts in the policing context. The fingerprints taken by police used to be collected and stored on paper. Figure 1.1 (left image) shows these hard-copy records stored at the Los Angeles Police Department's Records and Identification Division at the Police Administration Building (PAB, otherwise known as the LAPD's Headquarters). Just looking at the boxes of paper files is daunting. Today, fingerprints can be taken remotely, via a digital reader in the field, and then digitally stored and shared. They can be matched using an algorithm that often takes just fractions of a second to analyze millions of prints (right image).

Law enforcement's adoption of big data is part of a broader shift toward the use of big data and machine-learned decisions throughout the criminal justice system. From surveillance to pretrial determinations and sentencing, big data saturates American criminal justice. It is also the subject of contentious debate in policy, media, legal, regulatory, advocacy, and academic circles. The White House launched the President's Task Force on 21st Century Policing in 2014 and the (now defunct) Police Data Initiative in 2015, as police

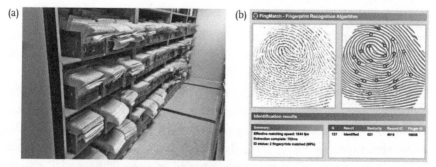

FIGURE 1.1 Paper fingerprint records at Records and Identification Division, LAPD (left), and fingerprint matching algorithm (right)
SOURCE: Author's Photo; figure by David Hallangen

departments across the country were taking up predictive policing.[9] A profusion of media articles, news stories, podcasts, and blog posts have addressed *Minority Report*–style policing,[10] and prosecutors and defense attorneys have begun to train in new police technologies. Legal scholars and regulators debate the suitability of existing law and regulations to govern police activity in the digital age, while activist and advocacy groups critique machine-learned decisions and technologically mediated surveillance as civil rights violations that discriminate against minority groups. No matter how quickly empirical research emerges, the technological capacities for data-intensive surveillance far outpace scholarship. Consequently, much discourse on the topic is speculative, focusing on the *possibilities*, good and bad, of new forms of data-based surveillance. We know very little about how big data is actually used by police in practice—and to what consequence.

Moving past hypotheticals and conjecture, this book offers an on-the-ground account of the LAPD's use of big data and associated surveillance technologies. This agency is undeniably working on the front lines, and it is actively policing with big data. In this account, I take a sociological approach to understanding the kinds of data the LAPD leverages, examining the concrete details of how and why this data is used, and illuminating what happens when data and advanced analytics are at work within institutions and social contexts. Along the way, I will ask: What's new about how law enforcement agencies are getting and using data? How are the meanings and implications of data contested? What do data sources and their selective use reveal about stratification and inequality, inclusion and exclusion, and claims about objectivity and subjectivity? And what does this all mean for the rule of law in the contemporary United States?

The Social Side of Big Data

Contrary to popular accounts, big data is not objective or less biased than discretionary "human" decision-making. More to the point: big data is fundamentally social.

Algorithms do not transcend the social, but are shaped by the social world in which they are created and used. The activities that generate and the technologies that analyze data are all embedded within social contexts and power structures, so the resulting data are anything but "natural," detached, or purely descriptive. Rather, people situated in preexisting social, organizational, and institutional contexts *decide* what data to collect and analyze, about whom, and for what purpose. So, just as individuals carry a range of implicit biases that affect their decisions, algorithms are loaded up with a scaffolding of implicit biases affecting the data they analyze and produce. What data can measure and quantify is not a technical question, but a normative one related to institutional priorities, organizational imperatives, and individual and group preferences. Nor does everyone have an equal ability to collect data, make decisions, construct policies, and intervene in others' lives based on that data.

Of course, the state has long used data to govern its citizens.[11] What is new and important is that the state is relying more heavily on private vendors and platforms to collect, store, share, and analyze data about its citizenry. This privatization is part of a broader neoliberal turn in statecraft, in which we have seen the privatization of services such as welfare,[12] education,[13] and punishment.[14] In turn, privatization has brought the logic of risk—actuarial calculations using proprietary algorithms—to bear in ways that increasingly structure life chances,[15] such as whether or not you get a loan, get released on bail, or get hired. The neoliberal shift lowers the state's accountability, in part, by pointing to the supposedly neutral data wielded by private enterprise.

Just as the state has long used data for governance, there is a long history of police using data to legitimate their function and signal accountability to external constituencies in the face of criticism over discriminatory practices.[16] But the growing role of the private sector in collecting and analyzing the growing suite of big data systems and predictive analytics is historically unprecedented. The LAPD is increasingly using data collected by private companies, storing their data on private platforms, and analyzing it using proprietary algorithms. Private vendors can hide behind trade secrecy and nondisclosure agreements, ultimately circumventing typical public-sector transparency requirements and lowering the accountability of the police by making it harder for scholars to study, regulators to regulate, and activists to mobilize for or against specific practices.

It bears repeating: although big data has the potential to reduce inequality and discrimination, as currently used it increases inequality while appearing to be objective. This applies not just to the policing case, but is part of a broader literature on credit, education, journalism, marketing, and insurance, to name a few.[17] We see a similar process tailored to the same ground-level processes and contingencies across cases. The policing case is a useful one because it puts the sociological dynamics in stark relief.

Policing via big data is supposed to make law enforcement practices more effective, fair, accountable, and objective—freed from biases of actors and organizations. Big data is, in this way, positioned as a panacea, the answer to constrained resources and claims about police bias and discrimination. However, the unintended consequences of algorithmic systems may be a Trojan Horse: the algorithms positioned as a gift to society actually smuggle in all sorts of biases, assumptions, and drivers of inequality. Existing organizational logics and power dynamics enable the use of—and resistance to—data analytics in policing.

In theory, big data can be used to improve the administration and accountability of justice. It has the potential to be used to reduce persistent inequalities in policing by replacing unparticularized suspicion of racial minorities and human exaggerations of patterns with less biased predictions of risk, and creating digital trails that can be used to police the police. In practice, big data technologies can have disparate impact. They are used in socially patterned, albeit inconsistent, ways with profoundly unequal, though often elusive, implications.

"Techwashing" inequality means appearing to replace subjectivity and legally contestable bias with "objective," "neutral," "color-blind" numbers produced through quantification, computation, and automation. In the words of one LAPD captain, it's "just math." But fetishizing computation as an objective process obscures the social side of algorithmic decision-making. Individuals' interpretation of data occurs in preexisting institutional, legal, and social settings, replete with power dynamics that become particularly visible when resistance emerges. For example, when the typical surveillance relationship is inverted and police officers become the *subjects* of surveillance, they tend to vigorously block, obfuscate, and contest data collection and interpretation.

The potential of big data is widely celebrated.[18] Proponents argue it is more objective and can eliminate inequality by stripping discretion from biased front-line actors. But when we actually look at big data on the ground, we see that the use of big data does not *replace* discretion, but rather *displaces* discretionary power to earlier, less visible (and less accountable) parts of the policing process. Quantification and computation obscures social processes, and the use of private, proprietary algorithms and platforms renders decision-making maddeningly opaque. The technological tools of police surveillance are far outpacing the laws that regulate them, resulting in a growing mismatch between law on the books and law in action. The legal protections regulating police activity are made anachronistic and ill-suited just as quickly as big data proliferates. Short of radical changes to the law, these new technologies will lead to a dramatic expansion of criminal justice contact and state intrusion into individuals' lives.

Studying Big Data Policing

In order to understand how police use big data and new surveillance technologies on the ground, I carried out fieldwork over the course of five years—two and a half years of intensive fieldwork between 2013 and 2015, and one follow-up site visit per year from 2016 to 2018. My fieldwork began with exploratory interviews with individuals in federal agencies and technology firms in Washington, DC. As I attended surveillance industry conferences and talked with individuals working in state, federal, and local law enforcement agencies, I learned that these agencies were starting to purchase licenses for analytic platforms originally designed for counterinsurgency efforts in Iraq and Afghanistan. One platform stood out early in my research—a platform designed by Palantir Technologies.

Its name a reference to the *"palantíri,"* omniscient seeing stones in Tolkien's *Lord of The Rings* trilogy, Palantir was founded by Peter Thiel, Alex Karp, Nathan Gettings, Joe Lonsdale, and Stephen Cohen in 2004. It is now one of the premier platforms for compiling and analyzing massive and disparate data by law enforcement and intelligence agencies. Originally intended for use in national defense, Palantir got partial start-up funding from In-Q-Tel, the CIA's venture capital firm. Palantir's clients have included federal agencies such as the Central Intelligence Agency (CIA), Federal Bureau of Investigation (FBI), Immigration and Customs Enforcement (ICE), and Department of Homeland Security (DHS); local law enforcement agencies such as the LAPD and New York Police Department (NYPD); and commercial customers such as JPMorgan Chase. It was valued at $20 billion in 2015.[19]

Just as I was starting to comprehend the migration of such defense technologies to local policing and local and federal agencies' data-sharing practices, whistleblower Edward Snowden began revealing classified National Security Agency (NSA) documents. The revelations uncovered an extensive NSA-led international mass surveillance apparatus, including warrantless monitoring of American citizens' phone and Internet communications. Suddenly, there was great national interest in the topic of government surveillance, especially the practices of federal agencies. However, local law enforcement agencies were largely absent from the conversation, despite local police being the ones that most enforce and shape individuals' everyday lived experiences of the law.[20] So that's where I shifted my focus.

Reaching out to 18 law enforcement agencies to try and figure out which police departments were using which data sources and which analytic platforms, I quickly learned that police departments tended to portray themselves as technically sophisticated when in reality, they were anything but. I was going to have to do my work with one of the "big guns": the NYPD, Chicago Police Department, or LAPD, all of which seemed among the most technologically advanced. I was particularly interested in the LAPD, because in addition to Palantir Gotham, the company's government intelligence platform, they were using PredPol, the world's largest predictive policing software. In the summer of 2013, I moved to Los Angeles to begin my fieldwork.

The LAPD is the third-largest local law enforcement agency in the United States, with 10,008 sworn officers and 3,112 civilian staff (as of 2019).[21] The department serves an area of almost 500 square miles and a population of just under four million. The LAPD has 1,650 cars, each equipped with its own laptop. Its four bureaus—Central, South, Valley, and West—are subdivided into 19 geographic areas. There are also two specialized bureaus, Detective and Special Operations.

Over the course of five years, I conducted interviews and observations with 79 individuals and conducted between one and five follow-up interviews with a sub-sample of 32 individuals to follow how certain technologies were disseminated and information was shared throughout the LAPD. Interviewees included sworn officers and civilian employees working in patrol, investigation, and crime analysis, as well as specialized sections and divisions, including Robbery-Homicide, Information Technology, Records and Identification, Fugitive Warrants, Juvenile, Risk Management, Air Support, and the Real-Time Crime Analysis Center (RACR, see Figure 1.2).

To see how officers deploy data in the field, I conducted observations on ride-alongs in patrol cars and a helicopter. I also shadowed analysts as they worked with data, responded to queries from detectives and supervisors, and proactively trawled the data for investigations and crime analysis.

My on-the-ground methods helped me understand that police departments are not monolithic. Like other organizations, they are replete with understudied heterogeneity. The fact that not all divisions adopted new technologies and started using new data sources at the same time was a source of analytic leverage, allowing me to observe considerable variation in when, whether, and how different big data technologies were taken up. It also meant I could probe how my respondents interpreted and felt about changes to their work as various big data analytics made their debuts across different divisions.

To supplement my research within the LAPD, I interviewed individuals within the Los Angeles County Sheriff's Department (LASD). LASD is an integral part of the ecosystem of public services in the region: it is the

FIGURE 1.2 Situation Room at the Real-Time Crime Analysis Center (RACR)
SOURCE: Author's Photo

fourth-largest local law enforcement agency in the United States and serves as the hub for a whopping 44 law enforcement agencies. I also conducted interviews at the Joint Regional Intelligence Center (JRIC). JRIC, in Southern California, is a "fusion center." Fusion centers are multiagency, multidisciplinary surveillance organizations that receive considerable federal funding from the Department of Homeland Security and the Department of Justice.[22] After 9/11, 80 federally funded fusion centers, including JRIC, were established across the country. JRIC was designed to enrich Suspicious Activity Reports (SARs)[23] and distribute them to appropriate county, state, or federal agencies. Today, its mission has expanded: it is meant to handle "all threats all hazards," and so JRIC conducts data collection, aggregation, and surveillance in conjunction with other fusion centers. It responds to Requests for Information (RFIs) from agencies across the country, including the DHS, FBI, CIA, and ICE.

In addition to conducting interviews and observations in police stations, cars, and administrative buildings, I tried to spend time where the police spent their time. I would eat meals with officers, hang out in the coffee shops they patronized, and go to sports bars to watch UFC fights with off-duty cops. I also interviewed individuals working at technology companies that designed the analytic platforms used by the LAPD, including Palantir and PredPol.

I supplemented my fieldwork with archival research, digging into law enforcement and military training manuals and surveillance industry literature. Using multiple methods and triangulating across various sources of data provided the analytic leverage necessary to better understand how law enforcement use and contest big data in theory and practice, as well as the ways they interpret and make meaning out of data's changing role in quotidian police work.

As the sociologists Michèle Lamont and Ann Swidler suggest, "Interviews often entail observation, and ethnography usually entails interviewing."[24] That is to say, there was considerable overlap between my observational, interview, and archival methods. I'd ask officers questions as we drove around the city during my ride-alongs, for instance. By putting my observational and interview data in dialogue with one another, I was able to compare my sources, ask clarifying or interpretive questions about my observational data in interviews, and examine the gaps between what people say they do and what they actually do.[25] Asking the same question of different people often yielded different answers—interesting data in and of itself. For example, when I asked a sworn officer in Fugitive Warrants a question about how they use social media data, he responded that it was "law enforcement sensitive" and declined to answer. When I asked the same question of a software engineer, he answered without hesitation.

Over the course of my research, I developed relationships with some of my respondents such that our regular communications (in person when I was in LA, or by phone or e-mail when I was out-of-state) grew less and less structured over time. We became more conversational: I would check in with engineers as I learned about new trends in data analytics, and officers would call if they had an experience during their shift that seemed relevant to my research. Depending on the respondent's preference, I audio-recorded my formal interviews (about half gave consent for recording) and had them professionally transcribed. Ride-alongs, on the other hand, involved no recording; that would violate privacy, since a recorder would pick up all of the information coming through dispatch as we went about responding to calls for service. It would also be impractical, as ride-alongs could be seven or eight hours long. Instead, I used my iPhone, laptop, or notebook to take notes, and I used a voice memo app to record my thoughts during my seemingly interminable commutes home via crowded LA freeways after a day or night of fieldwork.

Access behind the Blue Wall

One of the first questions I tend to get is how I obtained research access to the LAPD. The "blue wall of silence" is notorious, and it makes it difficult for researchers to secure the degree of access necessary to obtain in-depth qualitative data on day-to-day police practices. Thus, most ethnographies of policing focus on the subjects of police surveillance, rather than the surveilling agents. There are strong theoretical traditions and policy motivations for sociologists to study such structurally disadvantaged populations, but the methodological barriers are a less-discussed and crucial motivator for this choice. Disadvantaged populations have less power to exclude researchers from spending time with them. For example, the urban poor spend more time in public spaces than in private clubs or buildings with literal gatekeepers controlling access. Consequently, with a few notable exceptions,[26] privileged groups, organizations, and decision-makers such as the police are understudied, especially in the sociology of crime and punishment.

Among the classic police ethnographies that do exist,[27] only a handful of in-depth studies have taken us inside police departments since the rise of data analytics.[28] These studies offer important insights about the use of COMPSTAT and crime mapping, but they predate algorithmic policing. Consequently, we know little about how big data policing is exercised in practice, and even less about the contexts of reception.[29]

To protect my respondents' anonymity, I cannot describe my entrée in detail. However, in case it is helpful for future researchers, I want to share a couple of methodological points. I gained access to the department by starting high on the LAPD's organizational chart. Police departments are hierarchical organizations; if I could gain access at a point high in the chain of command, permissions would cascade down the ranks. The first six weeks of snowball sampling was by far the most difficult period of my fieldwork, as it involved a lot of awkward cold calls, ignored e-mails, and loitering around captains' offices. As time went on, I developed working relationships with individuals throughout the department and the dynamic shifted from struggling to get people to talk to me to having individuals routinely invite me to attend meetings or have conversations.

In the project's early stages, colleagues urged me to anonymize the department, which would permit me to write more freely. Yet I quickly surmised all the ways anonymity would be prohibitive for my project, particularly the ways it would limit my ability to provide meaningful historical context or specificity. Without identifying the department, I could not speak to the institutional context that catalyzed the adoption of big data analytics, the specifics of the department's analytic practices and platforms, or other relevant features of the department or city. Therefore, all respondents were told that the department would be identified, but their names would not be. Unless otherwise indicated, all names used throughout this book are pseudonyms. Still, the ranks remain the same, and I do not use any composite characters.

Most of my respondents assumed I knew very little about the everyday realities of police work, and, at the beginning of this project at least, they were correct. I struggled to understand what the dispatchers said over the radio, and I was constantly looking up acronyms and police codes on my phone. Occasionally, I had trouble explaining my presence in the field. In administrative or station settings, my role was usually clear: I was a researcher. My primary contact in any given division would typically spend some time ushering me around for introductions—although they tended to mess up the specifics with surprising regularity. In addition to being accurately presented as a sociologist from Princeton, I was variously introduced as a psychologist from Stanford, a senior from Harvard, and other inaccurate but perhaps not particularly meaningfully different positions. No matter: so long as a higher-up vouched for me, individuals tended not to question my presence in these settings. My social position was murkier on ride-alongs.

On one occasion, after a sergeant had arrested a teenage boy and was talking to the boy's mother in Spanish, the mother gestured at me sitting in the passenger seat and asked the officer something I could not understand. As we were driving back to the station to book the teenager, the sergeant revealed that she'd asked whether I was his daughter and if it was take your kid to work day. On another ride-along, I was with a sergeant responding to a veteran having a psychotic break in a church parking lot. As the veteran tore the pages from a Bible with his teeth, another officer at the scene strode over to ask if I was the man's wife.

Most commonly, when I was on ride-alongs, people assumed I was exploring joining the force. At one particularly grim crime scene, a teenager had been shot multiple times. An officer whose tattoos were partially covered by a long-sleeved shirt worn under his uniform, came over to quip: "That's [division] for ya. You still lookin' to join?"

The LAPD is clearly not a "typical" police department. In the United States, half of police departments employ fewer than ten officers, and the modal number of crime analysts is zero.[30] The LAPD, on the other hand, is an agency on the forefront of data analytics. As the sociologist Robert Zussman writes, "Successful case studies look at extremes, unusual circumstances, and analytically clear examples, all of which are important not because they are representative but because they show a process or a problem in particularly clear relief."[31] Indeed, the LAPD provides a strategic case study for understanding the interplay between technology, law, and social relations. It invests heavily in its data collection, analysis, and deployment capacities, and offers international training sessions on how law enforcement can better harness big data. Practices within this single, if sprawling, department may forecast broader trends that will shape other law enforcement agencies in the coming years.

Additionally, as a case study of policing, the LAPD is among the most extreme, emblematic cases of data wielded in the exercise of state power. No study of *policing* can separate out the practice from the actor and the institution. It is, necessarily, a study of the *police*, the institution and arm of the state that operates in high-stakes, sometimes literally life and death, impositions of policy. On the one hand, policing is a site where the state faces sophisticated, oftentimes rigid legal and organizational controls on its decision-making authority (e.g., the Fourth Amendment), but on the other, policing in practice means exercising an immense amount of discretion[32] in the application of state power in high-stakes environments. Police are the prototypical "street-level bureaucrat"[33]; they do not follow a policy of "full enforcement" where they strictly enforce all criminal statutes at all times against all offenders.[34] Rather, they are constantly using their judgment— informed by a variety of social factors—as they decide what to do, who to police, how to enforce, and what to record.[35] When big data is introduced into the exercise of state power, or the practice of policing, it has the potential to either ossify or upset existing organizational and legal dynamics. Like all social systems, the criminal justice system has all sorts of cracks and fissures. Big data can be thought of as the injection of a new technology, a dye that illuminates the cracks in the system. Big data analytics lay bare issues of classification, suspicion, and inequality in the exercise of state power.

Plan of the Book

The next chapter of this book begins by tracing the history of quantification in policing, from pin maps to predictive algorithms. In this way, we see that data has always been social. Chapter 2 surveys the surveillance landscape, starting with the "scientific turn" in policing in the early 20th century, then moving to the rise of evidence-based policing, the Information Sharing Environment that emerged after the terrorist attacks of 9/11, and the predictive algorithms and big data analytics put to work in modern policing. Historically, the police collected most of the information they use in the course of their daily operations themselves. However, this chapter highlights the growing role of the private sector—for data collection and the provision of analytic platforms—in policing. Both the past and present of policing are highly racialized, and so this chapter also describes how data is positioned as an antidote to racism and bias in policing. The chapter closes with an overview of data use and the technologies at work in the LAPD, providing background information for the rest of the book.

Chapter 3 takes a closer look at what big data policing looks like on the ground. It focuses on the first of two types of surveillance examined in this book—*dragnet surveillance*, meaning surveillance tools that gather information on everyone, rather than merely those under suspicion. Dragnet surveillance widens and deepens social oversight: it includes a broader swath of people and can follow any single individual across a greater range of institutional settings. Dragnet surveillance is associated with three key transformations in the practice of policing: (1) the shift from query-based to alert-based systems makes it possible to systematically surveil an unprecedentedly large number of people; (2) individuals with no direct police contact are now included in law enforcement systems, lowering the threshold for inclusion in police databases; and (3) institutional data systems are integrated, with police now collecting and using information gleaned from institutions not typically associated with crime control.

Chapter 4 shifts to *directed surveillance*, or the surveillance of people and places deemed suspicious. Big data has meant a shift from reactive to predictive policing, a useful shorthand for the technologically mediated directed surveillance used by many departments today. I analyze how the LAPD conducts person- and place-based predictive policing, why it adopted different forms of predictive policing, how it uses algorithms to quantify criminal risk, how the police do—and do not—incorporate insights from the algorithms into their work in the field, and how predictive policing serves as a foundation for ongoing intelligence gathering.

Taken together, Chapters 3 and 4 demonstrate that in the case of directed surveillance, the adoption of big data analytics is associated with mere *amplifications* of prior surveillance practices, but in the case of dragnet surveillance, it is associated with fundamental *transformations* in police activity. Figure 1.3 depicts the various degrees of transformation associated with the adoption of big data analytics. Each line represents a continuum of surveillance practices, from traditional policing to big data surveillance. The length of the solid lines represents the degree of transformation in surveillance

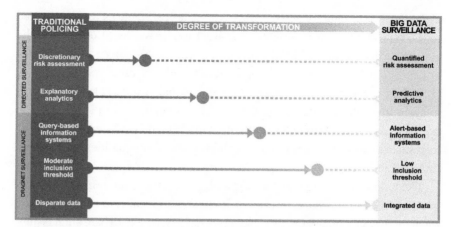

FIGURE 1.3 Degrees of transformation associated with big data analytics
SOURCE: Author; chart by David Hallangen

practices associated with the use of big data. This conceptual framework can be applied not only to the LAPD, but also to analyze the continuities and changes within a variety of institutions adopting new data sources and technologies.

Though I did not set out to examine police resistance in this study, I was quickly disabused of my assumption that cops would largely embrace the new surveillance and predictive tools being made available to them. In fact, I saw how wrong I was in my very first ride-along. Chapter 5 sheds light on how the police resist and contest big data analytics. Their resistance stems in large part from the proliferation of high-frequency observations and data collection sensors that result in the police themselves coming under increased surveillance. New developments are frequently viewed with suspicion, with officers believing technology is a means of deskilling, entrenching managerial control, devaluing experiential knowledge, and threatening their professional autonomy. Novel tech ultimately serves to reinforce old divisions—such as those between captains and patrol officers—even as it creates new distinctions within the department. Understanding these patterns of contestation underscores how big data is ultimately social. It also gives us a space to consider the extent to which data-based surveillance is—and is not—associated with deeper organizational change.

Chapter 6 discusses the implications of police use of big data analytics for inequality. On the one hand, big data analytics may be a means by which to ameliorate persistent inequalities in policing. Data can be used to "police the police" and replace unparticularized suspicion of racial minorities and human exaggeration of patterns with less biased predictions of risk. On the other hand, data-intensive police surveillance practices are implicated in the reproduction of inequality in at least four ways: by (1) deepening the surveillance of individuals already under suspicion, (2) codifying a secondary surveillance network of individuals with no direct police contact, (3) widening the criminal justice dragnet unequally, and (4) leading people to avoid institutions that collect data and are fundamental to social integration.[36] Crucially, as currently implemented, "data-driven" decision-making techwashes, both obscuring and amplifying social inequalities under a patina of objectivity.

Technological change is far outpacing the laws and regulations that govern police use of data, rendering foundational legal constructs anachronistic in the age of big data. Legal scholars have started to debate such issues, but their work is primarily theoretical. Chapter 7 grounds these debates in empirical detail and argues that the law (and its attendant scholarship) is thinking too narrowly about data-based surveillance.

My conclusion reflects on the major lessons I have learned about how big data is fundamentally social and how humans embedded in social institutions are central to the life course of data, from defining the problem to collecting and cleaning the data, selecting and deploying the model, and deciding what to do with data in the field.[37] We must find ways to curb institutions' craving for data, because that hunger too often outpaces our understanding of the intended and unintended consequences of a data binge. I offer guidelines for academics, lawmakers, and community groups regarding how data can be leveraged to promote efficiency, fairness, and accountability in criminal justice reform. I also discuss the future of law enforcement, identify policy and research priorities, and connect my findings on big data surveillance in policing to other sectors, including education, insurance, healthcare, finance, and immigration.

CHAPTER 2 | Policing by Numbers

The Public History and Private Future of
Police Data

PIRATE ATTACKS WERE TOP OF mind for a pair of shipping company owners, who explained that they were looking for predictive technologies to help protect their cargo, while an investment banker was hoping to find just the right tool to help track his employees. Tech-startup staffers gave demonstrations about their innovative approaches to catching human traffickers and ferreting out terrorists. One guy looked like a cop.

An acquaintance, having heard that I was studying surveillance technologies, had gotten me here: a surveillance industry conference in Washington, DC. I made my way over to the man who stood out: short-sleeved shirt, bulky digital watch, Oakley sunglasses pushed up onto his head, and shoes that landed somewhere between lug-sole boots and cross-trainers. Sure enough, he introduced himself by name, rank, and police department. He wanted, he said, to learn about technology to help "catch bad guys in my city," and the real innovations weren't being developed by law enforcement, but by tech startups and national defense. He'd come to DC to see whether there were any new counterinsurgency technologies that might be used in his department.

Our brief conversation hit on two of the key findings I explore in this chapter—that local law enforcement is embracing technological tools initially developed in military contexts, and that police are partnering with private companies to design tools and collect data. As the neoliberal turn has invited the private sector into more and more once-public endeavors, it should be no surprise that organizations like the LAPD are increasingly reliant on private vendors for the data and technology they use as they carry out their daily operations.

In turn, there is a long history of the state using data to legitimate its function. For instance, data has been mobilized across time to make claims about objectivity and efficiency in the face of concerns about, for example, wide policing disparities with regard to race, class, and place.

This chapter traces the role of data in the evolution of policing, then shifts to the unprecedented organizational change that has insinuated the private sector into the LAPD and the current form and function of police work.

From Pin Maps to Predictive Algorithms: The History of Quantification in Policing

The use of data for decision-making in law enforcement is not new: the police have, for instance, used crime-forecasting tools for almost a century, and data in one form or another has long legitimated the function of the American state. So documenting the history of quantification offers a useful corrective to the "disruptive" rhetoric in Silicon Valley around big data fundamentally transforming everything as we know it. The historical perspective suggests that the embrace of big data by police is part of a broader trend toward quantification and algorithmic risk assessment in the criminal justice system.[1] What is new and important about the current big data age and organizational form of policing we find ourselves in is the role of private actors in public policing.

The "datafication" of policing began in the early 20th century, alongside efforts to decouple local policing from politics.[2] In what scholars call the "Political Era," policing was characterized by pervasive political corruption and close ties between mayors and chiefs of police. Law enforcement professionals understood that they were lackeys for their mayors' political machines. Reformers among police leadership tried to insulate departments from direct political control and bring officers under the administrative oversight of central command in what would be dubbed the "Reform" or "Progressive Era." Their efforts created the hierarchical, bureaucratic structure of policing we know today.[3]

The professionalization of policing centered on three core ideas: crime control should be police departments' priority, police should fight crime objectively and free from political influence, and authority within any given police department should be centralized and rationalized.[4] The science of policing and criminology—and the data it required—emerged in support of fighting crime "objectively."

August Vollmer was instrumental in promoting the application of scientific principles to police service, earning him a reputation as the "father of modern law enforcement." He was the first chief of the Berkeley Police Department, served a short stint as the chief of the LAPD, and was brought into many police departments to train officers in the "scientific approach" to policing. Vollmer's scientific approach involved leveraging information and communication technologies like signal boxes and telephone kiosks, while developing new strategies for crime control. These included pin mapping, the process by which police would plot out a week's worth of crime by placing pins on maps, and then qualitatively assess and work to predict crime patterns (see Figure 2.1).[5]

Many of the tactics introduced into policing during the Reform Era were drawn from military practices. Vollmer had extensive personal experience in the military apparatus, working in counterinsurgency efforts in the Philippines, and he drew upon it heavily in designing and implementing police practices in the United States.[6] He wrote that principles of "military science," including information systems, intelligence, strategies, and communications, when correctly applied, could reduce crime and protect communities. The strategic and technological changes Vollmer and other military-minded reformers instituted gave the police greater power to surveil and collect and organize information on civilians. Tracing the history of the militarization of the police, the historian Julilly Kohler-Hausmann notes the following:

> [Urban areas'] struggles with state authority were easily interpreted with the same rhetorical devices used for insurgent populations abroad. Thus, it is not surprising that over time, more and more voices called for the state to use the same tools and techniques employed overseas to subdue allegedly dangerous domestic spaces. And so, by the mid-to-late 1960s, domestic law enforcement agencies had begun to interpret the conditions in inner cities as wars and had begun to turn for answers to military training, technology, and terminology.[7]

This creep of military hardware and organizational structure—from surplus military gear to SWAT teams—received a flurry of attention in the literature about police militarization in the 2010s.[8] Yet, as will become apparent later in this chapter, the creep of military *software* into police operations is both vital to contemporary law enforcement and largely overlooked.

CRIME AT A GLANCE : MARKING A MAP WITH COLOURED FLAGS
IN THE NEW MAP ROOM AT SCOTLAND YARD.

FIGURE 2.1 Crime pin maps at Scotland Yard, 1947
Copyright: Illustrated London News Ltd/Mary Evans

By the 1970s, following over half a century of attempts to reform law enforcement and reduce crime through police professionalization, there was a
growing consensus that "nothing works."[9] In the early 1990s, the orthodoxy
of "community policing" was ascendant. Under this banner, police attempted
to establish closer relationships between officers and the residents on their
beat, and they implemented "problem-oriented" policing strategies in which
law enforcement and community members jointly attempted to identify and
address the root causes of specific crime problems.

Meanwhile, the state tried to become more proactive than reactive via "evidence-based" policing. Partnerships between criminologists and police departments developed ways to use data to track, map, and predict crime and more efficiency deploy limited police resources. Based on the not entirely surprising observation that crimes are not randomly distributed, but spatially concentrated into a few, small geographic areas, "hot spots policing" emerged as a key patrol strategy.[10] A series of randomized experiments supported the notion that directed, place-based patrol of microgeographic hot spots could indeed reduce crime.

In 1994, Commissioner William Bratton established COMPSTAT in New York City. COMPSTAT, a management model linking crime and enforcement statistics, is multifaceted: it serves as a crime control strategy, a personnel performance and accountability metric, and a resource management tool. Crime data is collected in real time, then mapped and analyzed in preparation for weekly crime control strategy meetings between police executives and precinct commanders. At those meetings, trends are noted, and precinct commanders are instructed to use their discretion to deploy their resources to improve their weekly, monthly, and yearly crime stats. COMPSTAT spread quickly throughout major American cities in the 1990s and early 2000s.

Then came September 11, 2001. In the years following the terrorist attacks, the 9/11 Commission would describe that day as the result of a series of catastrophic information-sharing failures within the intelligence community. The commission's report found that various US authorities had relevant information that could have identified the threat and prevented the attacks, but there were no systems in place to share that information across agencies and platforms. The federal government's response to 9/11, which included congressional acts and new federal data-sharing programs, shaped the legacy of counterterrorism on local policing. Such initiatives include the Information Sharing Environment (ISE), established by the Intelligence Reform and Terrorism Prevention Act of 2004; Secure Communities, a deportation program that relies on integrated databases and partnership among federal, state, and local law enforcement agencies; and Centers for Excellence, Department of Homeland Security–sponsored consortiums of universities conducting research on homeland security issues (jokingly referred to as "Centers for Invasiveness" by a civilian employee working in LAPD's Information Technology Division). They also included fusion centers.

As described in the previous chapter, fusion centers are surveillance hubs built in the wake of 9/11 where federal, state, and local agencies come together to collect, aggregate, analyze, and share information. There are currently eighty fusion centers across the United States.[11] Although their original mission was counterterrorism, there was insufficient terrorist activity to keep fusion center analysts busy, so their mandate quickly broadened to include gathering and sharing information related to "all hazards, all crimes, all threats."[12]

SARs, or "Suspicious Activity Reports," are key conduits into fusion center databases. SARs are tips and leads from law enforcement and civilians, regardless of suspicion of criminal activity. In the era of "see something, say something," mundane activities like using binoculars, drawing diagrams, or taking pictures or "video footage with no apparent aesthetic value" can be recorded on SARs—and made into fusion center data.[13] Along with the SARs, fusion center data comes from criminal justice, public health, financial, motor vehicle, credit, immigration, tax, insurance, property, car rental, postal and shipping, gaming, and utility record sources. It also includes dossiers from third-party data brokers.[14]

Ultimately, 9/11 catalyzed and accelerated the emphasis on data sharing for the purposes of crime prediction and prevention across local and federal agencies. Through the infusion of federal dollars into efforts to wage the War on Terror, state and local law enforcement agencies gained powerful new resources to collect, analyze, share, and use a wide range of new data. DHS, for example, gave $35 billion in grants to state and local police between 2002 and 2011, $17 billion of which was allocated by one piece of legislation alone: the Homeland Security Act of 2002.[15] Local law enforcement agencies came to be viewed by federal agencies as "force multipliers," well situated to collect intelligence on the front lines of homeland security.[16] Officials in often underfunded local agencies recognized that the data they began to collect were, of course, also useful for their local, daily operations, surveillance, and crime control efforts.

Which brings us to the age of "predictive policing,"[17] in which the LAPD is a leader. William Bratton, of COMPSTAT fame and the former commissioner of the NYPD, became LA's chief of police in 2002. Bratton oversaw the process of merging previously disparate information systems to create a more data-based picture of crime in the city. In 2008 he began working with federal agencies to assess the viability of a more predictive approach, and in 2011 the LAPD started using PredPol. This predictive policing software was developed in partnership by Jeff Brantingham,[18] a UCLA anthropologist whose research was partially funded by grants from the Army Research Office, and George Mohler, a computer science professor then at Santa Clara University (now at Purdue).

A decade later, we can see that predictive analytics are used for a wide range of law enforcement–related activities in the LAPD and beyond. These include algorithms to predict when and where future crimes are most likely to occur,[19] network models predicting individuals most likely to be involved in gun violence,[20] and risk models identifying law enforcement officers most likely to engage in risky behavior.[21] Like PredPol, many predictive policing efforts are made possible by federal funds now targeted at improving and expanding law enforcement's use of technology. For example, the Smart Policing Initiative—a consortium of the Bureau of Justice Assistance, local police departments, and researchers—provides federal funds to more than 30 local law enforcement agencies (including the LAPD) to support new data-driven practices.

The police started using predictive analytics for many of the same reasons as other institutions did—they had the potential to improve efficiency and accountability. From a technical perspective, big data is a means by which the police can become more efficient: it aims at improving prediction, filling analytic gaps, and allocating scarce resources. An institutional perspective[22] goes further: law enforcement adopted big data analytics not because there was empirical evidence that it *actually* improved efficiency, but because there was immense institutional pressure to conform as other institutions began marshaling big data and algorithmic predictions for decision-making. Using predictive analytics and surveillance technologies initially developed in military contexts, for example, could confer a degree of legitimacy upon police departments. Moreover, data-driven policing may provide greater accountability as departments respond to criticisms over discriminatory practices. For example, as I will discuss in more detail later, law enforcement has responded to nationwide movements around police violence, including Black Lives Matter, and their calls for police reform by holding up data-driven policing as a partial antidote. Implicitly, these responses have promoted data as impartial and objective, though, as noted earlier, data are inescapably social.[23]

Whether the use of big data *actually* increases efficiency and accountability is a complicated question that will be grappled with throughout this book. For now, I will simply say that big data, predictive policing, and, most recently, "precision policing"—which focuses police resources on what data suggest are the highest-risk individuals and places—are integral parts of recent discourse around police reform.

Regardless of why big data analytics was adopted in the first place, data originally collected for one purpose tends to be "developed, refined and expanded as part of efforts to deal with new problems and situations."[24] The tendency for data or systems initially used for one purpose to be used for another, often unintended or unanticipated purpose, is known as "function creep" and is a fundamental component of the big data landscape. It is so central to organizational behavior that surveillance scholars Mark Andrejevic and Kelly Gates argue that " 'function creep' is not ancillary to the data collection process, it is built into it—the function *is* the creep."[25]

The Role of the Private Sector

Historically, the police have collected most of the information they use themselves, by stopping and questioning people while on patrol, taking notes during calls for service, and conducting interviews in the course of investigations. This information populates the criminal justice databases available to law enforcement: records of citations, collisions, and warrants; county jail data; sex offender registries; gang databases; and so on. However, one of the most transformative features of the digitization of policing is that law enforcement is increasingly securing routine access to a wide range of data from *nonpolice* databases.[26]

Referred to as "the biggest industry you've never heard of,"[27] data brokering is a $200 billion industry.[28] Over 4,000 companies[29] such as Acxiom, Cambridge Analytica, Epsilon, CoreLogic, Datalogix, PeekYou, LexisNexis Accurint, Spokeo, Zabasearch, and Thomson Reuters CLEAR, collect and aggregate information from public records and private sources, then make these data available to whoever can pay the fee for access. When you buy contact lenses and companies offer you a rebate if you tear off the box top and mail in? That's a data grab, a means of monetizing your data (more than covering the cost of your "rebate"). So a wide range of companies generates profits not only from their primary business, but also from a secondary business: selling their customers' information to data brokers.

Pizza chains, consumer health websites, repossession agents, payday lenders, liens, online surveys, warranty registration, rebates, Internet sweepstakes, loyalty-card data from retailers, social media, mortgages, bankruptcies, drivers licenses, professional credentials, charities' donor lists, magazine subscription lists, public records, Social Security death master files, and credit headers (the identifying information at the top of a credit report that includes name, spouse's name, address, previous address, Social Security number, and employer)—all these and more are involved in selling your data.[30] Yet it is hard to fully understand the scope of the data brokerage industry: even the Federal Trade Commission cannot find out exactly where data brokers obtain their information, because brokerages cite trade secrecy as an excuse to not divulge that information.[31]

Sometimes third-party data brokers provide law enforcement wholesale access to their data. But that is not the typical model, as scale is becoming a limiting factor with massive datasets, and brokers may consider the datasets proprietary assets. Instead, brokers commonly rely on metered pricing models, which give law enforcement agencies logged access for individual queries. And some data brokers go beyond simply making data available to law enforcement; based on over 1,500 documents obtained by filing FOIA requests with seven data brokers, the privacy scholar Christopher Hoofnagle has shown that some data brokers actually tailor their data for law enforcement agencies.[32] In the words of a vice president for DBT Online, a subsidiary of Choice Point (a data broker that was a spinoff of Equifax's Insurance Services Group),

> [A]fter 26 years with the DEA, I retired and joined Database Technologies, Inc. as a Vice President. My goal here is to introduce AutoTrack PLUS to every member of the law enforcement community throughout our nation. . . . To that end, every law enforcement agency is extended an automatic 33% discount on our service.[33]

As more and more information is digitized, and as personal records are linked across formerly separate institutional boundaries, the scope of data that brokers can make accessible to law enforcement increases exponentially.

In some instances, it is simply easier for law enforcement to purchase privately collected data than to rely on in-house data, because there are fewer constitutional protections, reporting requirements, and appellate checks on private sector surveillance and data collection.[34] Therefore, purchasing data from data brokers can be a way for law enforcement agencies to circumvent privacy laws.[35]

But law enforcement is not only using data *collected* by private companies; it is also using private sector platforms to *store, share,* and *analyze* police data. Companies such as PredPol, HunchLab, Coplink, IBM i2, Mark 43, and Palantir, to name a few, design predictive policing algorithms, data-sharing systems, intelligence and investigative analysis software, cloud-based records management, and data integration platforms for law enforcement use. Microsoft and Amazon design domain awareness systems and storage platforms for body camera footage, respectively. In short, programmed policing means profits.

One reason I was at the surveillance industry trade show mentioned at the start of this chapter was to better understand the political economy of data-based surveillance. At the conferences I attended, I was joined by local, county, and federal law enforcement agencies and representatives from federal agencies, including the FBI, CIA, and ICE. Private sector attendees included representatives from bail bonds companies, repossession companies, and international shipping firms. Neoliberal discourse[36] was pervasive; data-based surveillance was clearly being positioned as a site of profitable investment. Data was referred to as a "strategic asset," while "ROI" was used to mean not return on investment but *return on information*.

Prior to the first of these conferences, I assumed that law enforcement representatives would ask surveillance company representatives how their platforms could help police achieve their goals. I quickly saw, however, that the pattern was usually the inverse: software representatives would demonstrate the use of their platform in a non–law enforcement—usually military—context, then ask local law enforcement whether they would be interested in a similar application for their local context. In other words, instead of filling analytic gaps or technical voids identified by law enforcement, software representatives helped create new kinds of institutional demand to sell lucrative platform licensing agreements.

For large agencies like the LAPD, software vendors come directly to the department itself—much like the way pharmaceutical reps go to hospitals and doctors' offices—to try to sell their products. Ian, a civilian employee in the LAPD's Information Technology Division, told me that "all of these" vendors "come into the LAPD saying 'we want to do data-sharing with you, because you're LAPD,'" but "they all kinda almost do the same thing. . . . It's like they just want to get their stuff in place and get a license agreement." He was frustrated that command staff was, to his mind, too easily seduced by "something they see at a trade show or a vendor dog and pony show." Ian imitated LAPD staffers enthusing over the latest platform or technology: "*Hey! Look at this cool interface, it's the greatest thing in the world. You can do X, Y, Z—it's like* Minority Report, *whoa!*" Ian's colleague, Manuel, spoke up at this point, reinforcing Ian's comments: "Our command staff is easily distracted by the latest and greatest shiny object. But they don't know what it takes to get that integrated, and then nobody thinks about implementation. They just want it."

Tracing the corporate lineage of police surveillance technologies and the creep of military and corporate interests and practices into local law enforcement's daily operations is crucial for understanding the practice and institution of policing today. The growing role of the private sector in public surveillance matters for at least two reasons. First, it is wrong to assume that using data is necessarily "evidence-based policing," or that certain data and platforms are used because they are the most effective for improving public safety and solving crimes. Rather, path dependence is often the strongest force at play. Once a law enforcement agency is using a given platform, the time and money they've put into that platform are sunk costs, and they're likely to continue structuring their data to conform to that platform. Agencies may continue to use legacy systems, even if their efficacy has not been evaluated, sometimes even if they *know* those systems don't work that well. Research on welfare agencies nearly three decades ago showed that even when computer systems were ineffective, agencies continued receiving federal and city money for those systems, because the data platforms' primary value was political. In local government power politics, data pumped out by these systems was used to "enhanc[e] the welfare agencies' image when they dealt with federal funders and auditors."[37] The quality, reliability, or even accuracy of those records was only incidental.

Second, in contrast to administrative agencies, the private sector is subject to far less oversight. If public agencies such as local law enforcement are increasingly using tools and data designed and gathered by the private sector, they are able to work in ways that are less visible—a point to which we will return in Chapter 7, which focuses on the legal implications of digitized policing.

Police Use of Data Is Racialized

Data is increasingly positioned as *the* answer to policing challenges. However, the police use of data is as inextricably linked to race[38] as the history and present of policing itself. Media, policy, and academic discourse around data analytics may treat data as objective and color-blind, but one would have to ignore the social dynamics that shape the data to assume that *police data* are color-blind.

Since its inception, local law enforcement has been called upon to enforce racial suppression. In the antebellum South, slave patrols controlled the movement of Black bodies under the Fugitive Slave Act. After the Civil War, local police maintained the color line by enforcing racial segregation, peonage, and racially discriminatory laws. In "Sundown Towns," police prohibited Black people from being out after sunset.[39] And it is not only what the police did, but also what they *failed* to do. American police, well into the civil rights era, failed to stop lynching and other forms of violence against racial minorities, and they failed to protect civil rights protestors.[40] To this day, racialized policing enforces ideas of who is allowed to exist in what places and spaces.[41]

In an attempt to mobilize white opposition to the civil rights movement, law-and-order rhetoric was invoked in the late 1950s.[42] Tension between minority communities and the police continued to rise during the 1960s and 1970s, and repeated incidents of police brutality and racial bias ultimately triggered "race riots" in cities across America, including New York, Newark, Detroit, and Los Angeles. Racial resentment, coupled with the growing opposition to the Vietnam War and an increase in crime rates in the 1960s, brought to the surface a crisis of confidence in American policing.[43] Politicians capitalized on racialized fears of urban street crime, mobilizing support for the War on Crime and the War on Drugs. Sweeping criminal justice reform, from the streets to the courtrooms, brought zero-tolerance policing and harsher sentencing laws, and politicians vied to be the "toughest" on crime.[44] The 1990s proved a pivotal decade, with the passage of the Violent Crime and Law Enforcement Act of 1994—the largest crime bill in the history of the country—which provided funding for 100,000 new police officers, $9.7 billion for prisons, and $6.1 billion for crime prevention programs.[45] Law enforcement tactics pioneered in this era were later demonstrated to disproportionately target poor minority individuals and poor minority neighborhoods through stop-and-frisk and broken windows policing. These approaches were heralded by law enforcement as key contributors to the decline in crime in the 1990s, [46] though scholars have subsequently called the role of policing into question and attributed the drops to a wide range of other factors.

Ethnographic accounts of policing in the 20th century shed light on a persistent paradox—throughout history, minority communities have been simultaneously overpoliced and underserved. The sociologists Elijah Anderson[47] and Terry Williams,[48] for example, describe crime in the ghetto as largely ignored by law enforcement, while others[49] describe frequent raids and aggressive policing tactics deployed against poor and minority neighborhoods. Even now, well into the 21st century and despite facially race-neutral policies and reductions in intentional racial animus, the police continue to mete out differential treatment to people and communities of color.[50] Structural inequalities and implicit biases are entrenched and enduring. Consider that research has shown, time and again, that, relative to their proportions of the population, racial and ethnic minority groups are stopped by law enforcement more often than whites.[51] When they are stopped, racial minorities are questioned, handcuffed, and searched at higher rates than whites, but are less likely to be arrested.[52] Unsurprisingly, Black and Latino residents are more likely to perceive stops as unfair and report higher rates of distrust of the police.[53] Critically, not only does the racial gap in policing persist, but it is also widening.[54]

The most brutal form of police contact—killing—is also disproportionately distributed. Young men of color—especially Black men—are significantly more likely to be shot by the police than whites.[55] This grim reality has given rise to nationwide protests, the Black Lives Matter movement, and data activism (or "statactivism"). Statactivists count police-involved deaths, build databases, and mobilize statistics to build the case that racism is part and parcel of American policing.[56] In response to the lack of a federal database of shootings committed by law enforcement, for instance, statactivists in organizations such as Fatal Encounters, Killed by Police, and Mapping Police Violence, alongside the *Washington Post* Fatal Force project and *The Guardian*'s The Counted, have created and maintain databases of police-involved deaths. Transforming deaths to data creates what the science and technology studies scholar Bruno Latour calls "immutable mobiles," "objects which have the properties of being mobile but also immutable, presentable, readable, and combinable with one another."[57]

The solution proffered in response to so many of the problems of race and policing is "more data." Humans are subjective and biased, the reasoning goes, but data are objective and unbiased. Data carries promises of "mechanical objectivity"[58]: in contrast to an individual's personal account of an emotionally fraught event such as a police-involved shooting, data are ostensibly stripped of subjective interpretation, and presented as objective measures. Again, we run up against the stark fact that data are, no matter how they are presented, social products of social contexts.

Thus, there is reason to be wary when data-driven policing is offered as *the* antidote to racially discriminatory practices in police departments across the country. For example, as mentioned in the Introduction, in 2015 the White House launched the Police Data Initiative, which mobilized 21 jurisdictions across the country to use data and technology to respond to the challenges, ranging from trust and legitimacy to crime reduction, outlined by the President's Task Force on 21st Century Policing.[59] However, big data itself is not immune to direct action or social movements. Community activist groups such as the Stop LAPD Spying Coalition have mobilized *against* predictive policing, claiming that "[w]ith the move toward pre-emptive policing, domestic law enforcement is criminalizing people and communities for behaviors that law enforcement claim are precursors to a criminal or terrorist activity,"[60] and in May 2018 they successfully demanded the LAPD's Office of the Inspector General (OIG) audit the department's predictive policing programs.[61]

Data Use in the Los Angeles Police Department

As one of the largest and most technologically advanced departments in the country, the LAPD is a department on the forefront of data analytics. But the reasons it became a front-runner in data-driven policing go beyond the department's size and budget. The first reason relates to external pressures for transparency and accountability. To say the 1990s was a rocky decade for the LAPD would be an understatement. The department was embroiled in a number of high-profile scandals throughout the decade, starting with the Rodney King beating and ending with a federal consent decree.

Early on March 3, 1991, LAPD officers pulled over Rodney King, an unarmed Black motorist, for speeding. Officers ordered King and his friends to exit the vehicle and ultimately kicked and clubbed King 56 times, causing 11 skull fractures and a broken ankle. A 31-year-old plumber named George Holliday used a hand-held video camera to record the incident from his balcony and passed his tape to a local news station. The release of 81 seconds of video unleashed deep, long-simmering public resentments about the way the LAPD's officers treated the public, particularly when the public happened to be Black. When the officers involved in King's beating were found not guilty on criminal charges the following year,[62] the city erupted with massive riots. The rage poured out, and the riots went on for six days. All told, there were 63 deaths, 2,383 injuries, 7,000 fires, and almost a billion dollars in financial losses.

The next high-profile scandal involved the revelation of widespread corruption in Rampart Division's special operations anti-gang unit, C.R.A.S.H. (Community Resources Against Street Hoodlums). The Rampart Scandal— as it came to be known—and subsequent investigation revealed an expansive web of corruption and civil rights violations within the department. The misconduct ranged from unprovoked shootings and beatings to planting false evidence, stealing and dealing narcotics, bank robbery, perjury, and covering up evidence. In all, more than 25 officers were investigated or charged, and over 100 criminal convictions were overturned due to police misconduct.

Amid the discovery and disclosure of the corruption, training deficiencies, and civil rights violations, the Department of Justice imposed a consent decree on the LAPD from 2001 to 2013[63]. The consent decree, a binding court order that ends a civil litigation or accompanies the withdrawal of a criminal charge, came in response to a pattern of "excessive force, false arrests, and unreasonable searches and seizures."[64] It mandated, among other things, the creation and oversight of a new data-driven employee risk management system called TEAMS II, new field data capture systems, the creation of new databases, training reform, and the implementation of department-wide audits. An employee in risk management explained the legacy of the decree to me in simple terms: "We got sued. And so [now] we collect all this information on our employees to try to figure out if they're on the threshold of essentially becoming a risk to themselves and to the system at large." The new employee risk management system was a means not only to increase accountability at the organizational level, but also to predict risk at the individual level. For example, it should flag individual officers who engage in actions, like legally contestable stops or too many pursuits, that put the department at risk. Importantly, the legacy of the decree extends beyond employee risk management; it is also associated broadly with more information sharing, risk prediction, and data-driven decision-making across the organization.

The second factor contributing to the LAPD's use of data is the influence of state legislative decisions concerning offender management. In the wake of *Brown v. Plata*—a 2011 US Supreme Court decision stating that the overcrowding of California prisons and consequent lack of access to adequate healthcare violated the Eight Amendment—and the associated order to dramatically reduce the state's prison population, the California Legislature passed AB 109. This bill shifted the responsibility for supervision of released "non-non-nons" (nonviolent, nonserious, nonsexual offenders) from state to local law enforcement agencies and county probation officers. The "prison realignment legislation" also outsourced compliance checks to local law enforcement agencies, including the LAPD and LA County Sheriff's Department (LASD). As a result, local law enforcement agencies were responsible for approximately 500 additional individuals released into LA County each month.

The LAPD did not have the time or manpower to go knocking on every parolee's door. They needed a way to efficiently stratify the post-release community supervision population according to risk, so that they could better focus their limited resources. That meant new data integration challenges between state, county, and local agencies. For example, one crime analyst from the LASD recalled that some members of the supervised population were getting searched up to three times a day. Unbeknownst to one another, probation officers would go to conduct a search at a residence, only to have Los Angeles Interagency Metropolitan Police Apprehension Crime Team (LA IMPACT) officers come to conduct a search, only to have the LASD arrive to conduct a third search. Clearly, previously disparate information on the parolee population needed to be integrated. The LAPD, along with county and state agencies, pursued interagency data-sharing and risk-modeling initiatives across the region.

The third relevant factor contributing to the state of the LAPD's data analytics is the availability and adoption of new data integration technologies. In 2011 the LAPD began using a platform designed by Palantir Technologies, the CIA-financed surveillance software company introduced in the Introduction of this book. I first became familiar with Palantir through surveillance industry conferences. The Joint Regional Intelligence Center, or JRIC (the fusion center in Southern California), started using it in 2009, and the LAPD followed shortly after.

With some "arm twisting" from their contacts in Homeland Security, an interviewee at LASD explained, Palantir became the first company to gain direct access to LAPD data. The LAPD holds regular training sessions, and more divisions sign on to use the program every year. There are at more than 1,300 trained Palantir users in Southern California, owing partially to Palantir winning the Request for Proposals to implement AB 109 statewide in 2014. Expressing his faith in the platform, one of the first LAPD captains to use Palantir in his division told me, "We've dumped hundreds of thousands into that [Palantir]. They are so responsive and flexible about what we want. They're great. They're gonna take over the world." He paused and reiterated, "I promise you, they're gonna take over the world."

Before Palantir, officers and analysts conducted mostly one-off searches in "siloed" systems: one to look up a rap sheet, another to search a license plate, another to pull up field interview (FI) cards, and more still to search for traffic citations, access the gang system, view the AB 109 data, and so on. The Palantir platform helps overcome this fragmentation by integrating previously disparate data sources into a single search. A query takes mere seconds. As the captain explained, before Palantir, his data were "a mile wide but only an inch deep." Now, in Palantir's terminology, he can "drill down" much deeper on any one individual, address, car, or entity by accessing more data points collected from more disparate sources, all searchable in relation to one another. Seeing the data all together is its own kind of data.

So, specifically, what kinds of data are available?

The first thing to understand is that there is no *one* data source or analytic platform used by everyone within the LAPD. There is a patchwork of legacy systems, each brought on at different times, used by different people in different divisions, and often unable to operate in tandem or communicate from one platform to another. Further, despite my best efforts, I learned it was impossible to get a list of all of the different data sources—let alone who has access to each—because usage varies widely by role and division and there are formal and informal access controls, which means that not everyone in a given department has the same permissions to access every data source or analytic platform. This unevenness of knowledge and access first became evident during a conversation with an officer as I waited for my ride-along at a station. He was sitting at a computer, skimming his mouse over a Palantir mousepad. I asked him what he thought of Palantir and he looked up from the computer and replied, without irony, "never heard of it."

In the interest of providing a working inventory that can be built upon and cross-checked in future research and practice, I offer a list of databases, platforms, and sensors I encountered through the course of my fieldwork between 2013 and 2018 in Appendix D. Although the list is incomplete and data sources are constantly changing, this list gives readers an idea of the scope of the data sources, analytic platforms, and sensors at the LAPD's fingertips. Some of the databases are only available at police stations or at information hubs, such as the Real-Time Crime Analysis Center (RACR) or the fusion center (JRIC), while others can be searched remotely, using in-car laptops.

Although the vast array of data at the LAPD's fingertips is impressive, data use and integration are nowhere near seamless. Anyone who studies technological change in organizations could predict as much.[65] Adjacent counties use different geocodes, different criminal justice agencies use different individual identifiers, and there are hundreds if not thousands of individuals across agencies, toiling away, trying through their invisible labor to make systems interoperable. As they work, new systems and new versions of old systems are brought online. New people are trained to input data. New demands for outputs arise, and the data are shuffled in different ways. It's a persistent paradox of data analytics: the scope of data collected is broader and the analytics more complex than you could ever imagine, yet, no matter what, some data remain fragmented.

And lest we forget, data has errors, individuals use technology incorrectly, and institutional barriers to integration are just as prevalent as technical barriers. One person in the Robbery-Homicide Division described it as "very fragmented" and said "one of the big ongoing problems" with Palantir and other systems used for data-sharing is that, "each agency you go to. . . . Everybody's got their own ideas for what they're wanting to do and what serves their mission." He listed the FBI, the Secret Service, and the federal Marshals before adding, "And it's the same with local law enforcement as well." Another respondent, a civilian employee of the LAPD, said similarly,

> Law enforcement is very personality driven. So, people want their own signature. They want their own brand, in which "Bratton" is sort of like a brand name in terms of law enforcement. So, people will want their own signature or style, like [Sheriff Joe] Arpaio over in Arizona.[66]

The result of this piecemeal approach is considerable variation and unevenness in data coverage across even the divisions of this one organization, the LAPD. Data make certain policing tasks more efficient, but they're also an incredible source of frustration. One respondent in Information Technology Division described a data system that seemed awkwardly tacked onto another: "There is the current detective case management system, which is sort of like a pimple. . . It's a mess. It's terrible. It's like, 'Oh, we need a case management system,' and they just, like, stuck it on the top."

Complaining about the case management system, a frustrated detective in the Juvenile Division gestured emphatically, saying, "I want one special fucking unit that I can call and say 'This is what I've got, this is what I've done, what can you direct or guide me to?' I want a unit of experts to turn to!" Over and over, the people inside the LAPD sounded just like anyone who has ever furiously pressed "o" in an attempt to override an automated customer service menu and get a real person on the line. They lamented instances where they felt parts of their work were replaced by technical systems—and even worse, technical systems that didn't work very well, and certainly didn't play well with other platforms.

———————

Just like other organizations, the LAPD's decisions about which technologies to adopt, which data to collect in-house, and which data to purchase from external vendors are not made in a vacuum. Rather, they are shaped by political, economic, and social factors, and by an organizational context rife with power politics. Its nearly innumerable stakeholders include county, state, and federal law enforcement; the military; technology companies; and third-party data brokers. As the science and technology scholar Rob Kling argues, ideologies, developed through interaction in broader organizational fields, play a crucial role in mobilizing support for specific new technologies.[67]

Indeed, big data has become more than just an amount or type of data—it is a rhetoric, a mantra, and an ideology that has come to dominate discourse in a wide range of institutions.

Along with ideology, funding shapes law enforcement's adoption of new data sources and technologies. The LAPD spends hundreds of thousands of dollars on grant writers and criminal justice consultants. That spending often pays off—many of the new data-driven initiatives the LAPD is undertaking are funded by federal grants, including the Smart Policing Initiative, which is the primary funder of Operation LASER, one of the LAPD's most controversial predictive policing programs, which is discussed in detail in Chapter 4. Once the department secures federal funding, the funds becomes subsumed into the operating budget. And the department has a vested interest in maintaining that cash flow, regardless of whether the originally funded technology is effective. It's a process one officer described as the "budgetization of grants," and it's just one way that funding affects data in policing.

Although federal grants make many of the data-intensive initiatives possible, overreliance on grants may exacerbate the fragmentation of legacy systems. As one administrator from the Records and Identification Division explained, "We could get grant funding for one cool project integrating some data, but then the money's up and we can't maintain it, so it goes away."

Meanwhile, as the feds increasingly embrace big data surveillance tactics, policing is not merely a local issue, but a national one. In his 2018 remarks at the Project for Safe Neighborhoods National Conference, Deputy US Attorney General Rod Rosenstein referenced Operation LASER: "We also support 'predictive policing,' which involves analyzing data so police can anticipate crime and preempt it. We need to send police to disrupt criminal activity in response to data analysis, instead of just dealing with the consequences after crimes occur."[68]

Tracing the role of data throughout the history of policing sheds fresh light on the foundations of the data-intensive policing we experience today. The taken-for-granted narrative around big data suggests that it is new, transformational, and disruptive, as well as objective and unbiased. Contrary to narratives coming out of the tech industry that data and advanced analytics are disruptive and reshaping our world as we know it, data is better understood as a form of capital—a resource with shifting utility over time. From pin maps to predictive algorithms, the police have been using data in their daily operations for the better part of a century. That said, this is an important historical moment to analyze the data involved in predictive policing and other government initiatives. An unprecedented reliance on private sector data collection, storage, and analysis brings threats to transparency, and the mass digitization of information makes it possible to share data beyond the policing context—for example, with Immigration and Customs Enforcement (ICE). Whereas the police themselves used to be the primary collectors of the data they use, it is ordinary people going about their daily routines and leaving digital traces in a wide range of non–law enforcement institutions that now populate law enforcement databases.

CHAPTER 3 | Dragnet Surveillance
Our Incriminating Lives

You just need to give me enough data to catch the bad guy. That's all I need.

—Crime Analyst

THE LAPD'S REAL-TIME CRIME Analysis Center (RACR) is a hulking, institutional-gray building about a mile north of downtown. Its only marking is its address: 500. I had an early morning meeting scheduled, and so I walked up to the security gate, pressed the buzzer, and announced myself. The gate swung open. In the lobby, I identified myself again at reception, declining a donut the guard offered from a box on his desk. About 20 minutes later, Mary—the civilian employee who had helped schedule my meetings for the day—ushered me inside. We strode past dozens of nondescript cubicles, and I spotted a whiteboard listing today's date, the total number of homicides last year, this year's homicide YTD (year-to-date), last year's YTD, and the percent decrease since last year.

Mary handed me off to Doug, a "forward-deployed" Palantir engineer who waited for me in a training room. Palantir's clients need training in order to learn how to use the platform, and they need a point-person to answer their questions and challenges, and that's where engineers like Doug come in. He logged in to Palantir Gotham, the company's government intelligence platform, and pulled up the home page (Figure 3.1). For him, it was a banal moment, but I'd been eagerly anticipating this sight: there is virtually no public research available on Palantir, and media portrayals are frustratingly vague.

As Doug listed agencies using Palantir, he started running through some of the different ways the platform could be used. He patiently explained what he was doing as he queried, clicked, zoomed, narrowed, and filtered:

FIGURE 3.1 Palantir homepage
SOURCE: LAPD

So now, imagine a robbery detective who says, "Hey, you know what, I have a male, average build, black 4-door sedan." Like, they would [previously be able to] do nothing with that, right? So, we can do that.

Let's go take a look at vehicles that are in the system. Here is vehicles. So, I change my focus to vehicles. . . . Now, we're going to go look at color. . . . There are 140 million records in this system . . . we know it's a Toyota, maybe a Hyundai, right? Or a Lexus. . . . So let's say we think it's one of those types of vehicles, right? And that got us then to 2 million [vehicles]. And if we were to go look at, say, a color. We are going to lose about 100,000 records just by choosing a color immediately, just because certain records just don't have that information. And so, we know it was black. Maybe it was blue, 'cause it could have been blue. It could be dark green. . . . And we know it was a 4-door.

Do you see what's happening over here? In five hops, they're able to get down to 160,000. Now they're still not going to look at 160,000 vehicles. We didn't get into model and year, but we could do that, and we could chart it, which makes it easy. Now this is just one of the cool advantages of "object explorer" and being able to look at all your data. . . . So now I could say, I think it was between 2002 to 2005, drill down, now we're 23,000. Now it gets pretty manageable.

So now let's flip over and let's look at the people that are connected to these vehicles. And I know I'm looking for a male. And I'll just do one of them.

And I know that like let's say he was pretty short. And he was on the heavier side. Brick house. We just got down to 13 objects, 13 people. And you could say, "Okay, well, now let me take a look at—all 13 have driver's license numbers." So now we've narrowed it down to 13 potential people and they could take these 13 objects and go to the DMV and pull their DMV photos and go to the witness or victim and say, "Here you go."

In less than a minute, using partial information, Doug was able to narrow a search from 140,000,000 records to 13. He went on to show me how to look up which of the 13 had any citations or arrests, the divisions in which they received their citations or were arrested, and identify one person who had been cited in the same division in which the robbery occurred. If the person ended up not being the person who committed the robbery, officers could simply save this search formula and keep running it in the coming days, just in case any new data came in. I asked what happens when the system gives a false positive. What happens to the wrong suspect? Doug said bluntly, "I don't know."

In the introduction, I asked you to consider all the digital traces you leave as you move through the world in the course of your everyday life. Rapidly proliferating automatic data collection sensors record and save those digital traces, and make *dragnet surveillance*, or, the collection and analysis of information on everyone, rather than only people under suspicion, possible at an unprecedented scale. Dragnet data collection and analysis results in surveillance that is both wider *and* deeper. It includes a broader swath of people and can follow any single individual across a greater range of institutional settings. Technologically mediated dragnet surveillance shifts the surveillance ratio from 1:1 to 1:many and is increasingly suspicionless, programmatic, ongoing, cumulative, remote, invisible, automated, preemptive, and embedded into routine activity.[1]

In this chapter we will consider what dragnet surveillance looks like on the ground. Digitized policing is different from traditional policing methods in a number of ways: the proliferation of automatic alert systems and shifts from query-based to alert-based systems makes it possible to systematically surveil ever larger groups of people; individuals with no direct police contact are now included in law enforcement systems, effectively lowering the threshold for inclusion in police databases; and institutional data systems are integrated, such that police now collect and use information gleaned from institutions that are typically not associated with crime control.

The Power of a Platform

Data—particularly large, diverse sets of data—are relatively useless on their own. You need a good platform. And Palantir is excellent at processing, sorting, and analyzing data. With the right platform, searches that used to take hours, days, or even weeks may now only take a few seconds. Tracking a vehicle that previously required an individual detective physically following a car can be done by simply punching in a license plate and receiving notifications whenever an automatic license plate reader (ALPR) picks it up. Police stops that used to be recorded on paper cards and stored in a filing cabinet are now uploaded and can be integrated into a multimodal network that presents connections individual officers might never have been able to make. Not only is technologically mediated surveillance faster, it appeals to law enforcement because it promises to increase efficiency and save resources. As one detective put it, the kind of query that used to take multiple investigators searching multiple systems for a week can now be conducted almost instantly.

Trevor, a civilian employee working in the Information Technology Division, underscored the transformative role of technology in policing as he made this prediction: "If there is going to be improvements in the next 10 to 15, 20 years, it's going to be probably in computer technology of how it delivers information to the officer and the investigator in order to solve crimes and effect change, right?" Of course, Trevor and others working in information technology have a vested interest in making the case that information technology is a crucial component of law enforcement. But no matter how you quantify it—through increased federal and within-department funding for data-intensive policing, the proliferation of law enforcement contracts with tech companies, the increase in tech training sessions for police, or the rising number of data points the police access daily—data analytics *are* central to law enforcement operations today. Of course, as a sergeant noted, "information sharing is not a natural act." It requires institutional buy-in, infrastructure, personnel, and trust.

As mentioned in Chapter 2, the Southern California fusion center JRIC started using Palantir in 2009 to connect and analyze Suspicious Activity Reports (SARs). At the time, it was the largest law enforcement deployment of this software anywhere in the world. The LAPD, Long Beach Police Department, and LA City Fire soon adopted the platform, and there were over 1,300 trained Palantir users in the region by 2014. More users are onboarded every month. Sergeant Michaels, who coordinates some of the training sessions at JRIC, claims "they catch bad guys during every training class."

The LAPD's field interview cards and arrests were the first data sources integrated into Palantir. Both are geocoded, meaning you can plot where these police stops and arrests occurred. Because one of Palantir's biggest selling points is the ease with which new, external data sources can be incorporated into the platform, its coverage grows every day. LAPD data, data collected by other government agencies, and external data, including privately collected data accessed through licensing agreements with data brokers, are among at least 19 databases feeding Palantir at JRIC. The data include (but are not limited to) information from field interview cards, the Crime Analysis Mapping System (CAMS), traffic citations, crime alerts (including bulletins from other agencies), automatic license plate readings, the sex offenders registry, Burbank citations, Sheriff's incidents, county jail records (including phone calls, visitor logs, and cell block movements), collisions, warrants, crime stopper tips, California Law Enforcement Telecommunications System (CLETS), and foreclosure data.[2]

Though there was a lot of uncertainty among interviewees about exactly *what* data were in the databases they were accessing, a pair of civilian employees mentioned the use of LexisNexis's public records database Accurint and speculated that it contained documents like utility bills and credit card information. Indeed, LexisNexis has over 84 billion public records from 10,000 diverse data sources, including 330 million unique cell phone numbers, 1.5 billion bankruptcy records, 77 million business contract records, 11.3 billion name and address combinations, 6.6 billion motor vehicle registrations, and 6.5 billion personal property records. As their website states, by accessing this data, a user can:

> Identify relatives, associates and neighbors who may show up in photos or be mentioned in social media postings with a search of hundreds of networks and millions of sites on the open web. Find cell phone data critical to serving a subpoena such as associated addresses, carriers and an exclusive phone detail report with custodial contact information for the carrier. Reconstruct a person's job history with Employment Locator, which provides places of employment as well as contact information for employers.[3]

Palantir sits on top of old legacy systems, meaning it does not own the data the LAPD uses, but rather provides an interface that makes it possible to link data points across previously separate systems. For example, Palantir can transform data inputted as a familiar spreadsheet (with rows and columns) into objects and entities that can be visualized in relation with a single graph. Users can plot data on maps, as a network, as a time wheel, or as a bar graph with a timeline of phone calls and financial transactions, for example.

As discussed in Chapter 2, before Palantir, LAPD officers and analysts used to conduct mostly one-off searches in what respondents described as "siloed" systems: one for rap sheets, another for license plates, field interview cards, traffic citations, gang data, the AB 109 (community supervision) data, and so on. The goal of Palantir, then, is to create a single data environment, or "full data ecosystem," that integrates hundreds of millions of disparate data points into a single access module.

The platform even allows users to give order to structured and unstructured data content such as e-mails, PDFs, and photos through "tagging." The process of labeling and linking objects and entities like persons, phone numbers, and documents such as law enforcement reports, tips and leads, and calls for service also makes it possible to plot data on maps and graphs on which users can see data in context and make new connections. It can also make it easier to see what crucial data might be missing or what sorts of data might be useful for law enforcement to begin collecting. Whereas one piece of information may not be a useful source of intelligence on its own, Doug explained, the "sum of all information can build out what is needed."

Running Queries across Datasets

Most staffers who use Palantir Gotham use it for simple queries (what Palantir calls "drilling down using 'object explorer'"). Users can search for anything from license plates to phone numbers to demographic characteristics, and a vast web of information will be returned. One officer described the process:

> You could run an address in Palantir, and it's going to give you all the events that took place at that address and everyone who's associated to those events. . . . So if it's a knucklehead location where a lot of things are happening there, you're gonna get people documented on there one way or the other. . . . Either field interview cards, or they're on crime reports, whatever. . . . Otherwise you could search all of records within [LexisNexis's] Accurint. . . . and see who's living with who a lot of times.

It's not quite so simple as run a query, get a list of suspects. Doug might have made this look too easy, or too automatic. Notice, for example, how the officer says "knucklehead location"—he means that you can query an address, and if it's been listed as the address for many people or their car registrations, if it's been the site of multiple calls for service, or it's otherwise connected across the databases, a Palantir Gotham search is going to return a tangle of information. Some of it will be useful, some of it won't, but the presumption is that if criminal activity is going on at a location, *someone* or *something* will be in Palantir.

Another employee at Palantir demonstrated its use for retroactive investigative purposes: Law enforcement had a name of someone they thought was involved in trafficking. They ran a property search, which yielded the person of interest's address and date of birth. Then they ran a search for common addresses (whether there are any other people in the system associated with the same address). One turned out to be a sibling of the initial person of interest, which sent investigators searching again, this time coming up with a police report for operating a vehicle without a license. They also searched the address of a third sibling, who lived at a different address. A radius search revealed several tips concerning this same house: one neighbor had called in to report a loud argument, and another that a suspicious number of cars was stopping at the house. With this information, the police were able to set up in-person surveillance and subpoena phone records, which were run through Palantir's "time wheel" function to identify temporal patterns. Modeling revealed phone calls to one or two phone numbers at the same time each week; using those phone numbers, police got a new database hit. They found a name, a police report, and identified their suspect.

In another instance, I saw a user search for a car using just a partial license plate. They entered "67" and accessed all of the crime reports, traffic citations, FIs (field interview cards), ALPRs (automatic license plate readings), names, addresses, and border crossings associated with cars whose license plate contained these numbers in this order. An engineer demonstrated a search based on characteristics drawn from a suspect description:

> We can do things like . . . see if there's any people out there that . . . are male whites that have "November" somewhere in their record that's from an incident, a citation, an FI, that has "Snoopy" and the word "arm" next to each other, and see if that comes up [referring to a Snoopy tattoo on a suspect's arm]. It'll take a second. [Profile of an individual comes up]. So yeah, Arm. Snoopy. All this other stuff.

By structuring previously unstructured data through tagging and generating links among previously disparate data points, entirely novel searches can be performed. Snoopy and arm? This isn't the kind of thing a beat cop in the 1980s could make much use of, other than maybe checking out the tattoos collected on folks in their lockup. As Doug explained,

> It's about big data in that you want to quickly build up this profile, or the offender profile, or consolidate all the information you can real quickly about a person or about things like that . . . and figure out how do we make your decision based off of that information.

Now, for example, if the individual with the Snoopy tattoo gave a home address that was included on an FI, and if this address could be linked with calls for service and DMV data, it is possible that a Palantir user could link residential and vehicular data for all people associated with that address.

Advanced analytic tools on the platform include geo-, temporal, and topical analysis, each of which can be visualized differently. For example, users can plot (geo-analysis) all the types of crime they are interested in (topical analysis) in a given period of time (temporal analysis). Users can visualize the data on a map or along a chronological axis, as well as conduct secondary and tertiary analyses in which they analyze the results by, for example, modus operandi (e.g., using a bolt cutter) or proximity of robberies to a parolee's residence.

Another way to use the analytic suite is to paint a detailed picture of the population of interest in an area. One officer explained this:

> The big thing that Palantir offers is a mapping system. So, you could draw out a section of [his division] and say, "Okay, give me the parolees that live in this area that are known for stealing cars" or whatever [is] your problem. . . . It's going to map out that information for you . . . give you their employment data, what their conditions are, who they're staying with, photos of their tattoos, and, of course, their mug shot. [And it will show] if that report has [a] sex offender or has a violent crime offender or has a gang offender. Some are in GPS, so they have the ankle bracelet, and . . . we have a separate GPS tracker for that.

Associations among suspects are revealed in new ways via Palantir, too. Should officers suspect that a person of interest is co-offending, or committing crimes with other people, Palantir Gotham's link analysis system will be useful. A detective in Robbery-Homicide Division told me about this:

> Yeah, so, for example, I could run an individual today. And let's just say that that person comes up . . . ten times: three or four field interviews, couple arrests,

maybe two or three calls for service. When you run that name, all of that information will pop up, but it pops up in a visual manner. So, for example, you run my name now you see . . . that my name comes up ten times . . . it pulls up events that I might have been involved in, like a crime. And then when you take that crime and you expand out and you search the details of that crime, then you can see the other individuals that are associated with that crime. So now . . . you can start to build up a sense of whether or not you have this individual that has worked with other individuals in the past. And maybe there's a vehicle involved, you know, maybe the person that you just pulled up isn't your suspect per se, but maybe you see that that person was involved in another crime with another individual and that individual is associated with the vehicle.

Manuel, a civilian employee in Information Technology Division summed it up, saying that cops now "have better access into information that was always out there, but it was just hard to get to. And now when you can see that in context to our data, it just creates a better picture."

Shift from Query-Based to Alert-Based Systems

One of the most substantively important shifts that have accompanied the rise of big data policing is the shift from query-based systems to alert-based systems. By "query-based systems," I mean those databases that operate in response to a user query, such as when an officer runs your license plate during a traffic stop. In alert-based systems, by contrast, users receive real-time notifications when certain variables or configurations of variables become present in the data. High-frequency data collection makes alert-based systems possible, and that carries enormous implications for the relational structure of surveillance.

Imagine an officer wants to know about any warrants issued for residents of a specific neighborhood. In a query-based system, they would need to set up specific searches, and most of those would only be useful well after the warrant had been issued. There are 1.8 million warrants in LA County. All of those warrants are geocoded and can be translated into object representations spatially, temporally, and topically in Palantir. Through tagging, users can add every known association of a warrant to people, vehicles, addresses, phone numbers, documents, incidents, citations, calls for service, ALPR readings, FIs, and the like. All that information is cross-referenced in Palantir. Then, using a mechanism in Palantir that's similar to an RSS feed, an officer can set up automatic notifications for warrants or events involving specific individuals (or even descriptions of individuals), addresses, or cars to their cell phone.

For example, an alert can be set up by putting a geofence around a given area and requesting an alert every time a new warrant is issued within that perimeter. One sergeant had an e-mail alert set up in this way, and could even get the alert while he was out on patrol. "Court-issued warrant, ding!" As soon as he got the notification, he says, he was able to track down and arrest the suspect. Previously, the process was far slower. "Now," he explained excitedly, "you draw a box in Palantir and go about your business. Ding!"

A civilian employee echoed the officer's comment, describing the utility of ALPR alerts: "If you have an automated license reader, you can flag a plate or a partial plate and you could attach it to your e-mail. And if it ever comes up it will send you an e-mail saying, 'Hey, this partial plate or this vehicle, there was a hit last night. Here is the information.'" Real-time location was once only possible if law enforcement was conducting 1:1 surveillance, received a tip, or encountered a person of interest in the course of their work. Now they can access license plate reader data remotely and immediately. A software engineer spoke of the gang unit monitoring entire networks of people: "Huge, huge network. They're going to maintain this whole entire network and all the information about it within Palantir, as they're also working up each individual person that is of interest."

Relatedly, real-time notifications can be useful in operational planning. One sergeant described preparing to search a house suspected as a card mill (a place where fake credit cards are produced). Conventionally, an officer in his position would "run the guy, work up the house, see there's a gun registered, see he's a gangster, and that there was a call for service." Then he'd park his car three doors down, set up a few more cars to secure the perimeter in case someone runs out, and hope for the best. With Palantir, he can gather intel about all the surrounding houses, as well: he can draw a geofence to get all geocoded data points inside that radius, including calls for service, police reports, FIs, SCARs (suspected child abuse reports), warrants, and ALPRs. He could see that the house he was going to park in front of actually was linked to a warrant for assault with a deadly weapon, tipping the officer off that, if that resident saw the car, "they might go out and shoot you." So Palantir, he explained, is an "operational game changer," giving him the data he needs to protect his officers' safety by, for instance, locking down a neighborhood and positioning an airship overhead while law enforcement conducts that search. Of course, this situational awareness made possible by Palantir can, in addition to protecting officers, ratchet up their sense of danger and escalate an already tense situation. Such platforms provide an unprecedented number of data points supporting the "danger imperative," or the cultural frame officers are socialized into in which they may face lethal violence at a moment's notice.[4]

Alerts can also be used to break down information silos within the department. LAPD's jurisdiction is almost 500 square miles. A captain pointed out that it is difficult for individual detectives to spot series of crimes that span division lines:

> Let's say I have something going on with the medical marijuana clinics where they're getting robbed. Okay? And it happens all over, right? But I'm a detective here in [division], I can put in an alert to Palantir that says anything that has to do with medical marijuana plus robbery plus male, Black, six foot.

He continued, "I like throwing the net out there, you know? Throw it out there, let [the database] work on it while you're doing your other stuff, you know?" An interviewee in Robbery-Homicide gave a similar example:

> Another nice component of Palantir is that you can set up a search feed so that when, you know, if there are any particular sexual assaults or kidnappings in a particular area, I can set up a search feed so that it will search for this kidnapping, this type of assault in this particular area with this particular type of crime. And it's just running behind the scenes.

Palantir's isn't the only platform that can shift law enforcement from query-only to alert-based data-intensive policing. A crime intelligence analyst described a pilot project taking place in the FBI's ViCAP (Violent Criminal Apprehension Program) Web. Automated data grazing was being used to flag potential crime series across jurisdictional boundaries, he said. "You could get an alert that would say, you know what, your case is pretty similar to this case over in Miami." If the case reaches a merit score—a threshold at which a certain configuration of variables is present—the system flags the cases as similar. The system matches on fields such as suspect description, license plate, type of weapon, cause of death, motive, type of crime, narcotics- or gang-related crimes, the presence of a sexual assault or robbery, whether it's a domestic, and MO: "What kind of bindings were used . . . or was there torture involved? What type of trauma has occurred? Was there, you know, was there some type of symbolic activity?" Importantly, although the matching process is automated, the choice of which parameters the system uses for matching is left to ViCAP agents' discretion.

Taken together, the use of alerts represents not just a scaling up of existing police practices, but also a fundamental transformation in how patrol officers and investigators generate case knowledge. Under the traditional surveillance model, alerts about incidents and suspects are sent out from dispatch centers. However, as alerts are becoming automated, there is a decrease in human intermediation in broadcasting out these real-time alerts or conducting data grazing.

It is important to note that alert-based systems are supplementing, rather than replacing, query-based systems. Searches are still critical features of law enforcement information systems. In fact, one of the transformative features of big data systems is that *queries themselves are becoming data*. A Robbery-Homicide informant made this observation:

> I queried the system a certain way and then another person queried the system a certain way . . . we were looking for something very similar in our query, and so even though the data may not have connected the two, the queries were similar. Yeah, so then [the database] will be able to say "Hey, listen, there's an analyst in San Francisco PD that ran a very similar query as to yours," and so you guys might be looking for the same thing.

A detective in Juvenile Division noted that if he searched for the name of a person of interest in one national database, he could see how many times that name had been queried by other users. I wondered aloud why that information would be useful. "If you aren't doing anything wrong," he said, the cops are not going to be looking you up very many times over the course of your life. In other words, in auditable big data systems, queries are serving as quantified proxies for suspiciousness. He launched into an anecdote: A child was missing, and a suspect was starting to emerge from the neighborhood. The child had been over at the suspect's house, but, at face value, the "guy is as clean as a Safeway chicken. Suit and tie. Has a decent job." Yet this detective noticed that someone had run the man's name through NCIC (the National Crime Information Center) before. The suspect didn't have a criminal record, but the detective concluded, "Just because you haven't been arrested doesn't mean you haven't been caught."

The idea that the cops won't be looking you up unless you've done something illegal flies in the face of scores of empirical research studies that have demonstrated racial disparities in "hit rates," or the probability that being stopped by the police will lead to an arrest. For instance, the police are more likely to stop Blacks and Hispanics than whites, but when whites *are* stopped, they are less likely than minorities to be released without charge.[5]

Put another way, a higher proportion of whites who are stopped are arrested, suggesting police stops of racial minorities are more indiscriminate. It's easy to invalidate the statement that if you aren't doing anything wrong, the cops won't be looking you up in a database or stopping you on the street. Further, over time, criminal conduct and criminal justice contact have become relatively uncoupled: the relationship between committing crimes and being arrested for committing crimes has become weaker. This is especially true for Black people, who are increasingly likely to be arrested (and by extension, have the cops looking them up) without committing any crime.[6] So big data doesn't directly exacerbate racial inequality, but the *assumptions* around what big data can tell you—such as query counts—may do so by quantifying and reifying incorrect assumptions about policing, race, and crime.

No Police Contact Needed: Lower Database Inclusion Thresholds

Law enforcement databases have long recorded who has been arrested or convicted of crimes. Today, they also include information on people who have been stopped, as evidenced by the proliferation of stop-and-frisk databases. The real surprise may be that as new data sensors and analytic platforms are incorporated into law enforcement operations, the police increasingly utilize data on individuals who have not had any police contact at all.

The automatic license plate reader (ALPR) is perhaps the clearest example of a low-threshold "trigger mechanism,"[7] lowering the bar for criteria that justifies inclusion in databases. ALPRs are quintessential dragnet surveillance tools—they take readings on everyone, not just people under suspicion. Their data comes in the form of two photos—one of the license plate and one of the car, along with the time, date, and geo-coordinates attached to those photos, as read by ALPR cameras mounted on the tops of police cars and static cameras at intersections and other locations (see Figure 3.2).

Law enforcement–collected ALPR data can be supplemented with privately collected ALPRs, such as those used by repossession agents.

Just this one, relatively simple technological tool makes everyday mass surveillance possible on an almost unimaginable scale. The data produced by ALPRs give the LAPD a map of the distribution of vehicles throughout the city, and in some cases it may enable law enforcement to learn a given driver's typical travel patterns. For example, an analyst used ALPR data to see that a person of interest frequently parked near a specific intersection at night, and deduced that this intersection was likely near the suspect's residence or "honeycomb" (hideout). A captain reminded me that even a partial

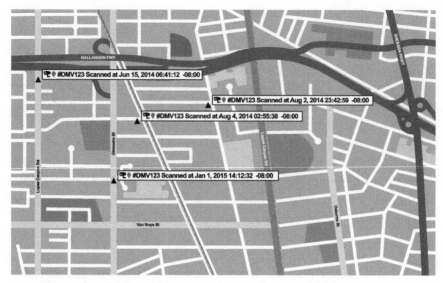

FIGURE 3.2 Plotted Automatic License Plate Reader (ALPR) readings
SOURCE: Palantir Technologies; map by David Hallangen

license place could help suss out a person's normal routes. An officer in South Bureau shared that he had used ALPR data on a car that he identified as "probably" a suspect's vehicle and

> saw this pattern that they have a lot of photographs [of the car] on Avalon Boulevard, and we pretty much established that they're hanging down in these projects, the Southeast Division. . . . So our detectives . . . what corridor are they gonna take? Avalon, because that's showing where a lot of the [ALPR] hits are. So, they're driving south to do some surveillance in this area, they see these guys going northbound on Avalon. So, our detectives make a U-turn, follow them, and videotape them conducting another robbery. And they take 'em down. Yeah.

There are several other ways law enforcement can use ALPR data. One is to compare them against "heat lists" of outstanding warrants or stolen cars. Another is to place a geofence around a location of interest in order to track cars near the location. For example, after a series of copper wire thefts in the city, the police found the car involved by conducting a "radius search" in Palantir to isolate the three geographic locations from which wire was stolen, setting up time bounds around the time they knew the thefts occurred at each site, and querying the system for any license plates captured by ALPRs in all three locations during those time periods. One captain explained,

"They [suspects] are creatures of habit. So, if a car is spotted all over the city, but near copper wire thefts, you have your guy."

However, the most common use of ALPRs is simply to store data for potential use during a future investigation. Recall the body dump described in the introduction to this book, where the ALPRs helped law enforcement track down cars spotted near the scene where the body was left. ALPRs can also be placed at strategic locations like hospitals, as one sergeant told me. He said that there was an emergency room known for "homie drop offs," where family and friends would quickly drop off shooting victims without sticking around for questioning. Previously, he explained, "some minimum wage security guard didn't notice the car make and model, let alone the license plate," but with an ALPR mounted in the ER driveway, police can now look up license plates and start to build out a network of the victim's associates. Clearly, there is investigatory value to this data, but, as will be discussed in more detail in Chapter 6, there is also the potential for a negative unintended consequence: individuals may avoid emergency healthcare because they fear police surveillance for one reason or another.[8]

ALPR coverage is rapidly expanding. There are all kinds of efforts to link ALPR data to data collected by non–criminal justice agencies. For example, a captain explained that he wanted to link ALPRs to data from Automated Traffic Surveillance and Control (ATSAC) cameras, electronic toll pass data, and cameras in pay-parking lots, hospitals, the University of California, Los Angeles, the University of Southern California, and LAX. "If we tied these cameras in for license plates," he explained, "it would dramatically increase the number of reads going into the bucket." Individuals at the Information Technology Bureau seconded the captain's idea, arguing that by merging these external data collection sensors, they would get "millions" more observations.

To be sure, ALPRs are plainly useful. I saw as much in my fieldwork. But I also saw instances when respondents overestimated their utility (and the utility of other technologies). One detective in Juvenile Division was enthusiastic about his use of ALPRs, explaining,

> predators that go to schools. For example, there was a guy in a red Toyota in [area] that kept bothering high school girls. LAPD put undercover female officers that look young, created a geofence around the schools, a bunch of creeps exposed themselves, and [ALPRs] found the same car in all locations.

Yet when I asked, "So you caught the guy?," he paused briefly before admitting that they hadn't. The ALPRs actually picked up six cars that had been to all of the schools, but none of them belonged to the original suspect in the red Toyota.

In addition to ALPRs, there are all sorts of low-threshold trigger mechanisms being leveraged by the LAPD. Much of the data is what's being called "collateral data collection," and it is a passive, pervasive way people are being caught up in the surveillance state. Figure 3.3 is a deidentified notional representation, based on a real network diagram I obtained from the LAPD.

The Carmen Sandiego–looking figure in the middle, "Stephen Thompson," is a person with direct police contact. Radiating outward, we see all the entities he is related to, including people, cars, addresses, and cell phones. Each line indicates the type of connection (e.g., sibling, lover, co-arrestee, vehicle registrant). The data needed to build this chart may be gathered by officers during a call for service or interview and recorded in the open-ended narrative portion of the FI cards, or during a crime scene investigation, and

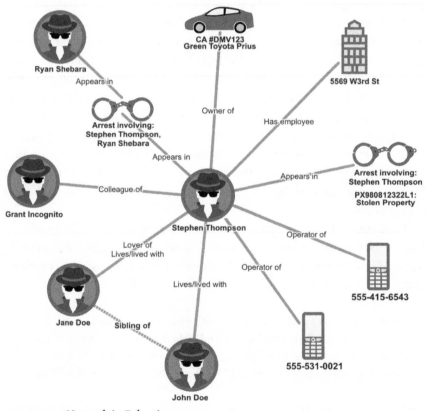

FIGURE 3.3 Network in Palantir
SOURCE: Palantir Technologies; diagram by David Hallangen

subsequently entered into the corresponding system for reporting or record-keeping purposes. To be in what I call the "secondary surveillance network," radiating out from the person of interest, individuals do not need to have direct law enforcement contact; they simply need a connection to the central person of interest. And once they are in this system, these individuals can be "autotracked," meaning officers can receive real-time alerts should they come into contact with the police or other government agencies.

Institutional Data Systems Are Integrated

Finally, the proliferation of digitized records makes it possible to merge data from previously separate institutional sources into an integrated, structural system in which disparate data points are displayed and searchable in relation to one another, and in which individuals can be cross-referenced across databases. This integration facilitates one of the most transformative features of the big data landscape: the creep of criminal justice surveillance into other, non–criminal justice institutions. Function creep—the phenomenon of data originally collected for one purpose being used for another—contributes to a substantial increase in the data used by police. Law enforcement follows an "institutional data imperative,"[9] or a mandate to collect as much data as possible, in part by securing routine access to a wide range of data on everyday activities from nonpolice databases. As we have seen, new data sources are incorporated into Palantir regularly. One captain commented:

> I'm so happy with how big Palantir got. . . . I mean it's just every time I see the entry screen where you log on there's another icon about another database that's been added . . . they now have been working with Palantir to develop a database of all the foreclosure properties . . . they just went out and found some public data on foreclosures, dragged it in, and now they're mapping it where it would be relative to our crime data and stuff.

Another interagency data integration effort is LA County's Enterprise Master Person Index (LA EMPI) initiative. If established, LA EMPI would create a single view of a client across all government systems and agencies: all of an individual's interactions with law enforcement, social services, health services, mental health services, and child and family services, would all be in one place under a single unique ID. After talking about the benefits of information sharing with an employee in the county's Chief Information Office, the conversation shifted to the legal frameworks that have long protected information silos to prevent privacy concerns with sprawling information systems like LA EMPI. Flatly, he told me "consent is anachronistic." Although the explicit motivation behind the EMPI initiative was to improve service delivery, such initiatives effectively serve the latent function of extending the governance and social control capacities of the criminal justice system into other institutions.

I encountered several other examples of law enforcement using external data originally collected for non–criminal justice purposes, including the aforementioned LexisNexis, but also TransUnion's TLOxp (which contains 100 billion public and proprietary data points), databases for repossession and collections agencies; social media, foreclosure, and electronic toll pass data; and address and usage information from utility bills. Respondents added that they were working on integrating hospital, pay-parking lot, and university camera feeds, as well as rebate data, pizza chain customer lists, and so on. One interviewee in the Information Technology Division said they had their eye on consumer data: "Other stuff, shopping data. You can buy it, you know, certainly other vendors are. So why not?" Truly, in some instances, it is simply easier for law enforcement to purchase privately collected data than to rely on in-house data. As mentioned in Chapter 2, there are fewer protections and less oversight over private sector surveillance and data collection.[10] Plus, private data can be more up-to-date than police-generated data.

———

Dragnet surveillance—and the data it produces—can be incredibly useful for law enforcement to solve crimes. As one officer explained, after any crime, "the first thing you're gonna do, always, is check the digital footprint." For many people, this could end up being entirely unproblematic. However, imagine if your locational information was collected at three different times. These data points might tell a different story than you would about why you were in those places at those particular times. Using a series of data points to reconstruct an individual's intentions and behaviors (whether incriminating or exculpatory) rests on the assumption of an infallible state, or the assumption that law enforcement will draw a correct conclusion. And, as the analyst above implied, you are not able to consent—or refuse consent—to the collection of your data at each point. When many streams of information flow together, they form a "data double,"[11] which can be a powerful tool in the hands of law enforcement. As a member of legal counsel at Palantir explained, digital traces can be knit together so that circumstantial evidence looks like a comprehensive picture: there is "usually not one smoking gun document but we're able to build up a sequence of events prosecutors might not previously have been able to do . . . [we can integrate] data in a single ontology to rapidly connect illicit actors and depict a coherent scheme." As will be discussed in Chapter 7, this reconstruction may be invisible to civilians (and their lawyers, if they end up being charged).

Digital traces are also indelible. Once your information is available, it stays that way. One LAPD employee told me that they planned to purge their ALPR data, for instance, when they run out of server space. They "have not needed to purge any information yet."

Our quotidian activities are being routinely accumulated and codified by law enforcement, and files are lying in wait. In that sense, we lead incriminating lives. But indiscriminate data collection is not the inevitable outcome of technological advancement. More simply: technological determinism is a trap. Mass surveillance is not the "natural" result of mass digitization. Instead, what we *allow* to proliferate and become the objects of massive data collection efforts are *choices* that reflect the social and political positions of the subjects and subject matter that we feel comfortable surveilling. As a counterpoint, consider guns in the United States: we do not permit the mass tracking of guns. There is no federal gun registry, and the National Instant Criminal Background Check System (NICS) is *required* by law to destroy the audit logs of background checks that go through its system within 90 days. We certainly have the technology to track guns, and we could easily leverage existing technology to do more tracking, but gun owners are powerful political subjects. They have the resources to assert that their guns should not be tracked. As we will see in Chapter 5, so, too, have police officers routinely invoked their authority and legitimacy to undermine attempts to surveil *their* work lives. They have the power to resist in ways that their more usual subjects, disproportionately low-income, minority folks with little political capital and no small amount of fear, cannot. In that way, even dragnet surveillance serves to reinscribe inequality.

| Directed Surveillance

Predictive Policing and Quantified Risk

IN 2008 THE LAPD's chief of police, William Bratton, coauthored an article with one of his lieutenants, Sean Malinowski, envisioning the future of law enforcement: "predictive policing." In their prescient piece, Bratton and Malinowski—who has a PhD in public administration—wrote that "experts foresee the expanded use of streaming data analysis, pre-programmed threshold alerts and improvements in the way in which we visualize the data analysis that the computer performs on its own." Further, "We will move from near real-time analysis to true real-time analysis and then to a 'predictive policing' posture wherein more accurate and reliable probability modeling will be utilized to forecast potential crime trends over an increasing time span."[1] By 2014, 38 percent of departments in a national survey responded that they were using predictive policing, and a majority are expected to be using it by 2020.[2]

The centrality of predictive policing to the LAPD's approach to crime control was apparent on my very first day of fieldwork, as I sat in a captain's office. Middle-aged and soft-spoken, he was also clearly excited as he described what he called a shift from "intuition-based" to "data-driven" policing. The captain had done his research—even suggesting multiple articles that might supplement *my* research—and rattled off a dizzying array of technologies that collect real-time data for his investigators and enthused over the incorporation of automated alerts into new iterations of analytic software. None of this was theoretical: the "future" of policing was here.

———

Contrary to the *Minority Report* analogy used in many media accounts,[3] today's predictive policing is not part of a dystopian control regime in which people are arrested for crimes they have not yet committed. At the moment, at least, it's considerably more boring than that. Predictive policing simply refers to analytic techniques used by law enforcement to forecast potential criminal activity. It involves using data to determine current crime patterns and direct patrol resources, such as where officers should go and who they should stop. It is informed by a large body of research that demonstrates crime is not randomly distributed across people or places. Rather, patterns of place-based environmental conditions,[4] situational decision-making,[5] repeat offenders,[6] and social networks[7] shape when and where crime is likely to occur, and who is likely to be involved. The technology takes advantage of these known patterns to aid in law enforcement.

In general terms, the stages of predictive policing are collection, analysis, intervention, and response.[8] The first stage involves marshaling data, which may include the kinds of basic crime data included in official reports as well as more complex environmental data such as seasonality, neighborhood composition, or environmental variables associated with crime, such as vacant lots, parks, schools, and ATMs. The second stage is data analysis, an umbrella term for methods ranging from basic arithmetic to algorithmic approaches like risk terrain modeling, and near-repeat analysis, to network models. The third stage is police intervention. Crime forecasts are distributed to patrol officers and supervisors to decide where to deploy officers in the field. With the right data, the logic goes, cops can use their uncommitted time (i.e., when they are not responding to calls for service or booking someone at the station) to surveil the people and places the models suggest are likely to be associated with future criminal activity. The fourth stage, described by law enforcement as "target response," refers to the reaction of individuals being policed, and it is evaluated as desistance (the police intervene and the person does not commit a crime) or displacement (the police intervene and the person moves on to find another place to commit the crime, and in the process some attrition typically occurs and some crime is prevented).[9] Highlighting both the cyclical nature and the military roots of predictive policing, one captain called it a "battle rhythm" that grows increasingly complex over time. Critically, the very act of predictive policing creates new data and shapes future forecasts.

Different criminological theories inform person- versus place-based predictive policing. Person-based predictive policing is premised on the idea that a small percentage of people are disproportionately responsible for most violent crime. Therefore, if the cops can identify and focus their resources on the "hottest" people, they should be able to dramatically reduce violent crime. Data is used to identify individuals or groups most likely to be involved in crimes as victims, offenders, or both, via a wide range of analytic approaches, including social network analysis and regression-based risk assessment.

Place-based predictive policing, by contrast, draws from canonical events-based, place-based, and opportunity theories of crime. Events-based theories use the criminal event—such as a robbery—as the unit of analysis, while place-based theories focus on the location. Situational opportunity theories focus on how certain physical and social environments provide opportunities to commit crime.[10] The basic underlying assumption for all is, again, well supported by empirical data: crime is not randomly dispersed. Factors such as routine activities and soft targets (originally a military term referring to unarmored or undefended targets, now used in criminological theory to denote individuals, objects, or places that may be easy to victimize) make crime cluster in particular areas. That clustering can often be explained as a function of environmental factors that create certain vulnerabilities at certain times.

An algorithm or a series of algorithms built into a platform processes data to predict risk of crime. Location-based predictive policing algorithms are typically used to predict property crime, and person-based algorithms are more commonly used to predict violent crime. Both guide police decision-making about where and whom to police.

Predictive policing is promoted as a technical solution to long-standing social issues relating to efficiency and accountability. A rationalizing impetus guides the adoption of algorithmic technologies in resource-constrained police departments, because predictive policing proponents argue that by relying on "less-biased" assessments, algorithms may help deploy resources more objectively.[11] The efficiency and accountability justifications are often used in tandem to emphasize the benefits of constructing, acquiring, and implementing algorithmic technologies to replace or, minimally, complement human decision-making.

The Shift from Reaction to Prediction

In the early 1980s, faced with evidence that reactive policing strategies were ineffective at reducing crime, there was a paradigm shift toward more proactive, problem-oriented policing strategies, including hot spots policing.[12] By plotting crimes, creating heat maps, and focusing police resources on hot spots—smaller units of geography and specific locations where crime is densely concentrated—police could more effectively address crime.[13]

During his first term as NYPD commissioner, Bratton led the development of COMPSTAT, a command accountability system now employed by hundreds of police departments across the world. COMPSTAT uses computer-mapping technology and timely crime data to identify crime patterns and target police responses. As described in Chapter 2, departments that adopt COMPSTAT hold regular performance measurement and accountability meetings in which officers and supervisors discuss crime problems and officer behavior in light of the week's numbers, and supervisors are called to account for crime rates.

In 2004 the LAPD implemented COMPSTAT Plus, a second-wave variation of COMPSTAT that Bratton and Malinowski described as "less confrontational."[14] COMPSTAT Plus was based on three strategies: diagnosing the causes of police underperformance, fostering stakeholder dialogue about the key problems, and tasking commands with developing action plans to address those problems. Beyond COMPSTAT, Bratton oversaw the merging of previously disparate information systems in order to create a more data-based picture of crime in LA. By focusing on past crimes to shape future police deployment, he emphasized a shift from reacting to crime to proactively preventing it.

In many American cities, violent and property crime rates began a steady decline in the 1990s—a decline that has largely continued into the 2020s. Law enforcement usually takes credit, but scholars debate the extent to which policing drove down crime rates. Still, Los Angeles experienced a particularly precipitous decline after 2000. Its homicide rate dropped twice as fast as New York City's: there were 1,231 homicides in LA in 2000, but just 253 in 2019. And the brass pressure LAPD officers to push crime rates even lower. One captain described his division's now low crime rates as a sort of Catch-22: "My problem is, do we continue going down? Because we could, I mean, we could go to European levels of crime or something. But at some point we're gonna see this . . . area is where the friction happens."

The captain drew a straight horizontal line and an asymptote approaching it, gesturing at the point where the two lines came together. That was the point of "friction." He continued, comparing low crime rates to low unemployment rates. "Someone figured out—an economist or somebody—what the natural rate of unemployment is, and there's always going to be that," he explained. "There's going to be like 4.5 percent unemployment just because of people changing jobs and that kind of thing. So, they kind of look at it like you're always going to have 4 percent rate, so if you're 9 percent, we're in trouble. If you're at 4.5 percent, that's probably natural. We don't have that for crime." It seemed misguided, the captain told me, to continue to try and beat YTDs (year-to-dates), when they might be approaching the "natural" rate of crime. Shaking his head, he lamented, "A business wouldn't run that way." In a different division with higher—albeit also declining—crime rates, another captain explained, "Chief said, in no uncertain terms, 'We *will* reduce crime.'" The problem, he said, was that "sooner or later, the low-hanging fruit will be gone. So, you need to innovate."

Innovating has increasingly meant more data and finer-grained analysis—intensifying predictive policing by extending hot spots policing through the temporal density of big data (that is, high-frequency observations). So while the use of data and statistics for predicting crime is nothing new, today's data is far more granular than it once was. Increasingly, records are detailed and data collection is automated. Bratton wrote, "American Police Chiefs used to look at crime numbers annually, in response to the FBI's Uniform Crime Reports data collection efforts. Beginning in the 1990s we began to critically analyze crime data on a monthly, then weekly, then daily basis. When I arrived here in LA, we developed methods to draw down data several times per day for analysis."[15] By late 2011 the LAPD was implementing a predictive policing software designed by PredPol. As mentioned in Chapter 2, PredPol was cofounded by Jeff Brantingham, a UCLA anthropologist with military grant funding whose parents were foundational scholars in the field of environmental criminology, and George Mohler, a computer science professor. Now their company's software is used in almost 60 police departments, the largest of which is the LAPD.

Even so, predictive policing proponents have recently begun to talk about the need for a paradigm shift in performance metrics, where cops "coming in at the end of the shift with a zero" tally for arrests is counted not as a failure, but as a success. A captain in Central Bureau explained that if cops are using data to prevent crime rather than just "chasing productivity" by reactively arresting people for crimes they've already committed, that *should* be considered a win. This may mean adopting a territorial imperative of "staying home," or continuing to police areas that are apparently low-crime in order to prevent criminal activity.

Person-Based Predictive Policing

Newton Division covers a predominantly residential area of nine square miles and about 150,000 people. Although the area experienced a steep decline in violent crime since the early 2000s, the division is still home to considerable gang activity and has the third-highest rate of gun violence in the city. Its nickname, "Shootin' Newton," and unofficial logo, a three-leaf clover riddled with bullet holes, were emblazoned on division officers' T-shirts and internal PowerPoint presentations. As I headed out for a ride-along, the officer working the front desk in the division building said sarcastically, "Be careful, it's boring out there."

Newton was an early adopter of a predictive policing strategy called Operation LASER (Los Angeles' Strategic Extraction and Restoration Program). Initiated in 2011, LASER was federally funded through the Smart Policing Initiative, a national initiative encouraging local police departments and researchers to partner and use data to reduce crime. Almost a million dollars' worth of grants came from the Bureau of Justice Assistance ($499,959 in 2009 and $400,000 in 2014).[16] $413,141.57 of it flowed to Justice and Security Strategies (JSS), founded and directed by the former Justice Department senior executive Dr. Craig Uchida, for designing Operation LASER. JSS is just one of many third-party companies contracted by enforcement agencies to develop data-intensive police strategies, and it routinely works for law enforcement, correctional and social services agencies, state and district attorneys, and homeland security.

Uchida's presence loomed large during my fieldwork. He was hired by the LAPD in 2009 and given free rein to implement Smart Policing in Newton in 2011. As we talked about data analytics, officers and civilian employees would often say, "You really need to talk to Dr. Uchida about that." I spoke with him a few times and saw him present on his law enforcement work at academic conferences. In one of his articles, Uchida and a coauthor likened their data-driven strategy of targeting violent repeat offenders for policing to "laser surgery, where a trained medical doctor uses modern technology to remove tumors or improve eyesight."[17]

Indeed, a recent discursive shift has moved away from prediction to *precision*, as evidenced in Bratton's Twitter feed: "#PrecisionPolicing is how law enforcement is continuing to drive down crime in the 21st century, focusing on the few in society causing violence," he tweeted in 2018. Operation LASER is emblematic, premised on targeting "the violent" with "laser-like precision." This approach includes both place-based and person-based (specifically, offender-based) strategies.

LASER's place-based strategy uses data on all gun-related crime to create heat maps. Gun-related crime includes all Part I and II incidents with a gun, as recorded in the FBI Uniform Crime Reports (UCR).[18] Supervisors then carry these heat maps with them every day on patrol. On one ride-along, the sergeant explained that she looks at hot spots and tries to determine whether they overlay "chronic locations" like liquor stores, hotels, or other criminogenic places. As available time permits, officers spend extra time in the hot spot corridors, recording their "dosage" (time spent in predictive boxes) in their Daily Field Activity Reports (DFARs). In short, LASER's place-based strategy closely resembles long-standing hot spots policing strategies.

The more significant policy change is LASER's person-based predictive policing strategy. It begins with the Crime Intelligence Detail (CID)—three sworn officers and a civilian crime analyst—gathering intelligence from daily patrols, the Parole Compliance Unit, field interview cards, traffic citations, release from custody forms, crime and arrest reports, and criminal histories. They use that information to generate a list of twelve "chronic offenders," about whom the CID then uses Palantir to generate "Chronic Offender Bulletins" (see Figure 4.1). To be clear, people listed on the bulletins are not necessarily wanted for any crimes, nor do they have outstanding warrants. Rather, as one officer explained as he gave me a paper copy of a recent bulletin, they are "information-only" documents. They include a person's name, date of birth, CII number (California Information and Identification number, or rap sheet number), driver's license number, physical descriptors, physical oddities (such as tattoos or scars), arrest history, CalGang designation, parole and probation status, warrants, vehicles, recent stops, and police contacts. Bulletins are posted in the roll call room, distributed to officers during roll call, and uploaded to patrol officers' in-car laptops. As the copy reads, officers cannot use this information as the sole basis for probable cause in order to detain the individual; instead, they are instructed to seek out and gather intelligence on these chronic offenders during the course of routine patrol work.

A key goal of the bulletins is to improve "situational awareness" and "remove the anonymity of our offenders that are out there," one officer explained. When I asked whether he had grounds to stop and question people on the bulletins, he replied, "Yeah, not the probable cause but the awareness. . . . The awareness of what the individual is about." The ambivalence and ambiguity in his answer felt crucial.

During the initial pilot of the Chronic Offender Bulletins, officers quickly realized that too many individuals were being designated "chronic offenders." It would be practically impossible to keep track of that many people. So Operation LASER rolled out a point system in which each chronic offender was assigned a point value and ranked accordingly: five points for a violent crime on their rap sheet, five points for a known gang affiliation, five points for prior arrests with a handgun, five points for being on paper (under parole or probation supervision), and so on. An officer described the point system as a way to "pull them apart" and "decide who's the worst of the worst." He continued, saying that "this is really what gives the importance of

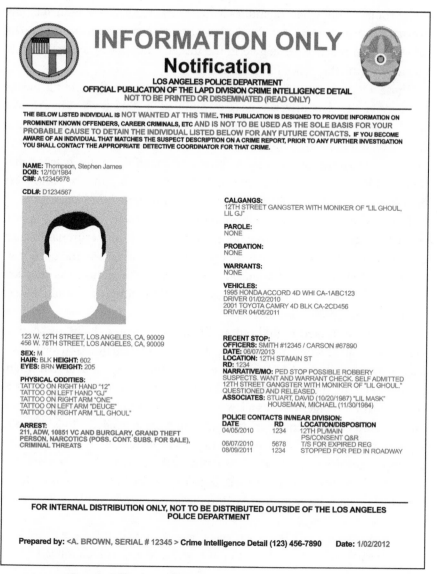

FIGURE 4.1 Chronic Offender Bulletin
SOURCE: LAPD; rendering by David Hallangen

FI-ing someone [filling out a field interview card] on a daily basis, instead of just saying, okay, I saw that guy hanging out, I'm gonna give him two weeks, and I'll go FI him again. *It's one point for every police contact.*"[19] What he meant is that each time an individual comes into contact with the police, a point is added to that person's LASER score. In fact, departmental materials about Operation LASER sometimes clarify that it's one point for every *"quality* police contact," but what constitutes a quality contact is never defined in any official documents, nor was there a consistent answer given to me across interviews. In practice, it seemed to me that "quality police contact" simply meant any time the police filled out an FI.

Those FI cards (see Figure 4.2) are the fundamental building blocks to many of the data-driven strategies outlined in this book. They're just small, double-sided index cards, and they have to be manually entered into databases, but their importance cannot be overstated. Cops may use them to mark bullet casings for crime scene photos and stuff them into gates so that they can't lock behind them as they enter a property, but they are also a *key* intelligence tool—one of the first data sources integrated into Palantir.

FI cards include personal information such as name, address, physical characteristics, vehicle information, gang affiliations, and criminal history. On the back of the card, there is an open space for officers to include a narrative or additional information on persons with the subject. As they are entered into the system, every FI is tagged with the time, date, and GPS coordinates of the police contact.

Officers are trained to pull out an FI card and "get a shake" as soon as they interact with someone in the field. Similarly, a Palantir software engineer working with the LAPD explained how little pieces of data that might seem innocuous at the time of collection can eventually be pulled together to create useful intelligence: "It's a law enforcement system where that citation can, the sum of all information can build out what is needed." In addition to inputting the *content* of the cards, one captain explained, there is an incentive to simply "get them" (individuals stopped in the course of police work) "in the system" as entities that future data points can be linked to. Similarly, an officer who had been with the LAPD for almost a decade, explained:

> It's such a huge intelligence, you know, document that we have. Because it incorporates so much. And on top you have the person with the subject . . .

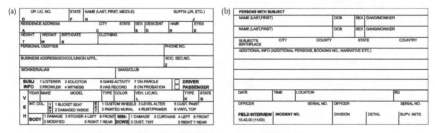

FIGURE 4.2 The front and back of field interview (FI) cards
SOURCE: LAPD; rendering by David Hallangen

an FI will give you the person that they're associated with. Even down to the clothing. . . . And it's just really: the work you put into the FI just is what you get out of it. So it's so important to really have a good, clean FI.

I witnessed supervisors urging officers to "get a strong FI" every time they talked to someone in the field. On a ride-along, one sergeant explained that she uses it "basically to tag all the personal information I can get . . . these things come into play later on in ways you could never even imagine." Respondents seemed to be saying that even if the value of information collected on an FI is not immediately apparent, it may help the LAPD in future investigations. One officer offered a hypothetical:

> If I stop you and Steve, I would write that you were with Steve in the narrative part of the card, and then two years later, if Steve is arrested, I could pull up all the FIs on Steve, and if they are looking for a female white, they can say "Oh, look, maybe it's Sarah."

Regardless of whether or how well you know someone, being stopped with them is an indelible association in the digital age. It can be recalled instantaneously with a search in Palantir (or another similar system), and it can be leveraged by law enforcement, prosecutors, and judges for crime charges or gang sentencing enhancements. Another thing I found interesting about this hypothetical was that this officer, like so many others I would speak with over the course of my research, has discursively incorporated the form of information officers enter into forms and databases into their everyday lingo. They describe people as "female whites" or "male Blacks." Because we know that language both shapes and is shaped by how we see the world,[20] the choice of data entry fields is not simply a technical question, but a normative and epistemological one, too. What we measure affects what we look for and read as important.

One way FIs are proving useful is in documenting gang affiliations. A sergeant explained that an individual may have gang tattoos all over his body, but "nobody wants to claim anymore because of enhancements"—that is, with sentencing enhancements in place for crimes committed by gang-affiliated individuals, fewer gang members are going to own up to their gang affiliation when they are arrested. So if law enforcement can FI an individual multiple times and record that that person was, on multiple occasions, with a known gang member, police can classify that individual as a documented gang member and enter his or her name into CalGang, the state's gang database.

Returning to the chronic offender strategy, after individuals are scored, they are rank ordered according to those risk scores (see Figure 4.3).

At the top of the Chronic Offender List is the division and the date; on the left is the chronic offender's name, CII number, and DOB; and on the right is their alias and photo. A corresponding Excel spreadsheet lists their name, DOB, home address, point score, gang, RD (reporting district), date assigned, date checked, unit assigned (e.g., GED [Gang Enforcement Detail]

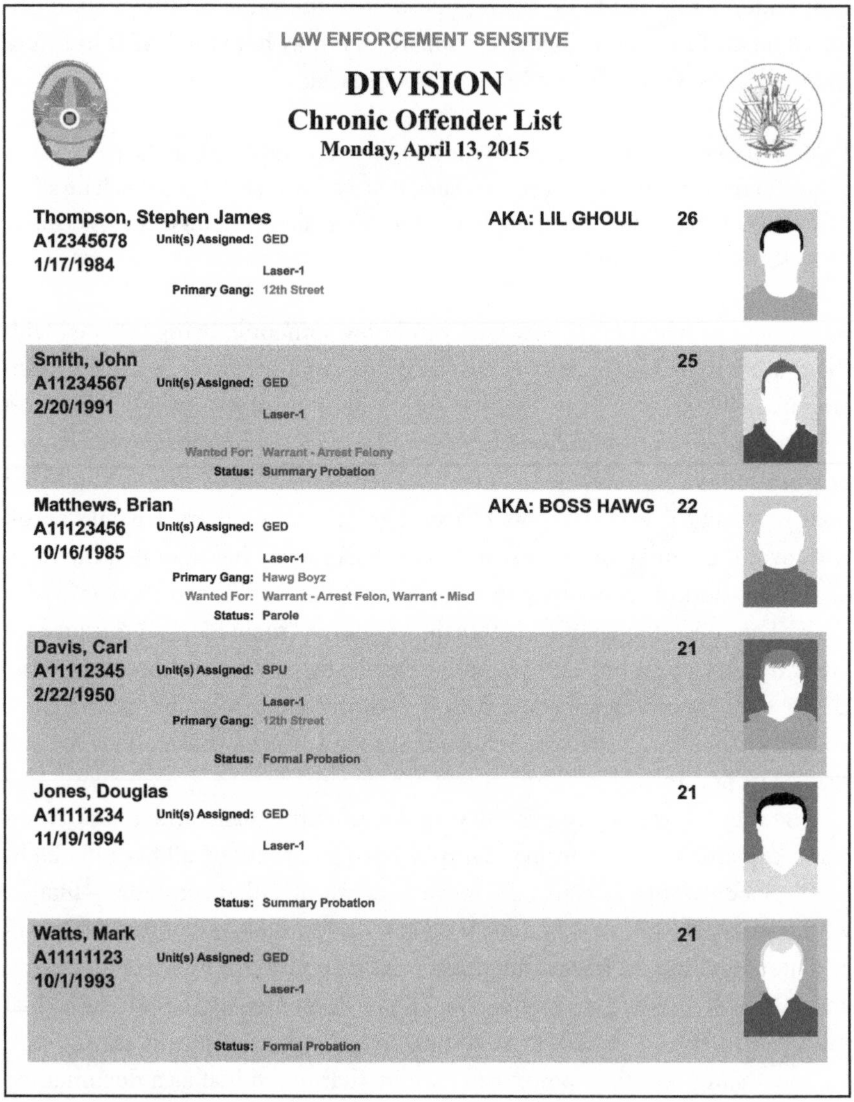

LAW ENFORCEMENT SENSITIVE

DIVISION
Chronic Offender List
Monday, April 13, 2015

Thompson, Stephen James   AKA: LIL GHOUL 26
A12345678   Unit(s) Assigned: GED
1/17/1984
                 Laser-1
      Primary Gang: 12th Street

Smith, John   25
A11234567   Unit(s) Assigned: GED
2/20/1991
                 Laser-1
         Wanted For: Warrant - Arrest Felony
             Status: Summary Probation

Matthews, Brian   AKA: BOSS HAWG 22
A11123456   Unit(s) Assigned: GED
10/16/1985
                 Laser-1
      Primary Gang: Hawg Boyz
        Wanted For: Warrant - Arrest Felon, Warrant - Misd
             Status: Parole

Davis, Carl   21
A11112345   Unit(s) Assigned: SPU
2/22/1950
                 Laser-1
      Primary Gang: 12th Street
             Status: Formal Probation

Jones, Douglas   21
A11111234   Unit(s) Assigned: GED
11/19/1994
                 Laser-1
             Status: Summary Probation

Watts, Mark   21
A11111123   Unit(s) Assigned: GED
10/1/1993
                 Laser-1
             Status: Formal Probation

FIGURE 4.3 Chronic Offender List
SOURCE: LAPD; rendering by David Hallangen

or PCU [Parole Compliance Unit]), which officer they are assigned to, and the latest status (i.e., whether they are in custody, for how long, and at what facility). The area commanding officer decides which field personnel to assign to a given chronic offender.

"There are a lot of chicken-shit violations you can stop someone for," one sergeant explained during a ride-along. Every officer said that the stops still have to be constitutional, but that you could always find *something* to stop someone for if you wanted to. When it comes to stopping chronic offenders with high point values, another officer offered examples:

> Yesterday, this individual might have got stopped because he jaywalked. Today, he mighta got stopped because he didn't use his turn signal or whatever the case might be. So that's two points . . . you could conduct an investigation or if something seems out of place you have your consensual stops.[21] So, a pedestrian stop, this individual's walking, "Hey, can I talk to you for a moment?" "Yeah what's up?" You know, and then you just start filling out your card as he answers questions or whatever. And what it was telling us is who is out on the street, you know, who's out there not necessarily maybe committing a crime, but who's active on the streets. You put the activity of . . . being in a street with maybe their violent background and one and one might create the next crime that's gonna occur . . . So by doing them [stopping them and filling out an FI] on a daily basis or whenever you come in contact, [it] really sets him above the other guy that may not be out as much.

FI cards, among their many functions, are a means of gathering ongoing pre-warrant intelligence on people's locations, social networks, and activities. Ideally, an officer explained, law enforcement could put one officer on every individual on the list, and "odds are [you're] probably going to find them committing another crime." Practically, when budget cuts and personnel shortages loom, there aren't enough police resources for that level of supervision. Therefore, instead of having one officer on every chronic offender, officers engage in a process I term "stratified surveillance," or differentially surveilling individuals according to their risk score. In one officer's words, they utilize undercover operations and then "sit our surveillance on some of the higher point offenders and just watch them on a daily basis." He continued,

> And you start building either, you know, there's two ways of looking at it. Either kind of conducting your investigation to see if maybe there was a crime that had just been committed. Or, "We know who you are, you know, I just called

you Johnny, I've never really met you before, but I know who you are now," so maybe it's put in his mind, "Oh, they're on to me, they know who I am."

It seemed that Operation LASER was not simply about removing violent offenders with "laser-like precision." It was also functioning to justify ongoing intelligence gathering, and functioning as a deterrent, signaling to people on the street that they were being tracked by law enforcement.

The mass collection and dissemination of data associated with the chronic offender program also systematizes previously particularized information. Whereas law enforcement conventionally would police individuals based on their personal familiarity with an offender, area, or crime, the systematic codification and dissemination of rank-ordered lists of people based on point values reshapes police surveillance practices. Officers used to need to be familiar with a particular case to know who someone was "capering" with, but now big data codifies that information and makes it available to anyone in the department.

When I asked an officer whether they were criticized for the practice, he quickly replied, "No." In fact, he explained, the department actually implemented the point system in part as a *legal compliance* mechanism:

> The Code of Federal Regulations. They say you shouldn't create a—you can't target individuals especially for any race or I forget how you say that. But then we didn't want to make it look like we're creating a gang depository of just gang affiliates or gang associates. . . . We were never criticized that much, but we were just trying to cover and make sure everything is right on the front end.

As work from sociolegal studies and organizational theory has shown time and time again, organizations construct compliance in ways that fit their interests.[22] The way that the officer stumbled over his discussion of race and gangs sheds light on how the operationalization of legal standards on policing in practice is particularly messy. It also shows how "data-driven" policing is seen as offering a legal solution for law enforcement: it does the same old thing, but faster and in a supposedly race-neutral, quantified way. Put differently, coding people as "likely offenders" looks race-neutral and makes disparate treatment more legally defensible.

Although the LAPD's person-based predictive policing practices have come to public attention in recent years, in part due to the efforts of advocacy organizations and a department-wide audit of predictive policing practices that will be discussed in this book's conclusion,[23] at the time of this interview, it wasn't surprising that the department hadn't been widely criticized for these practices. It was 2013, and, quite simply, nobody knew about it. In all my informal conversations with LA residents, journalists, and activists at the time, I couldn't find a single person who knew the details of Operation LASER.

Even within the department, there was massive variation in how the person-based system was implemented. At the time of this writing, LASER had been implemented in 16 of the Department's 21 area divisions.[24] However, there were inconsistencies in how risk scores were calculated, and even whether risk scores were used when classifying someone as a chronic offender. In 2019, for example, there were 637 individuals on the Chronic Offender List, 112 of whom had zero points.[25] It turns out that some divisions, like Newton, used the point system to develop their list of chronic offenders, whereas others came up with the lists simply by talking to patrol officers. In terms of interventions, some divisions explicitly directed officers to stop chronic offenders on a daily basis, whereas others conducted "door knocks," and others sent letters to chronic offenders informing them that they were on the Chronic Offender List, encouraging them to not engage in further criminal activity, and providing them with information on organizations that were available to assist them in getting jobs or removing tattoos.[26]

Much like strategies, opinions of Operation LASER varied widely within the department. When I asked a captain what he thought of person-based predictive policing, he told me that he had no plans to adopt it in his division, calling it a "civil liberties nightmare." Under new leadership, officers in that division started using it two years later. This remarkable within-department inconsistency was present throughout my fieldwork, and is a point that receives far too little attention in sociological research on the police, which tends to characterize "the police" as a homogeneous monolith.

On balance, the points system can quickly turn into a feedback loop and produce a ratchet effect[27] wherein individuals with higher point values are more likely to be stopped, thus increasing their point value, justifying their increased surveillance, and making it more likely that they will be stopped again in the future. Some individuals on the LAPD's Chronic Offender Lists were stopped as many as four times in one day. And despite one of its goals being to avoid legally contestable bias in police practices, Operation LASER hides both intentional and unintentional bias in policing. The point system may ultimately serve to prevent individuals already in the criminal justice system from being further drawn into the surveillance net, while obscuring the role of police practices in shaping risk scores. In other words, person-based predictive policing places individuals already under suspicion under new and deeper forms of surveillance, while appearing to be, in the words of one captain, "just math." Moreover, the point system is not used in lower-crime areas of the city. Therefore, individuals living in low-income, minority areas like South LA have a higher probability of their "risk" being quantified than those in more advantaged neighborhoods where the police are not conducting point-driven surveillance. Spatial and social inequality are replicating through this tool, a point to which I will return in Chapter 6.

Place-Based Predictive Policing

The LAPD began conducting predictive policing in Foothill, a division in the San Fernando Valley, in November 2011. Malinowski, coauthor of the paper with Bratton discussed at the beginning of this chapter, who had since been promoted to captain of Foothill Division (and later chief of detectives), started using PredPol to try and reduce property crime, primarily car theft. As discussed in Chapter 2, PredPol uses a patented and once-proprietary algorithm that leverages three inputs as training data used to predict future crime: official crime data on location, type, and time of crimes.[28] It is predicated on the near-repeat model, a type of location-based predictive model, which suggests that once a crime occurs in a location, the immediate surrounding area is at increased risk for subsequent, similar crimes.[29] PredPol uses ten years of data, weighting more recent crimes more heavily than older crimes, in order to produce 500-square-foot "boxes" that overlay division maps. These boxes indicate the places and times that crimes are most likely to occur over the next 12 hours. With "risk-based deployment," officers receive printouts at the beginning of their shift (see Figure 4.4) and are encouraged to spend time policing the predictive boxes.

It's all about "placing cops in the right place at the right time," commented one Foothill respondent. PredPol outputs informed deployment during uncommitted time, such as when officers were not responding to calls or "booking a body" (booking someone at the station). Many of the boxes highlighted areas officers already knew were high crime, so the unexpected boxes drew attention. For example, when driving away from the station after booking someone during a ride-along, the sergeant I was riding with saw a box in what he thought was an odd place and decided to go check it out. He chuckled when we arrived: it was an empty lot with nothing but a small pile of dirt on it. Clearly, he pointed out, he knows where crime's at better than a computer could.

Once they get to one of the predictive boxes, officers are trained to identify criminogenic anchor points, such as buildings, parks, ATMs, or convenience

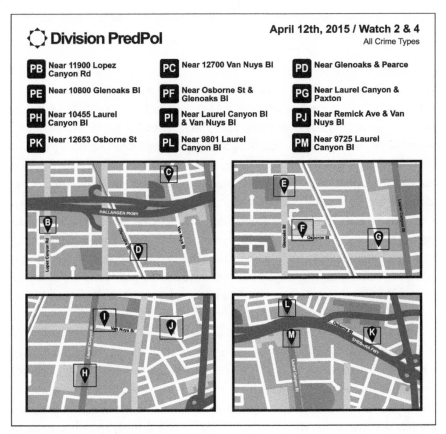

FIGURE 4.4 PredPol printout
SOURCE: LAPD; rendering by David Hallangen

stores. Note that although "data drives deployment," what officers do once *in* the predictive box—and how long they stay there—remains within their discretion. Those officers who engage with PredPol (as we will see in Chapter 5, not all police use the tools available to them) record their self-reported minutes on their in-car computers. That data is integrated into Palantir to measure the association between "dosage," or time spent in predictive boxes, and crime rates in specific predictive locations.

By relying on data, rather than human interpretation, of crime patterns, one supervisor believed he could use predictive policing to allocate his resources more efficiently:

> There's an emotional element to it, and you think right now, with crime being this low, a cluster could be 3 or 4 crimes. Clusters used to be 10, 12 crimes. Now 3 or 4 and they jump on it, you know. So, there could be overreaction.

Because, there's, you know, I mean it's a human doing it. And they cannot sort out what's noise.

I was able to observe predictive policing not just on the ground, but also in the air. True to the Air Support Division's (ASD) motto, "the mission is the same, only the vehicle has changed," ASD does not use PredPol, but rather the more conventional heat-mapping approach, and the division is viewed as a "force multiplier" for on-the-ground policing. LAPD's ASD receives ground maps, does fly-overs to patrol and look for suspicious activity, and uses heat maps to view property crime, violent crime, or both. On my fly-along, as the command pilot flew over a hot spot for property crime, we saw someone kicking in a door and the pilot called in ground support. I was surprised by how much you can actually see on the ground from a low-flying helicopter—small movements and interactions might not be visible, but it still provided a unique perspective. From the same spot where we observed someone kicking in a door, we could also see people in a park passing something from hand to hand and a car driving erratically.

The LAPD has two choppers—or, as they are more commonly called in the department, "ghetto-birds"—up in the air at all times, except from 4:30 a.m. to 8:30 a.m., because, one ASD respondent explained, they "don't want to keep people awake." One is based over the valley, and the other is almost always over South LA. A supervisor explained that after tracking airship presence and crime rates, they found that they needed to fly over hot spots in Newton 51 *times per week for there to be a reduction in crime*, so they often flew over hot spots 80–90 times. Take a moment to think about that. In order to have an impact on crime, a low-flying LAPD helicopter flew overhead nearly 13 times a day. Helicopters are an expensive and invasive intervention. According to one ASD respondent, there are never shootings when the airship is overhead. That's not particularly surprising; it seems imprudent to shoot someone in public when there is a LAPD helicopter flying directly overhead. At 9:00 p.m. the previous Thursday, he explained, when they flew away for a pursuit, there was another shooting. He said he was "convinced if we were above it wouldn't happen."

The use of location-based predictive policing is expanding rapidly within the department. It started in one division in the valley as way to combat property crime, had spread to 11 divisions by 2015, and is now available department-wide.[30] One captain expressed frustration that if one strategy is successful, there is political pressure to proliferate it through the department as quickly as possible. He sighed as he said that that kind of pressure to expand what seems to work, even in only preliminary launches, "is something that we deal with constantly." After its success with property crime, leadership wanted to use PredPol to predict violent crime. It wasn't effective, an outcome they attributed to the unit of analysis. Property crime is based on *location*, but violent crime's victims and offenders are *people*. The legacy of predictive policing more generally extends far beyond the LAPD. As just one example, Malinowski works with other police departments to teach them how the LAPD uses predictive analytics and how they might leverage data and technologies in new ways. While with the LAPD, he worked as a consultant for the Chicago Police Department, and has since retired to work part time at the University of Chicago and run his own private consulting company. In March 2019 he won a $635,000 contract to work with the Baltimore Police Department.[31]

So far, this book has focused on how the police use data to surveil civilians. However, an unexamined consequence of the proliferation of data-based surveillance is that the police themselves come under increased surveillance, particularly by their managers. In the next chapter, we will examine why and how some officers are pushing back against algorithmic control.

| Police Pushback

When the Watcher Becomes the Watched

Cops hate two things. We hate the status quo and we hate change.

—Lieutenant

You think there would also not be a search if you put a GPS device on all of [the Justices'] cars, monitored our movements for a month? You think that you're entitled to do that under your theory? . . . you could tomorrow decide [to] put a GPS device on every one of our cars, follow us for a month; no problem under the Constitution?

—Chief Justice Roberts During Oral Argument in *United States V. Jones*

I SPENT MOST OF my first ride-along freezing, despite it being 95 degrees outside. LAPD officers wear wool uniforms year-round. Consequently, Sergeant Ramirez, in his crisp blues, had the air conditioning blasting for the duration of my seven-hour ride-along.

The sergeant was easygoing and engaging. He told me that Tommy Lee Jones's character in *The Fugitive* inspired him to be a cop. He peppered me with pop quizzes, asking me whether I knew what street we were on, what direction we were going, or saw the group of day laborers we passed. While we were waiting at a traffic light, he ran the license plate of the car in front of us, the car to the front left, and the car to the front right. Nothing came up, but he asked if I thought that should be allowed. I shrugged and tossed the question back. "Well, is it?" He didn't answer. (It is.) Instead, he explained that situational awareness was key to being a good police officer: you always have to be alert, aware, observant.

Quipping that he felt like a "mother hen" looking after her chicks, Sergeant Ramirez piloted us to a scene where one of his "most proactive" supervisees, an officer who was working alone, had pulled over a teenage boy for skateboarding down the wrong side of the street. We were there to offer backup. When we arrived, we learned that the teenager was a registered sex offender and had an outstanding warrant for his arrest for failure to report to his "PO" (parole or probation officer). Ramirez put the teenager in the backseat of his cruiser and drove over to the arrestee's mom's house. He told me that if we didn't drop the backpack off, it would be stored at the station—which meant it would be a hassle for the kid to get it back.

About halfway through the shift, Sergeant Ramirez pulled into an In-N-Out drive-thru and ordered us two Double-Double meals, animal style, and a pair of Diet Cokes. He heard over his radio that there was a guerilla grow-op bust in progress nearby, so we drove to the site and enjoyed our burgers from under a freeway overpass, watching cops drag marijuana plants onto a flatbed truck.

Near the end of the ride-along, Sergeant Ramirez pulled up to a vacant house. Someone had called 911 about a possible break-in. When we got there, he manually typed into the in-car computer, "Code 6 at [the address]," meaning that a police unit had arrived and officers were investigating. Considering how technologically advanced the department seemed, I expressed surprise that there was not an automated mechanism for tracking the location of patrol cars. In fact, he explained, every police unit *is* equipped with an AVL, or, automatic vehicle locator, that should ping the location of each LAPD vehicle every five seconds. The AVLs weren't turned on, though, because of resistance from the police union.

———

So far, this book has focused on how law enforcement surveils civilians. This chapter flips the analytic lens to ask, what happens when the watcher becomes the watched? Police officers' reactions to the prospect of being surveilled are incredibly revealing, particularly when it comes to the power dynamics embedded in the practice of surveillance. To more fully understand big data policing, one must attend not only to how it is applied to civilians, but also how the police contest and subvert it.

Surveillance is fundamentally relational. The extent to which it is an exercise of power depends on the organizational contexts in which it is deployed, and how people feel about it depends on where they are in the organizational hierarchy. By focusing on the contexts of reception among police officers, this chapter offers a new angle on the claim that data-intensive surveillance is a social—rather than merely technical—process. Because it takes place in preexisting social, organizational, and institutional contexts, it reflects existing power asymmetries—in this case, between command staff and line officers, or, in more general terms, between management and workers.

Starting my fieldwork, I was ambivalent about how police might respond to being observed, not necessarily by me, but by the new surveillant technologies. On the one hand, media portrayals of law enforcement draw connections to *Minority Report*, characterizing the police as having a voracious appetite for new technologies and more data.[1] Perhaps the police would enthusiastically embrace big data analytics because it enhances their surveillant capacity. On the other hand, research by work and employment scholars would predict resistance from officers, who might be wary of possible entrenchment of managerial control and deskilling.

In this chapter, I first outline the technologically mediated surveillance of officers big data makes possible, and then officers' individualized and organized resistance against it.

Technological Adoption and Resistance

There are strong theoretical traditions and policy motivations for focusing research on the usual subjects of police surveillance rather than on the officers who find themselves under various forms of technological oversight.[2] Access is another reason scholars have more often researched the predominantly poor racial minorities frequently subjected to heavy police surveillance—these groups have considerably less social power to exclude researchers from studying them than do the police, whose departments are notoriously closed systems. As a result, we have a much better understanding of how the urban poor respond to surveillance than how those with more social power, such as the police, do.

Still, the police are, at the end of the day, employees. They work within an organization, and they are subject to managerial surveillance just like everyone else who has a job. Workplace surveillance and managerial control operates, in part, through information systems.[3] Worker behavior is made legible to management through informating, or the process of translating the measurement and description of activities, events, and objects into information that's useful and visible to management.[4] The organizational scholar Stephen Barley describes this process when it comes to the quantification of technicians' on-the-job activities and how it creates the "signs, symbols and indices"[5] that commonly mark the entrenchment of managerial control through electronic surveillance.

Across fields, technology, work, and organizations have become inseparable. As Wanda Orlikowski and Stephen Barley argue, combining institutional analysis from organization studies and information technology research, which focuses on the material properties of technologies, can help us understand technological change in the workplace.[6] Some technologies, they explain, are introduced with the explicit purpose of monitoring workers. But many more are introduced to perform other functions and only incidentally afford managers the ability to surveil workers. As this chapter will show, in the LAPD it was that "function creep," wherein technologies initially introduced for one purpose, such as to reduce crime, were repurposed to surveil officers themselves, that led to the most vehement resistance.

Worker resistance to managerial surveillance is, of course, nothing new.[7] Occupational identity and cultural context influence the forms that resistance takes.[8] For example, truck drivers, like police officers, often view independence, or being "out on the open road," as a central tenet of their occupational identity, so they have contested and resisted electronic logs that put them under increased surveillance.[9] Individuals are more likely to engage in resistance when they feel their identity[10] and occupational community[11] is threatened. For police, notoriously committed to their professional identity and authority, and willing to close ranks should they feel threatened, resistance to their own surveillance makes sense—an ironic sort of sense, in that they end up resisting the very tools they regularly use to surveil other people during the course of their work.

Another reason it's important to look at this particular case of technological change in the workplace carefully is that the bulk of the scholarship on the topic predates the introduction of big data analytics. Consequently, there is little scholarship on how individuals respond to the introduction of big data analytics as a means of surveillance in organizations. By recording an on-the-ground account of the adoption of—and resistance to—big data analytics within one of the world's largest, most influential police departments, we can attempt to tease out active resistance from the baseline level of resistance to authority that exists in any organization, reveal additional conflict concomitant to organizational change, and consider grievances specific to the introduction of big data analytics into the LAPD.

Whether and how new technologies and operational practices entrench or disrupt existing power structures depends on a number of factors, including who has access to data and for what purpose, as well as the extent of, sophistication of, and variation in worker resistance. Which is to say, the adoption of and resistance to big data analytics is far from inevitable or uniform.

Responses to Data-Intensive Surveillance

When Sergeant Ramirez told me the AVLs weren't turned on, it was the first form of officer resistance to technology I'd encountered during my field-work with the LAPD, but it wouldn't be the last. Throughout the department, I would see considerable variation in resistance to advanced analytics and new surveillant technologies. It appeared that whether individuals contested or embraced big data analytics varied along two axes: individuals' position in the organizational hierarchy, and their function in the department.

Three related, but analytically distinct, grievances, all of which relate to managerial oversight, emerged from my data. First, the fact that police come under increased surveillance is a collateral consequence of new data-intensive police surveillance tools. Second, officers feel that the increased emphasis on "data-driven" decision-making devalues their experiential knowledge. Third, algorithms are opaque, which impedes buy-in. An additional theme, unre-lated to managerial oversight, included contestation around privacy and civil liberties, and is discussed before I consider how big data became a form of capital within the department, entrenching old divisions and creating new distinctions and channels for promotion.

Objections to Their Own Surveillance

By far the most common complaint I heard from officers was that the prolif-eration of high-frequency observations and data collection sensors resulted in their own surveillance. Some saw it as an entrenchment of managerial control and a threat to their professional autonomy—the kind of friction that's always occurred between front-line workers and officer managers but has become more acute in the age of big data. For instance, supervisors have always been able to *tell* officers where to go, but now they can triangulate data to *see* and *record* where officers actually go.

When I followed up with management about the AVLs being turned off in squad cars,[12] multiple captains told me that the issue was frustrating. They wanted, one captain explained, to activate all the AVLs, because they could serve a basic but important function: visualizing division deployment and quickly pinpointing the closest unit to a given call. Describing what he called the "politics of pinging," he added:

> [I]f somebody has a help call and they need us, I can think of circumstances in my career where had we had that, someone would have not bled out. But

there are times when they put out a help call on radio and they put out parallel streets because of the stress [i.e., instead of saying an intersection as their location, officers accidentally say two streets that run parallel to each other]. The ambulance can't find them. If everybody had GPS then we'd just say, "They are at the corner of [intersection] and they're 500 feet from the corner."

Indeed, the use of AVL data for this purpose was uncontroversial in my conversations across the department's ranks. A second motivation behind activating AVLs met more resistance. As the captain above put it:

[T]he thing I'm really interested in with the GPS is the tracking of how much time they're spending on our missions. So, it's a measure of minutes on mission is what I go for . . . so that then we give them a mission in the [location-based predictive policing] predictive boxes instead of getting self-reported, it's a little Mickey Mouse, right? But via the computer—and I don't think they're lying to us 'cause they're all paranoid about getting in trouble—but I'd like to have GPS tracks because there are times when the officers are in the area, they're not on a mission to hit the boxes but they're on a radio call in the box. And we're not capturing any of that time. And I think if we get this done the right way . . . I'll have Palantir or somebody go in and pull it out and show me, "here is where the predictive boxes were over the course of the week, and here is how much time people spent in those boxes." And then I gather that for a year or something. Then we get to the real part that I'm interested in, which is how much dosage [police presence] do you need to affect a crime problem? That's the key.

Although AVLs were originally created to visualize units to streamline deployment, their data introduce an opportunity for function creep. Once the data exist, people in the organization may want to use it for different purposes. So although the captain was careful to explain his interest lay only in conducting aggregate-level analyses in order to learn what level of police presence was needed to reduce crime within PredPol's predictive boxes, he understood he would need to be strategic about how to deal with officers' wariness of tracking:

I'm not gonna tell on people in the department too much about that because it's just, well, that's not what it's built for. . . . The problem with the police officers is they're like, you know, they think we're gonna nickel-and-dime them on, "Where are you at? Oh, you guys are at Starbucks too long," or you know? And I have no interest in that.

Patrol officers expressed skepticism that supervisors could resist using the data in these more invasive, managerial ways. While I was on a ride-along in a low-crime division, I asked a sergeant about AVLs. She smirked and said, "The way I see it, they know where I'm at at all times." She continued, "The fastest way to get fired is lying. If your log says you're here and GPS says you're there, you're lying." Likewise, a sergeant in one of the highest-crime divisions told me on our ride-along that he actually suspects the cars are *already* pinging their locations and management just hasn't told patrol yet. I asked a Police Officer II in yet another division whether his AVL was turned on and what he thinks of them. "Apparently we have those, but I don't know if they run them all the time," he responded, elaborating:

> They were talking about that, and we heard rumors. Because the thing is—here's how most things go: They'll [management] basically tell us, "Okay, this [new technology] is coming down the pipeline." But then some old-timer will pretty much immediately go to the negative thing about that that he thinks about and then start, you know, rumormongering about it. And who knows if it's true or not, but you always think worst-case scenario because you've seen people get burned by the department before. You want to believe that they're going to stand by you, but lots of people get screwed over. . . . Perfect example: that pinging thing [AVLs]. It's like yeah, the rumor was they're going [to put] GPS in the cars now, and if your car goes over 80 miles an hour, it automatically is going to send an alert to your captain and somebody else and the watchman that night. It's automatically going to show that this vehicle is going over 80 miles an hour and then you're gonna have to justify why you're going that fast. Like, okay, and so [another officer] was like, "What the fuck? Oh, they're going to monitor us now? Come on."

Officers' resistance did seem to focus on the tools and technologies that lent themselves to function creep. I heard similar skepticism and suspicion around the use of DICVs (digital in-car videos), the front- and rear-facing cameras in police cars. The front camera turns on automatically after six seconds when the car's lights and sirens are activated, while the rear-facing camera records what's happening in the backseat of the car. Echoing the patrol officer's belief that the AVLs have actually been running for some time, another officer confided that he thinks the DICV cameras are always on.

Dylan, a Police Officer II, explained how, in the divisions with DICVs, two officers are tasked with auditing the footage. Their job, ostensibly, is to look for any discrepancies between DICV footage and written reports. They also work to spot problems such as a failure to turn on DICVs by compiling the serial numbers of all officers who worked a particular shift, then using the officers' electronic nightly logs (previously paper) to compare against the video database and see that there was a corresponding video for each traffic or pedestrian stop. That way, they can watch the video to look for discrepancies. Much like AVLs, DICVs afford law enforcement the technology to surveil civilians, but also give managers the ability to surveil patrol officers.

So, what if there is a discrepancy between DICV footage and the logs? Dylan told me that these mismatches are recorded as "failures," and a certain number of failures will mean getting a notice to go talk with a supervisor. He imitated a manager telling an officer, "I noticed you've got eight times where you don't have it [the DICV] turned on beforehand." The consequence of such a violation is what he described as "an informal training kind of thing," but "it kind of progresses from there." The issue can go up the chain of command, leading Dylan to conclude, "It's like ridiculous, though. It's like does it really matter? . . . All of a sudden we have to worry about putting my stupid microphone on." Dylan sighed and said that all the different data sources about officers' on-shift behavior were getting out of control. To him, the tech seems like it only serves to get officers in trouble.

Interestingly, not all bureaus are equipped with DICVs. At the time of my fieldwork, they were only installed in divisions in South Bureau. An officer in South Bureau seemed exasperated by the uneven roll-out, telling me that their division had already had the cameras for about five years, though other divisions had yet to get them. He lamented, "We've been the only fucking bureau to have this . . . you tell me how it's possible to have a department but yet a quarter of the department's gonna be under one set of rules or possible sanctions where the other ones aren't? Like, how does that fucking work?" The officer complained that he works under the threat of sanctions and reprimands around not turning on the DICV per department policy, while "the other 75 percent of LAPD doesn't have to worry about it at all. So we're on an unequal playing field. Right?" Musing about why he thought South Bureau had been singled out for DICVs, he continued:

Number one: South Bureau geographically is the smallest area for distance and so it was the cheapest to implement . . . they need to set up the system, deal with antennas and everything and make sure everything's right, yada yada. So, South Bureau was the cheapest. But also, because they wanted transparency to South Bureau, because that's traditionally where the most [civilian] complaints have come from. Now mind you . . . of course there's a relation. It's also where the most violent crime happens.

Hearing how the officer made sense of within-department variation in surveillant technologies was illuminating because, although he had hypotheses about costs and legitimacy and accountability, at the end of the day, he didn't really know *why* the cameras were rolled out in some divisions and not others. That lack of transparency came up in multiple interviews, and it contributed to the distrust many officers seemed to have toward the brass.

Resistance came in a number of practical strategies. Officers thwarted their own surveillance, for instance, by trying to obfuscate or block data collection.[13] Subsequent to a "rash of antennae malfunction" in South Bureau, an internal investigation discovered that officers deliberately removed the antennae from approximately 50 cars in order to tamper with the voice recording equipment and prevent management from being able to hear what they were saying in the field. Similarly, I noticed on my ride-alongs that officers on patrol frequently used their cell phones, rather than going through dispatch, to communicate with one another. I asked a sergeant how he decided which to use, and his initial explanation was that it is sometimes just easier to call or text a colleague. A slightly more complicated calculus emerged later that night, when we were at a crime scene. I watched the sergeant use his cell phone to call another officer who was at the hospital after transporting the victim, a young man who had been stabbed. The sergeant asked the officer to estimate the probability that the "vic" would die ("is it 50/50?"). Later, when I inquired why he'd made the call on his cell phone, he said that it was the middle of the night, and he did not want to go through official channels—which could be audited—and call in homicide detectives before he was sure it was actually a homicide. Detectives, he said, would be annoyed if they had to get out of bed if nobody was dead.

Officers also resisted the technology by producing *more* data, on their own terms. For example, one sergeant showed me how he carries his own audio recorder everywhere, because he does not trust the department's recording equipment. If he has his own audio, then should someone accuse him of wrongdoing, he reasoned, he has his own proof. He went on to describe technology as a "double-edged sword"—on the one hand, technology such as vehicle cameras can clear officers of wrongdoing, but on the other hand, if they don't turn the camera on, the assumption will be that the officer was doing something wrong.

This surveillant gaze represents an uncomfortable inversion of officers' usual surveillance work and is part of the crisscrossing attending function creep: no one, not even the police, is exempt from surveillance today. The police are, however, differentiated from individuals on the street in their ability to resist, and the ways they can reasonably frame their own resistance, by virtue of their occupational position as police officers. This ability is in stark contrast to citizens who wish to avoid surveillance.

The Devaluation of Street Knowledge

A second grievance officers expressed about the way big data is reshaping their jobs is their sense that the emphasis on big data devalues the local, experiential, street knowledge they accumulated from their time observing and interacting with individuals in the field. Cops regularly talk about the importance of "street smarts," with more than one officer contrasting himself with "eggheads" or "pencil geeks" (which, a few reminded me, is what they considered me) who only know about policing from books and numbers. Patrol officers expressed frustration that spreadsheet jockeys were out-of-touch, too focused on the abstract and theoretical. The use of predictive models to conceptualize risk of crime serves to lower the value of sworn officers' existing competencies and raise the value on the competencies of other classes of employees, even civilian employees within the department. One blunt sergeant said of the data-intensive activities at the Real-Time Crime Analysis Center (RACR), "Looks bitchin', but it's worthless."

The technocratic oversight threatens a deskilling of police work for some. Policing, to them, is a craft, not a science. They worry that they will become nothing more than line workers and insist that their years of accumulated experiential knowledge is irreplaceable. On one ride-along, a sergeant told me that it was "ridiculous" that managers would consider telling them where to go based on predictive boxes, because patrol officers were the ones "out there, pushing the black and whites" (driving around in police cars).

A captain, weary from the effort of trying to incorporate predictive analytics into his daily operations, lamented, "There's so much resistance." He explained how a typical exchange plays out with his officers:

> They're like, "You know what? I know where the crime's occurring." This is the biggest thing you hear from us is when they [say], "I know where crime's occurring." And I show them the [predictive policing] forecast and they say, "Okay, so [at intersection], I know there are crimes, I could have told you that. I've been working here ten years! There's always crime there." I go, "Okay, you're working here ten years on that car, why is there still crime there if you're so knowledgeable?"

A Palantir engineer underscored the sentiment:

> Law enforcement also has ground truth of "they know where the bad areas are."
> Does that also open up a potential for not being diligent and open minded?
> Does that close you off to being willing to look at your area without that filter?
> Are you saying, does that necessarily have to happen in that location? Could it
> happen elsewhere?

Resistance around the perceived threat to their expertise is not limited
to patrol, but occurs in investigations as well. After a detective zeroed in on
a suspect using Palantir, I asked him how important the platform was for
solving the case. He said, a bit defensively, that without the program, he
"probably would have still found [the suspect] eventually."

Effective managers implemented data-driven policing by highlighting—
rather than minimizing—their officers' experiential knowledge and ap-
pealing to the reasons those officers joined the force in the first place. Of
course, management has always given patrol officers directions regarding
where to go. What is different is that management can now track and triangulate where officers went and where officers say they went. As they
began to use PredPol dosage data tracked in Palantir to see whether and
how much time their officers spent in predictive boxes, and as monitoring
became more procedural (*how* did officers patrol) than outcome-based
(did they make any arrests), one captain who was an early adopter gave a
warning:

> When it's not successful with predictive is when . . . they overdo it. They'll
> mandate time in a box and if you don't do it they'll penalize you. And that
> throws off the result and it pisses everyone off. This has to be voluntary com-
> pliance, which the police department is not great at. They have to *want* to.
> You have to convince them. You gotta go back to why they came on the job,
> see? "If you came on the job to prevent people from being victimized, I'm
> giving you a way to do that, and you need to get in these boxes that have the
> highest probability of a crime occurring and prevent it." So, it's a different
> way of selling it.

Emphasizing that he is careful to defer to officers' judgment, this captain
explained how his officers are sometimes "still confused about 'What do you
want me to do in the box?' And I'm careful to not say. I say, 'What I want you
to do is go there and use your knowledge, skills, and experience to identify
what the problem is and then have a visible presence there to deter the suspect from wanting to commit that crime.'"

I learned that most individuals making deployment decisions at the management level in the LAPD are aware of officers' concerns about the possible subversion of their experiential knowledge in favor of data analytics. Multiple captains and sergeants carefully noted that they were not privileging one form of information over another. Rather, they were seeking to "supplement" officer knowledge and experience with data. Examples included respondents who said officers "don't want patrol with their heads buried in the computer"; that "you have to use your grey matter, . . . the system is designed to augment the human, not the other way around, . . . [and a] person can recognize a pattern faster than a machine"; "What's the best data storage system? Your brain. Because it integrates everything"; and "[You] can't fight crime from a computer. [You] gotta drive to the big red dot you saw on the heat map. See with human eyes."

Part of why it might be difficult for officers to accept data-driven decision-making is that data analytics threaten a sacrosanct, independent, and autonomous law enforcement identity. As I mentioned earlier, research suggests individuals are more likely to resist change when they feel their identity[14] and occupational community are threatened. Emblematic of this, one officer told me he prefers night watch because, on that shift, there are fewer people at the station checking in on him and the road is "all mine." Thus, being under strict supervisory surveillance undermines officers' self-conception that they are independent and uniquely qualified agents of the law. More generally, the idea that data analytics conflicts with the culture of and ideal-typical[15] personalities in law enforcement came up in multiple interviews. Law enforcement, one officer said, is "predisposed" to dislike being surveilled due to its "culture." "It's like, why are you going to look at what I'm doing?" He described his fellow officers as being "all paranoid about getting in trouble."

Civilian employees offer an interesting analytic comparison to sworn officers. They are part of the same organization and sometimes engage in similar tasks, such as crime analysis, yet they have not gone through the socialization and training process of the police academy, and they do not have power of arrest, a badge, or a firearm. Therefore, civilian employees in the LAPD are professionalized differently and hold distinct professional identities from sworn officers. A civilian crime analyst, Richard, described himself as an "outsider" to law enforcement and noted a certain "hostility" to concepts and ideas that did not originate within law enforcement. He called the cultural attitude a "not-invented-here type attitude" and characterized sworn officers' mindset as being, "If we haven't thought about it, it's obviously no good." A second civilian employee said, of the officers, "The personality types we have, they're not willing to accept that somebody could be doing it better. You know? Or that there's a better way of doing it. Because [they think] 'I certainly would be doing it if there was a better way.' You know what I mean?" And a third stated flatly, "Cops are skeptical of everything."

These civilian employees' characterizations of sworn officers' mindsets were largely consistent with characterizations those officers made about themselves. One captain said, "By nature we're skeptics, pessimists, we know how to do it ourselves," while another told me, "Because they [sworn officers] didn't come up with [PredPol] a lot of guys are like . . ." and dramatically rolled his eyes and sighed. When talking about PredPol, yet another captain explained that he "didn't buy in right away. . . . At first, I was all like, 'Whatever,' but now I've seen firsthand, it actually does work." That helped him sell the program to his officers—he could show them that "people like him," who he described as "more operational, less intellectual," think it is legitimate.

Many officers' resistance to learning how to use Palantir's platform was described by a captain as the result of them being "reluctant to learn because of the culture, and the mentality is nobody wants to be first. Because 'I don't want to have to learn anything. And I don't want to be the person asking the stupid questions.'" Interestingly, another captain described how he harnesses that same stubbornness to bring officers on board with Palantir. He explains, "Now that they see some of their peers in it and having success, their mindset also is 'I don't want to be the last one on the boat. I don't want to get left behind.'"

Opacity Impedes Buy-In

It's hard to trust what you can't understand. Predictive algorithms are opaque, shrouded in "algorithmic secrecy."[16] Partially, this is because algorithms—such as Google's "secret sauce," risk assessment tools such as COMPAS, or PredPol's predictive policing algorithm[17]—are usually proprietary. However, even those that are "transparent," in that they are publicly available, tend to be difficult to interpret. Algorithmic opacity is particularly relevant in the case of law enforcement, as it exacerbates the base-level skepticism that exists about the value of data-driven policing. For law enforcement—or anyone for that matter—to evaluate the fairness or efficacy of an algorithm, it must be understandable and interpretable.

Consider the following example: Hot spots policing, a predecessor to location-based predictive policing, involves plotting crimes, creating a density map, and directing patrol to the "hottest" areas. It's a straightforward, intuitive, and transparent system. Officers may think it is redundant—they say they know where the hot spots are, after all—but at least when they go to a hot spot and do not find a crime, it does not invalidate or undermine their faith in the entire system. By contrast, predictive policing involves an unseen algorithm (itself an undefined concept for most officers), and few cops will understand why the predictive box has been drawn in one location over another beyond their intuition about the high-risk areas in their division. Asked to explain how PredPol works, one captain replied that it involves a "mathematical equation I know nothing about." Machine learning is also unfamiliar to most officers—for most people, for that matter—and it is not covered in the police training academy. Therefore, when an algorithm does not "work"—when officers drive to a predictive box and see no crime—it can be easily discounted as nonsense. Recall that on one ride-along, the predictive policing box overlaid an area the sergeant I was with did not recognize. When we got there and it turned out to be a pile of dirt, he said, "See? I knew that wasn't right."

Emblematic of the idea that data-driven policing is cloaked "in a veil of technological wizardry,"[18] one officer dismissed PredPol, saying, "I think that's just witchcraft." Another, a captain using predictive policing in his division, gestured at a cupboard in his office, eventually walking over to rummage through it, saying, "And then there are people that think it's like voodoo science, you know like—you know, if another fucking person gives me a Ouija board." Sure enough, his officers had bought him Ouija boards to make light fun of his commitment to the "voodoo science" of algorithms. This lighthearted ribbing was based on officers' real fear that their naturalized knowledge, developed through personal, on-the-job experience, was being pushed aside for the supernatural promise of algorithms. A seasoned sergeant explained on our ride-along how "situational awareness is second nature" to him, because he had been "pushing the black and white for over twenty years."

Privacy and Civil Liberties

A fourth point of contention regarding the influx of big data analytics in policing had little to do with deskilling or managerial oversight, but came up surprisingly frequently—how new technologies infringe on individuals' rights to privacy.

In initial interviews, I avoided asking direct questions about the implications of predictive policing or big data analytics for privacy and civil liberties. I did not want to prime my respondents to think about such issues, nor did I want them to become defensive about how their own practices may infringe upon those rights. Nonetheless, these issues arose in about a third of my interviews, with both sworn officers and civilian employees independently raising privacy concerns about mass data collection.

As we spoke about general trends in data collection, a civilian employee set the scene:

> So, here's the trend, right? What's the ongoing trend? Collect more and more information, right? Piling up mass amounts of information, eventually being able to get what you're seeing in the media, in films and movies. The ability to be able to see a mass of information about somebody and somebody's life. And then there are privacy implications. Just with our license plate recognition, one of the concerns is how long are we keeping this data for? For what purpose? How long can we fish out this data? Most of the data collected is of no particular consequence to us. But yet we're keeping it so that perhaps later on we can, who knows? Find out what somebody was doing six months ago and where they traveled and you could essentially be extremely invasive in exactly what you're doing. But the feds have not established guidelines about that. So essentially every law enforcement agency is pretty much doing everything on their own.

Another civilian employee referred to the automatic retention of license plate reader data, joking, "It's all good! No, it's not." Sometimes, they explained, you could see the people in the cars in the license plate reader photos, and that's important data:

> Who's that with you next to you in the car? Yeah, I mean, it's awful. I mean I guess—[laughter] it is, it is. I mean it is, it doesn't matter until it's you, right? It doesn't matter until it's you. And that's the basic thing. Until it's one of us realizing that the agency that we're living with, right, let's say, you know, down in Orange County, is collecting all this massive information about what we're doing, right. . . . Yeah, it's fine when it's about other people. But it's when it's you, you realize how invasive it is about you then you're like, okay, then you have a totally different mindset.

My respondents were also concerned that individuals making decisions about new data collection practices did not articulate a clear enough purpose. Ramin, a civilian employee, criticized the seductiveness of new data and technology, regardless of whether there was any mechanism for evaluating whether the trade-offs between privacy and crime prevention outcomes came out even:

> What are the metrics that we're seeking to improve with big data, right? What exactly are we trying to improve? We know very generically that we should

reduce crime. Right? By collecting all this data and making use of it, we should see some impact. What happens when we're collecting all this information and you're actually not seeing that?. . . . I mean, what are we actually matching up? This data collection, the massive data collection and the outcomes? . . . We tend to just say, "Let's just go for the sexy tool," right? "This *looks good*, we're collecting all this data." We just never think about to what end. Right?

Ramin's colleague, Ian, who dryly referred to the Homeland Security Southern California "Center of Excellence" as the "Center of Invasiveness" and described the "collect now, analyze later" mantra pervasive in the department, reflected on "data greed," stating,

I guess the unasked question has been after all this massive effort is, "Has that data collection essentially led to these certain metrics that we've all agreed are preferable?" . . . Nobody actually analyzed it. And we actually do a lot of data collection and never actually decide that we need to just collect the bare minimum so that we can get the end result that we want, rather than, "Let's just collect as much as we can and maybe some good end result will occur." That's essentially where we are right now.

Ian emphasized his sense that the department needed to identify metrics that could measure the efficacy of current practices. He explains that "maybe we shouldn't collect this information, maybe we shouldn't add consumer information. Maybe we shouldn't get everybody's Twitter feed in. You know, because it's actually not panning out." Later, Ian would lament, "All we're doing right now is, 'Let's just collect more and more and more data and something good will just happen.' And that's, I think, that's kind of wishful thinking. You have to be ends-led. Led by the ends that you're trying to achieve." The implication I was hearing from my interviewees was that they wanted to know that the ends—the policing outcomes of data collection—really did justify the means—the exponential expansion of surveillance.

As discussed in Chapter 2, most of the platforms used by local law enforcement are designed by private companies and licensed by the agencies. In a group interview, a civilian employee drew attention to external vendors' "system arrogance." "Every vendor wants to be everything to everybody." That means,

Every single vendor comes in and says, you know, just give us the data so that we can present this stuff. Because what they're sold on is something they see at a trade show or a vendor dog-and-pony show, which is 'hey look at this cool interface, it's just the greatest thing in the world. You can do XYZ, it's like *Minority Report*, whoa, whoa'—that's the sort of stuff that's . . .

Another civilian employee interrupted to say, "Our command staff is easily distracted by the latest and greatest shiny object. . . . But they don't know what it takes to get that integrated and then nobody thinks about implementation. They just want it. But then it's implementation that actually makes it work."

Within my sample, civilian employees raised more general concerns about *privacy*, whereas sworn officers more frequently expressed concern over practices they thought could be *legally contestable*. For example, some officers I interviewed supported the offender-based point system, while others told me that they thought it was legally problematic. One captain, who does not use the strategy in his division, said "I wouldn't touch it with a ten-foot pole." Mike, a patrol officer in a different division, made a prediction:

> You know what's gonna happen with this, somehow some way it's going to end up where their client was specifically targeted and then as a result of that there's some new form of entrapment—it's like the 2010 version of entrapment. Somehow, like, you know, "you're unfairly targeting my client due to his past history which has nothing to do with his current performance," and somehow you just happened to be focusing on him when he was here and he shouldn't have been there.

I probed further about Mike's perceptions of the legality of the offender-based strategy:

> Here's the thing: the protective shield is the probation/parole aspect of it, because probation/parole, you're subject to conditions at any time and so that's kind of a green light as far as [data collection and surveillance] goes. But everything else is like you're basically targeting somebody based upon *what?* . . . What if I was just in a car, you know, a bunch of times, and I just happen to get pulled over? What if my brother's a gangster, but he's my family? I'm not gonna turn my back to my brother but yet I'm with him all the time. So, all of a sudden I pop up on your list for what reason? You know what I mean? That to me is—oh God.

In other words, to Mike, if someone is on parole or probation, stopping those high-point individuals is fine. It's justifiable. But it's a bridge too far for police to engage in similar practices with individuals who aren't "on paper" (on parole or probation).

A captain in a division using place-based predictive policing expressed his concerns about the location-based strategy: "Some officer somewhere, if this gets big enough, is going to say, 'Ok, everybody in the box is open season,' you know? I mean, it'll be a court case someday." He also said he was "not that keen" on geocoding FIs, and was careful to state that "we need independent reasonable suspicion that then leads to probable cause that then leads to an arrest." Where the practices seemed liable to land them in court one day, officers expressed reservations toward big data policing.

Within-Department Differences in the Reception of Big Data

There is a tendency in sociological research on the police to treat departments as monolithic organizations. Scores of sociological studies say "the police do X" or "the police do Y." But homogenizing cops obscures variation on a variety of axes within law enforcement organizations, including the differing ways individuals respond to the introduction of big data analytics into their daily operations. How do patterns of contestation of big data analytics map on to existing divisions in the department? Do they entrench old divisions? Do they create new distinctions? The remainder of this chapter analyzes how data was embraced unevenly in the department and how levels of enthusiasm for big data varied according to individuals' positions in the organizational hierarchy and functions in the department.[19] Big data's differential uptake reflected three preexisting divisions within law enforcement: local versus federal agencies, civilian employees versus sworn officers, and management versus patrol officers.

Local versus Federal Agencies

Interagency rivalries are as old as the institution of law enforcement itself.[20] The tension between local and federal law enforcement agencies was heightened after 9/11, which was framed as a case of agencies failing to share information, and the resulting mandate to share more information.[21]

Individuals in local law enforcement agencies—in my study, the LAPD and LA County Sheriff's Department (LASD)—expressed disillusionment and frustration with what they perceived to be an asymmetrical data-sharing relationship with the federal agencies. This became especially apparent in discussions about JRIC (the Southern California fusion center). The LAPD liaises with JRIC through the Department of Corrections in order to share information and increase "situational awareness." However, multiple interviewees in local law enforcement said JRIC is "useless" to them, because data sharing only goes "up" and never goes "down." For example, one sergeant within the LASD said that they routinely send information they gather to JRIC, but are unable to access information from the fusion center for their own daily operations. A civilian employee within the LAPD elaborated on that point:

> Well, yeah, there's a lot of the data that JRIC will not trickle down to the general agency because it's intel, right? So, it'll go only to our anti-terrorist section . . . that's what I don't like about JRIC, is it's hyper-focused just on Homeland Security issues. And I think there's a lot of opportunity there just on crime issues. So, they jumped in on like that Dorner case[22] just because it was such a high profile [case], and I think it was a huge benefit to us, because we didn't have the skillset to do what they did. But on a crime series, no, that's not so much their jurisdiction. And we're pouring in hundreds of thousands of dollars into these centers. But they're really focused in on just a small minority of what we're responsible for. And a lot of data's going there but, again, it doesn't necessarily come back out to patrol. Because [patrol's] not supposed to know certain things.

Other respondents, ranging from a detective in Fugitive Warrants to captains in South and Central Bureau, echoed the idea that federal agencies have access to more privileged information than local enforcement agencies. The captain in South Bureau stated simply, "It's annoying. They don't tell me anything."

Such information asymmetry has the capacity to produce and reinforce power in organizations. A civilian employee who had spent time at JRIC said the lack of transparency makes it difficult to evaluate federal agencies' efficacy. He explained,

> It's hard for us really to make sure how effective they are, because even though I work with a lot of major crimes, I don't try and get so much into the details, because it makes people suspicious and uncomfortable, because they all have top secret clearance and you don't. So, there's that mentality.

He described walking through JRIC with a colleague and gestured to imitate JRIC employees covering the papers on their desks so he couldn't see anything.

Alongside LAPD and Sheriff's Department personnel protesting their inability to access the data stored and shared at the federal level, some are skeptical about whether the feds even have any information locals might want. Speaking about data at JRIC, a different civilian employee called it "ineffective" and a "sporadic mess," because "most of the time it's like the locals know stuff before the JRIC actually gets to them." And during an interview with an officer at the division station, his captain interrupted to ask a few questions about my research. When I mentioned I had spent time at JRIC, he told me that he sends stuff up to JRIC, never to hear from them again. He explains, "I won't tell Eric Holder that, but it's no help to me at all."[23]

Sworn Officers versus Civilian Employees

Within the LAPD, there are just over 10,000 sworn officers and 3,000 civilian employees. Sworn officers have a strong legal and philosophical commitment to the identity of being a cop, a fact that previous work has attributed to their socialization and training at the academy and during the "breaking-in" period on the job.[24] On at least four occasions, I asked sworn officers a question and they refused to answer, but when I asked the exact same question of civilian employees, they answered without hesitation. To me, this suggested that some civilian employees may be less protective of information than their law enforcement colleagues. For example, before our interview, a detective in Fugitive Warrants warned me, "I have to be honest in that most of the methods we use are confidential and we cannot share." I proceeded with the interview and, for half an hour, this detective and his investigator sat across from me, offering one-word answers or responses like "that's law enforcement sensitive" and "Mmm, yeah, see we can't tell you that." I couldn't write about how they track down fugitives, he insisted, because then the fugitives would know how the cops track them down. By contrast, a civilian crime analyst who works with Robbery-Homicide (among other specialized and area divisions) offered up incredibly detailed explanations of the ways the LAPD leverages data to track homicide suspects.

I detected an "us vs. them" mentality that cut both ways. In addition to officers contrasting themselves with "egghead types" that sit behind a computer all day, as discussed earlier in this chapter, information technology staff indicated that they felt underappreciated. One data analyst complained, "You always forget about the data guy. But [the] law enforcement industry is that way," and the "guy that does all the dirty work is usually forgotten. I'm that guy." Another civilian, in Information Technology Division, told me, "IT is always just a support role. So, whatever the primary business, we're always just sort of like, you know, Santa's helpers. And we're kinda like, just there. Sometimes more of an annoyance than a benefit." A third argued that civilian employees deserve more credit: "I mean, if you think about it and why I'm sort of harping on the whole IT thing in law enforcement is in the last 20 years, the biggest improvements in law enforcement are computer technology driven. Right? That's the basic reality."

Civilians tend to be the first ones in the department affected by budget cuts, in part due to sworn officers' union protections. Cuts to civilian employee budgets, coupled with the increasing need for skilled data analysts, help explain the increase in outsourcing and contracts awarded to criminal justice consulting firms like Justice and Securities Strategies, Inc. and technology firms like Palantir. Cuts place analysts in a difficult position: fewer civilian employees are handling ever-more data. One explained that not only is he responsible for preparing materials for COMPSTAT, but now supervisors in every division want weekly data analytics on crime rates and the geographic distribution of crimes. As more complex analytics are incorporated into investigations, supervisors want analysts to keep them abreast of how cases are progressing—a request that one civilian analyst contends is "a little bit unfair." He now has to keep tabs on what detectives are doing, what is happening with every case, how many people are in custody, perform COMPSTAT preps, and, above all, be accountable to management. His role, he said, was the starting point in a "trickle up" process. If he does not provide data to the captain, the commander starts asking the captain for the data, and then the chief starts asking the commander. It was a lot of pressure and seemed to earn little respect.

The difference in resources made available to sworn officers, as opposed to civilian employees, was apparent early in my fieldwork. When I introduced myself and my research, explaining that I had selected the LAPD as a case study because it is one of the most technologically advanced departments, I got a markedly different reaction from civilian employees and sworn officers. Sworn officers at RACR (the Real-Time Crime Analysis Center), for example, agreed wholeheartedly, and proudly showed me the various programs at their fingertips. Meanwhile, a civilian employee in Records and Identification Division scoffed at the idea that the LAPD was a technology leader ("We are? Funny you think that"), and then pointed out the old mainframe systems still used in her division. Part of this variation can be explained by the specialized divisions the officers and civilian employees were working in—Robbery-Homicide is higher status than Records and Identification, for example—but even within divisions, there was variation along sworn/civilian lines.

Competing demands on analysts' time are also seen as potentially compromising data quality. "There are times when an analyst says 'I just want to make sure those locations are properly geocoded. That's not enough to cut it.' The pressure to get everything done in real time is real. 'You want me to get that done by *when*?'" This analyst's sentiment echoes what Barley[25] found in his work on technicians, where "caretaking" tasks like cleaning data were seen as crucial to the front-line workers, but often downplayed by their managers. Barley writes that "technicians complained that administrators often made technical decisions for political or personal reasons without appreciating the practical implications of their actions."[26] But, in the words of one captain, "Old news is useless." This creates tension between data quality—which necessitates spending time carefully cleaning and cross-checking the data (for accurate geocodes, for example)—and data timeliness.

So as technology's roles in law enforcement practices multiply and gain importance, data's new primacy is not reflected in the organizational structure of law enforcement agencies. In contrast to the strong officers' union, there is no group that organizes IT people across agencies. Ramón, a bookish civilian employee, commented that, for "all of us who are doing big data stuff, there's actually no coordination state wide, county wide, or even across the nation, right? . . . That's what militates against the success of it." Ramón's colleague rolled his eyes and put his hands up to gesture "stop." "Can you back up for a second?" he asked. "You used a word there." "Which one?," Ramón asked. "Militates." Ramón laughed and looked at me knowingly, in some kind of bookish solidarity. "*She* understands."

Managers versus Front-Line Workers

Tension between managers and front-line workers is ubiquitous in organizations, and it existed prior to the introduction of big data analytics. As such, some of the tension between law enforcement managers and front-line workers is merely a transposition of chronic tensions onto the new digital environment. Other tensions have been exacerbated by the function creep of data originally collected for one purpose being used for another.

The most common friction cited in my interviews was when data on officer behavior that was originally collected for risk management was used for performance evaluations. In order to understand the creep of accountability measures into performance metrics in the LAPD, it helps to have a bit of context about how data is used for risk management within the department. As discussed in Chapter 2, the 2001–2013 federal consent decree mandated that the LAPD implement an early warning system, TEAMS II, to flag officer behavior patterns that may put the organization at legal risk. TEAMS II's capstone is its Risk Management Information System (RMIS), a database of information about LAPD employees that can be used for supervising and auditing individual employees, units, and divisions. Supervisors can request a TEAMS II report on an individual by his or her serial number. The resulting document is similar to a credit report, and it will have consent decree–mandated information like action items or risk-related activities, including uses of force, personnel complaints, civil litigation, vehicle pursuits, and on-duty traffic collisions.

The intended use and primary function of RMIS is to reduce risk and give management access to data to manage risk among their employees. However, once managers had TEAMS II data, they began using the information for performance evaluations. For example, in addition to the mandated monitored events, the department incorporated productivity factors, such as stop and arrest numbers, into TEAMS II. Those productivity factors are then leveraged in promotion decisions.

TEAMS II is fundamentally comparative—for both risk assessment and promotion, it is used to compare peer groups of employees who have equal standing or duty assignment, rank, and classification. If individuals fall more than three standard deviations above the mean of their peer group on an action item—such as vehicle pursuits or use of force—they are flagged as a risk, and supervisors are notified. Supervisors can then choose to take no action, have an informal meeting, mandate training, do special evaluation reports, modify the officer's field duties, assign them to nonfield duties, or, most seriously, refer them to the Risk Management Executive Committee (RMEC), a panel of commanding officers who ultimately decide whether the officer should stay in the field. When I asked how three standard deviations was chosen as the threshold, an interviewee in Risk Management explained that it was basically an ad-hoc decision. Initially, they thought two standard deviations would be the "magic number," but too many people were getting action items. So they increased it to three.

Officers' frustration with function creep kept coming up. When talking about what TEAMS II data is used for, a Police Officer II described what he viewed as a frustrating case of managerial overreach: "Now it's like oh, well, we're monitoring for every little thing. It's like, that's not what it was originally sold to us as. Now it's almost like we're going too far with it like, like trying to get officers in trouble." He continued, explaining that TEAMS II data were figuring into promotions:

> It has a performance metric in that, too, where it'll compare you to your peer group. So, it'll compare me to not only [division] officers but also [adjacent division] officers on my particular watch, and then also department-wide officers in my general experience range. So it's like compare and contrast. Like, okay, this guy has two arrests but this guy has 500 arrests. And which one is the outlier? And then if 95 percent of people have 5 arrests, then that 500 will obviously be the outlier so that he is either exceedingly great or exceedingly bad.

The RMIS data made it possible to compare across officer groups in ways that were impossible before system integration, when officers' files had to be reviewed individually for promotion. Technically, action items that generate flags (e.g., pursuits, use of force, complaints), are not supposed to be factored into promotions or pay grade advancements (e.g., from a Police Officer I to a Police Officer II). However, multiple interviewees explained that commanding officers can run anything they want in the system, and they can look at all the action items in TEAMS II in any circumstance, including promotions.

In line with trends toward automated decision-making in a wide range of organizations, "flags," or warning signs, that were previously only manually reviewed are now automatically generated. An officer recalled an instance when he thought the automatic flagging misrepresented what had happened in the field. After being involved in three pursuits within "a few months," he received a letter indicating that if he was involved in any more pursuits, the system would automatically generate a report and send it to his supervisor for review. That is, the supervisor would be prompted to check that he wasn't "doing anything shady." The officer pointed out that he works in a high-crime division. These automatic data flags provided no context as to why he got in the pursuits in the first place, and therefore obscured the particulars of the incidents. For example, on one of the pursuits, he said he was secondary (meaning he did not initiate the pursuit, but was called in for support by another unit). With exasperation, he insisted that he was only on backup for about 20 seconds. He thought the automatic flag put him under unfair scrutiny, because he was not *actually* being overzealous or putting the department at risk when he was involved in high-speed chases. He was just doing his job and helping out his fellow officers.

Few of the officers I interviewed complained about basic risk management practices. Rather, they frequently objected to the repurposing of data originally intended for risk management into performance metrics, a frustration that exacerbated distrust and division between managers and officers.

———

It may initially appear as if officer complaints about and resistance toward data collection, analysis, and surveillant technologies fall into roughly two categories: worries about being monitored for either (1) disciplinary purposes or (2) the allocation of resources. Put differently, at first glance, it could seem that officers simply objected to having departmental risk management systems used to collect data on officer behavior for personnel management, and that they resented being told how to do their job effectively by algorithms rather than their own intuition. Instead, I found that the most vehement opposition was to function creep and quantified assessment when technologies and data originally designed for one purpose—such as risk management or crime reduction—were used for another, namely managerial assessment of job performance. Underpinning officer distrust is the sentiment that arbitrary decisions were being made by higher-ups whose methods and motivations were opaque. This poses a dilemma for management: insist on either outcomes or process. Inevitably, technologically mediated management is always a compromise between the two.

The inversion of surveillance also reveals a great deal about power relationships. Whereas much of this book focuses on the power asymmetry between the police and the communities they police, this chapter reveals a different type of surveillant asymmetry, between management and employees. However, ironically, in their complaints about managerial surveillance officers identify the very same fairness and inequality questions other chapters of this book consider: officers lamenting having to account for their whereabouts echoes the idea of individuals leading incriminating lives through their decontextualized digital traces; the opacity of algorithms is a point where the interests of the police and activists unexpectedly align; and the grievance about not all officers being subject to the same surveillance and scrutiny as those in higher crime divisions makes salient issues of equal protection.

Interestingly, it did not seem like officers' experience with managerial surveillance affected how they viewed their role in surveilling society more generally. The exercise of flipping the lens of surveillance and talking about how they were experiencing many of the uncomfortable or perceivably unfair aspects of surveillance did not build some kind of "surveillance empathy." Rather, I heard a cognitive dissonance in which sworn officers did not recognize (or at least did not verbalize) the irony that their discomfort and resistance is toward the same technology they are imposing on other communities.

When law enforcement officers become the subjects of surveillance, their relative power enables them to engage in more effective individualized and organized resistance than most civilians. Some of the front-line workers' techniques of resistance[27] are collective and organized, like union opposition to the use of AVLs. Others are more informal, such as evading technology and blocking data acquisition (using alternative communication channels, like cell phones instead of dispatch), vandalism (tearing tracking antennae off cars), or producing *more* data on their own terms (carrying their own recording devices). All these tactics to evade surveillance would, if performed by people outside law enforcement, be viewed as suspicious. Why are the same actions not damning when police engage in them? As one officer explained, "We're the good guys." The broader worldview of state legitimacy and police exceptionalism, in which cops do not have to be subject to the same rules as everybody else, seems to serve as their justification. The world is made up of good guys and bad guys, and if you're the good guys, you do the surveilling, but if you're the bad guys, you get surveilled. That's just the way it is.

Understanding patterns of contestation with regard to big data analytics helps us understand how new practices are adopted, resisted, and deployed. It also helps us understand professional identities, roles, and interactions within the deeper patterns of organizational change and continuity. Despite resistance, big data analytics and surveillance technologies are becoming more prevalent in the daily operations of the LAPD, in large part because people in managerial roles and other positions of authority support that spread.[28] In that sense, the use of technology has a reifying or entrenching effect. Data and technology are used as sources of control to reinforce preexisting power relationships.

To a certain extent, the introduction of big data analytics into the LAPD served to transpose age-old complaints about managerial control and organizational change onto new technologies. In research on computerization, Kling argues that technological change usually results in those with the most resources gaining the most influence: computerization projects tend to keep "important authority relationships . . . untouched."[29] In much the same way, in the case of law enforcement, I find that big data analytics and emerging surveillance technologies serve to entrench managerial control and put frontline workers under more fine-grained supervision and scrutiny.

To the extent that big data analytics have been disruptive to the internal organization of the LAPD and LASD, it is that they have reshaped channels for promotion. The new emphasis on proficiency in data analytics means that individuals who are promoted to supervisory roles in the department are increasingly individuals who have a working understanding of and are conversant in data analytics. I heard certain individuals repeatedly called Palantir "rock stars" or "power users." One captain who is enthusiastic about big data and has moved up the ranks rapidly over the past five years explained that some officers complained about his promotions: " 'What is this bullshit that [he] is trying to get promoted about?' . . . And I'm not kidding. . . . They really do. And unfortunately, I have been promoted because of it."

This chapter has examined surveillance through the lens of the employment relationship. But officer resistance is not merely an *outcome* of data-based surveillance. Rather, the practice of resistance actually *shapes* future data, which has important implications that will be explored in the next chapter.

CHAPTER 6 | ## Coding Inequality

How the Use of Big Data Reduces, Obscures,
and Amplifies Inequalities

> Although bigness is generally a good property when used correctly,
> I've noticed that it can sometimes lead to a conceptual error. For some
> reason, bigness seems to lead researchers to ignore how their data was
> generated. While bigness does reduce the need to worry about random
> error, it actually increases the need to worry about systematic errors, the
> kinds of errors that . . . arise from biases in how data are created.
>
> —Matthew Salganik,
> *Bit by Bit: Social Research in the Digital Age*
> (Princeton University Press, 2017)

MUCH OF BIG DATA's appeal stems from its aura of objectivity. Proponents of big data policing argue that in contrast to human discretion, algorithms and other automated data management systems reduce bias and increase efficiency, insight, neutrality, objectivity, accountability, and fairness throughout the justice system. This overlooks the basic fact that even new analytic platforms and techniques are deployed in preexisting organizational contexts[1] and embody the purposes of their creators.[2] Further, algorithms are tools that humans use to outsource their decisions—or at least streamline their decision-making processes—but human discretion remains central to their operation, from programming to data entry to the weight analysts assign to their results and recommendations. What data law enforcement collects, what methods they use to analyze and interpret it, and how it informs their practice are all part of a fundamentally social process.

Rather than eliminating human discretion, big data is a form of capital, both a social product *and* a social resource. For that reason alone, big data cannot possibly obviate inequality: like other forms of capital, it is transactional, some people and groups have more of it than others, and it can be extracted from already disadvantaged populations.

Still, empirically, to what extent the adoption of advanced analytics will reduce organizational inefficiencies and inequalities or serve to entrench existing power dynamics remains an open question. This chapter analyzes the promises and perils of police use of big data. Surveillance is always ambiguous; it is implicated in both social inclusion and exclusion, and it creates both opportunities and constraints. When debating the merits of a new algorithm or surveillance technology, it is always important to remember that its openness and fairness are relative questions: Is the use of big data better or worse than the inequalities created by existing models of policing? Can big data be used to reduce bias and improve public safety? What are the trade-offs? What are the intended and unintended consequences? How do the digital traces we leave shape our life chances?

As previous chapters of the book have detailed, big data and associated technologies permit unprecedentedly broad and deep police surveillance. The depth and breadth of surveillance has ambivalent implications for social inequalities. On the one hand, big data analytics may be a means by which to ameliorate persistent inequalities in policing. Data can be used to "police the police" and replace unparticularized suspicion of racial minorities and human exaggeration of patterns with less biased predictions of risk. On the other hand, data-intensive police surveillance practices are implicated in the reproduction of inequality in at least four ways: by (1) deepening the surveillance of individuals already under suspicion, (2) codifying a secondary surveillance network, (3) widening the criminal justice dragnet unequally, and (4) leading people to avoid "surveilling" institutions that are fundamental to social integration. As currently implemented, police use of big data exacerbates inequalities more than it remediates them, because data is collected, analyzed, and deployed in socially patterned, asymmetrical ways.

How Can Big Data Be Used to Reduce Inequality?

The vast majority of big data policing efforts are directed at tracking and predicting crime and criminal activity. Inverting the focus of big data surveillance and directing it toward the police themselves may generate new insights. Digital trails are susceptible to oversight. Therefore, aggregating data on police practices may shed light on systematic patterns and institutional practices previously dismissed as individual-level bias, ultimately providing an opportunity to police the police by increasing transparency and, potentially, accountability.

One limitation to this function is that there are so many holes in our current data on police activity. For example, after the shooting of Michael Brown and subsequent protests in Ferguson, Missouri, journalists and activists and academics alike cried out for data. How could they make more generalizable statements about police use of deadly force in the United States when there was no single law enforcement database recording all such incidents? Attorney General Eric Holder called the situation a "troubling reality" and declared that it struck "many—including me—as unacceptable." Holder concluded: "Fixing this," by creating a national database of officer-involved deaths, "is an idea that we should all be able to unite behind."[3] Another blind spot in the data concerns racial profiling: there is no national, government-run police database that can be used to measure and compare race and police interactions across jurisdictions.

Recent efforts to remedy the situation so that policing data can be collected, codified, and studied include the Obama administration's 2014 creation of the President's Task Force on 21st Century Policing and the 2015 establishment of the Police Data Initiative, which would create a community of law enforcement agencies, technologists, and researchers committed to using data to increase transparency and accountability and improve police–community relations. By September 2017, however, the Trump administration announced it was shutting down the Task Force.

That we cannot rely solely on data generated and maintained by the police or the government is not a total limitation, however. The mass digitization of information has begun to afford academics, journalists, politicians, and activists the opportunity to collect, merge, and analyze a wide range of new data sources, such as online public records, data collected from streamlined Freedom of Information Act (FOIA) requests, national news databases, and crowd-sourced content. The Center for Policing Equity, for example, has established the National Justice Database, which is the first database tracking national statistics on police behavior, including stops and use of force, and standardizing data collection across many of the country's departments.[4] Organizations such as the *Washington Post*, *The Guardian*, Fatal Encounters, Killed by Police, and Mapping Police Violence have begun to collect and publish information on police killings. And data collection on policing is now being crowd-sourced through, for example, apps in which citizens can use their cell phones to record, store, and upload footage of police to a local ACLU office.

The LAPD is ahead of the curve in using data to track their own officers' activity, in large part due to the federal consent decree imposed from 2001 to 2013 (see Chapter 2 for a more detailed discussion). The early intervention system, TEAMS II, comes out of the reasoning that only a small number of officers are responsible for a disproportionate number of use of force complaints. Therefore, if managers could predict who those officers will be and intervene, they may be able to dramatically reduce such complaints. As explained in Chapter 5, TEAMS II compares peer groups of individuals grouped together based on equal standing or similar qualities such as duty assignment, rank, and classification. If individuals are more than three standard deviations above the mean of their peer group on any action item—such as vehicle pursuits or use of force—they are flagged as a risk, and their supervisors are notified.

TEAMS II is an example of a system designed with the explicit purpose of monitoring the police. However, in the age of big data, many other tools typically used for surveilling civilians can be used to surveil the police. For example, Palantir is equipped with "immutable audit logs" that show who accessed what data when. In order to use the platform, users must log in and enter a reason for their search (when employees demonstrated the platform for me, they typically typed in "demo" as their search reason). These searches, along with tagging, resolving, and other data edits, can be audited. In other words, if an officer is using the Palantir platform inappropriately, there are digital traces the department can use to hold that officer accountable. However, accountability is not automatic. Just because technological capabilities exist does not mean they are used. Organizations need both the will and capacity to hold people accountable, and if my interviews are any measure, resource constraints are a perennial concern in the LAPD and LA County Sheriff's Department. Not one person I spoke with could identify a single instance in which a Palantir use audit had been conducted.[5]

Automatic vehicle locators (AVLs) provide another possible technology that can be leveraged to police the police. These in-car tracking devices were intended, in part, to help supervisors measure the effectiveness of dosage—raising or lowering police presence—in predictive policing boxes. Historically, sergeants and captains had a rough idea of where their officers drove on patrol. Now, with AVLs, the generation and collection of location data can be automated, granular, and uniform: the data is automatically GPS-coded every five seconds and available in real time. It is entered automatically and in the exact same format, every time. Management can now immediately and retrospectively corroborate where their officers are directed to go, where their officers say they are going, and where they actually go.

Another critical area data can shed light on is bias in police stops. How big data can be used to improve accuracy and fairness in stops is not simply a data question, but also a normative question. We must first ask, what is a defensible hit rate? For example, if the police stop 100 people, releasing 99 of them without charge, that is a 1 percent hit rate. That's a low payoff, and so that level of police intrusion would probably be considered indefensibly high. Indeed, judges typically examine historical hit rate percentages and include them in Fourth Amendment analysis. But say we change the context of our question: at airport security, for example, every single passenger getting on a plane is searched, and the TSA has a hit rate far lower than 1 percent. Here the risk of finding a bomb or other weapon is considered high enough to justify a lower hit rate for intensive policing. Hit rates also differ across racial groups: when the NYPD was conducting mass stop-and-frisks, for example, officers had to fill out a UF-250 form for each stop. Researchers have gained access and analyzed the magnitude of racial disparities in hit rates under stop-and-frisk, finding that 80–90 percent of individuals were released without charge and hit rates were higher for whites than Blacks. Specifically, this confirmed that, controlling for precinct variables and race-specific baseline crime rates, Blacks and Hispanics were stopped more frequently than whites, even though whites who were stopped were more likely to be carrying weapons or contraband than were Blacks.[6] Researchers have not yet been able to access the data necessary to conduct a similar analysis in Los Angeles or most other jurisdictions, but the data allowed reformers in New York City to effectively challenge stop-and-frisk policies on the basis of these indefensible hit rates. The ends (including racial disparities and low hit rates) did not justify the means (racial profiling and high rates of police intervention).

The use of big data may help limit the number of unwarranted police stops, especially of young men of color. One of its perks is that big data can be used to retroactively diagnose a problem—such as racial disparities in police stops—as well as to predict and prevent the problem in the future. A group of data scientists and lawyers—Sharad Goel, Maya Perelman, Ravi Shroff, and David Sklansky—used data from almost three million NYPD UF-250 forms to calculate a "stop-level hit rate" (SHR), or the pre-stop calculation of the numerical likelihood of a successful search. They developed a model that could correctly predict whether the stop would yield a weapon 83 percent of the time.[7] Their review of the retrospective data showed that 43 percent of stops had less than 1 percent chance of turning up a weapon, and that hit rates were unevenly distributed by race: 49 percent of Blacks and 34 percent of Hispanics stopped under suspicion of carrying a weapon had less than a 1 percent chance of carrying a weapon, compared with only 19 percent of whites stopped. Therefore, police could reduce their number of stops, while maintaining the number of recovered weapons and reducing racial disproportionality. But how?

Goel and colleagues[8] argue it is possible to construct statistically derived heuristics to replace uninterpretable black box algorithms. In fact, they suggest, simple, transparent, and easy to understand heuristics often work as well as complex statistical models. If officers focused on just three signals—a suspicious object (three points), the sight and sound of criminal activity (one point), and a suspicious bulge (one point)—the researchers believed they could reduce racial discrimination, increase constitutionality, and increase efficiency (i.e., hit rates). In deciding whether to make a stop, officers could add up their heuristic score and check whether the sum exceeded an area-specific threshold. That said, much like the LAPD's points system (described in Chapter 4), this method could lead to a feedback loop and obscure the role of police activity in producing risk scores. Implementing any such quantified risk assessment must consider the "human in the loop" and be validated in an ongoing manner.

Another example of big data analytics being used to offer insight on (and potentially reduce) inequality in policing is found in research conducted by Stanford social psychologists in conjunction with the City of Oakland.[9] Researchers statistically analyzed almost 30,000 stop forms, officers' written narratives, and linguistic data from body-worn cameras (i.e., words spoken by Oakland Police Department [OPD] officers during stops). Net of neighborhood crime rates, demographics, and officer race, gender, and experience, they found that OPD officers stopped, searched, handcuffed, and arrested more African Americans than whites. Importantly, the difference was not only in the *quantity* of the stops, but also the *quality*. OPD officers offered fewer explanations for African Americans' stops and used more severe legal language (e.g., mentioned probation, parole, and arrests), were less likely to use honorifics ("sir" or "ma'am"), and were less likely to apologize in conversation with African Americans. There was little evidence of overt bias or purposeful discrimination; instead, subtle cultural norms, beliefs, and practices sustained disparate outcomes.

There is a saying that sunlight is the best disinfectant. Shedding light on systematic patterns of bias in policing is a great first step in increasing accountability. However, we also need institutional change. Policing is embedded in power structures, and the outcomes of struggles between law enforcement, civilians, and information technology companies—which increasingly own the storage platforms and proprietary algorithms used in data analysis—will play a role in determining whether big data policing will ameliorate or exacerbate inequalities. Creating data on police activity is possible and paramount, as is directing that process with careful attendance to issues around privacy, confidentiality, and law enforcement–sensitive information. Without such structural change, inequality in data access will continue to thwart opportunities to reduce inequality in police treatment and outcomes.

Another way that big data could be used to reduce inequalities in the criminal justice system is by helping correct for incomplete information. Police—like all of us—operate with incomplete information. Social psychological research demonstrates that humans are "cognitive misers"[10] who rely on shortcuts—such as the conflation of Blackness and criminality[11]— to understand the world. Stereotypes like these become more important, or have the most cognitive utility, in situations in which decisions need to be made quickly and with incomplete information. Therefore, if big data can be utilized to fill information gaps, it may improve police interaction with, in this instance, minorities, by creating new "priors" or pieces of data to be considered in subsequent interactions. This learning could allow police to rely less on racial stereotypes. In other words, providing more— and more accurate—data may reduce unparticularized suspicion of specific groups and prevent the human exaggeration of patterns by replacing them with less biased predictions of risk. In theory, it could reduce categorical suspicion of young minority men, ultimately reducing the scatter-shot hyper-surveillance of minority neighborhoods and the consequent erosion of community trust.[12] Note the word "accurate": more data does not always mean more *accurate* data. As described throughout this book, data are not merely mechanical reflections of the world; they are shaped by social processes. Although it may be possible to reduce inequalities by making data more perfect, it will never eliminate them, because inequality is baked into the input data.

In sum, the mass digitization of information paves the way for two new avenues to reduce inequalities in policing and increase accountability: big data policing offers the ability to track individual police behaviors at a more granular level, which can fill informational gaps and be aggregated up to identify systemic patterns in the data. To make good on these promises, to actually use big data to reduce inequalities in policing, will require more. Of the four steps needed to make a change, we have only considered the first two: diagnosing the problem and identifying opportunities for interventions. We have a long way to go in terms of the third and fourth steps: implementing interventions and evaluating their efficacy.

Reinforcing Inequality through Big Data

Biased Training Data and Hidden Feedback Loops

The surveillance scholar David Lyon describes surveillance as a process of "social sorting" in which people are classified and stratified into categories for differential treatment.[13] With regard to crime, police surveillance classifies some people and places as high risk and others as low risk. The premise behind both person- and place-based predictive policing is that we can learn about the future from the past. That holds both for crime and for inequalities. When we hold up a mirror to the past, those inequalities are reflected into the future.[14] And if our data are incomplete or biased, algorithms will not only mirror, but also amplify inequalities.

The "past," for algorithms, is historical data—what is known as training data. Machines are trained to discover useful patterns of statistical relationships in existing data, then accumulate those sets of relationships into a model used to automate the process of predicting the future from new data.[15] What a given model learns and what it is trained to look for in the future depends on the kinds of data and outcomes programmers provide. Consequently, an algorithm is only as good as its training data.

Let me be more concrete. Consider the person-based points system the LAPD uses to identify people who are high risk. Recall that individuals receive five points if they are on parole or probation, five points if they are documented as having a gang affiliation, five points for a violent criminal history, five points for a prior arrest with a handgun, and one point for every police contact. Officers are instructed to find reasons to stop the highest-point people in their patrol areas. But this process obviously leads to a feedback loop: if individuals have a high point value, they are under heightened surveillance and therefore have a greater likelihood of being stopped. Because they gain points for police contact, each time they are stopped, their point value rises. In that sense, the LAPD's predictive models have created a behavioral loop: they not only predict events (e.g., crime or police contact), they also actually contribute to those events' future occurrence. Put differently, the mechanisms for inclusion in criminal justice databases and risk assessment programs determine the surveillance patterns themselves. And because even arrests that do not result in charges or convictions count toward risk scores, the point system can create a ratchet effect in which surveillance is increased absent any evidence that it is warranted.

The point system is supposed to focus scarce police resources on the "hottest" offenders. It should also help avoid legally contestable bias in police practices. However, in the process of quantifying criminal risk, the system hides both intentional and unintentional bias in policing and creates a self-perpetuating cycle. As the legal scholar Frank Pasquale writes, "bias can embed itself in other self-reinforcing cycles based on ostensibly 'objective' data."[16] The data that feed the person-based predictive policing model include past stops, arrests, and classifications (e.g., gang affiliated or on parole or probation). A recent report by the LAPD Office of the Inspector General (OIG) found that the racial/ethnic makeup of chronic offenders on the LAPD's high-points lists in August 2018 was 49.8% Hispanic/Latino, 30% Black/African American, 12% White, and 1.3% Other; the gender breakdown was 93.1% male and 6.9% female.[17] Moreover, individuals living in low-income, minority areas have a higher probability of their "risk" being quantified than those in more advantaged neighborhoods where the police are not conducting point-driven surveillance.

We don't know what distortions are present in the data, or how the data differ from actual offense rates. So we can't know the degree to which we're measuring crime or measuring enforcement. Simply put: bias in, bias out. Points-driven surveillance can serve to legitimize and techwash the biased police practices that produced the original data. Again, we are reminded that, in the words of the media historian Lisa Gitelman, "Raw data is an oxymoron."[18] *There is no such thing as raw data*, because data cannot be divorced from social context.

These concerns are dismissed all the time. What's the harm in stopping someone regularly who is not wanted for any crime? First of all, it would be wrong to assume that all people labeled "chronic offenders" are, in fact, chronic offenders. The same OIG report found that 44 percent of people assigned point values by the LAPD's system had either zero or one arrest for a violent crime. Half had no gun arrests. Almost 10 percent had *no* documented police contacts.[19]

All this is to say that the points system puts individuals already under suspicion under new and deeper forms of surveillance, while appearing to be objective or, in the words of one captain, "just math." The police have long been rounding up the "usual suspects." What's different is that now they are quantifying suspicion in ways that feed back on themselves. Such practices simultaneously amplify and obscure preexisting inequalities. They hinder the ability of individuals already in the criminal justice system to avoid being drawn further into the surveillance net, and they hide the role of enforcement in shaping risk scores.

Whereas person-based predictive policing has implications for racial and class inequality, unthinking reliance on place-based algorithms may exacerbate neighborhood inequalities, (which, of course, correlate with racial and class inequalities). Official crime statistics are incomplete; estimates of unreported crime range from less than 17 percent to over 68 percent, depending on the offense.[20] For example, there is little bias in homicide data—there is almost perfect overlap between homicide data, hospital records, and victimization records—but triangulating across those data sources with regard to rape suggests that only about 30 percent of sexual assaults are reported to the police. What's more, crime data are not missing at random—crimes that take place in public places are more visible to police and therefore more likely to be recorded,[21] individuals and groups who do not trust the police are less likely to report crimes,[22] and police focus their attention and resources on Black communities at a disproportionately high rate relative to drug use and crime rates.[23] Social dynamics result in systematic bias that becomes training data fed into predictive policing algorithms, yet once they are input as data, the predictions *look* impartial. Human judgment is hidden in the black box[24] under a patina of objectivity.

For example, if historical crime data are used as inputs in a location-based predictive policing algorithm, the algorithm will identify areas with historically higher crime rates as high risk for future crime, officers will be deployed to those areas, and will thus be more likely to detect crimes in those areas, creating a self-fulfilling statistical prophecy while obscuring the role of law enforcement in shaping crime statistics.

Directing resources toward people and places statistically more likely to be associated with criminal activity increases the probability that such people (and people in such places) will be caught if they do something wrong, while reducing the probability of discovering and prosecuting wrongdoing by other people in other locations—the ones from whom the algorithms distract police attention.

Quantified practices may thus serve to exacerbate inequalities in stop patterns, create arrest statistics needed to justify stereotypes, and ultimately lead to self-fulfilling statistical prophecies.[25] Unchecked predictions may lead to an algorithmic form of confirmation bias and, subsequently, a misallocation of resources. They may justify the over-policing of minority communities and potentially take away resources from individuals and areas invisible to data collection sensors or subject to systematic underreporting. Moreover, using police contact as the entry point into the criminal justice system means the digital feedback loops associated with predictive policing may ultimately be the best justification anyone can offer for the growth of criminal justice surveillance.

It is important to consider how actual offense rates and official crime statistics may differ, because understanding each step of data collection and analysis is crucial for understanding how data systems—despite being thought of as objective, quantified, and unbiased—may inherit the bias of their creators and users. For example, place-based algorithms are most effective (and least biased) when predicting crimes with high reporting rates, such as motor vehicle theft.

Individuals working at predictive policing software companies are increasingly aware of these feedback loops. For example, HunchLab—a main competitor to PredPol—has introduced some randomness to its algorithm, which now occasionally directs officers to medium-risk locations as well as high-risk locations. Jeff Brantingham and George Mohler, PredPol's cofounders, coauthored an article with Matthew Valasik in which they report that although there are more arrests in predictive boxes, there are no significant differences in the proportions of Latinos, Blacks, and whites arrested in treatment or control conditions; therefore, they conclude, PredPol does not lead to racially biased arrests.[26] However, there are two key limitations to the study—it does not consider stops, searches, and detentions short of an arrest, all of which are found to be highly consequential in procedural justice literature,[27] and it "does not provide any guidance on whether arrests are themselves systematically biased. Such could be the case, for example, if "black and Latino individuals experienced arrest at a rate disproportionate to their share of offending." There are many studies that demonstrate that this is *precisely the case*.

To say that predictive policing exacerbates inequalities because it enhances the surveillance of disadvantaged minority communities is an oversimplification. Many sources of data that are not historical crime data—such as victimization data, public health data collected by hospitals on gunshot wounds, and citizen-initiated data like 911 calls, suggest violence does concentrate in particular communities. The question, then, becomes a normative one—are the police the primary lever we should use in violence reduction? If not, what other types of targeted service interventions could we use prediction to direct?

Codifying Social Relationships into a Secondary Surveillance Network

The mass collection of data and linkage abilities that new platforms afford extend police surveillance beyond individuals with high point values or those suspected of engaging in criminal activity. Individuals are subject to collateral data collection. Remember the analysts who worried that automatic license plate readers sometimes clearly showed the faces of passengers? Or the items on officers' field interview cards that indicated not only the individual they stopped, but also individuals who were stopped *with* a person of interest? That data is not just discarded. Even if you do not consent to providing your information, by virtue of your network tie, you might be included in data systems. To be gathered up in what I call the "secondary surveillance network," individuals do not need to have any police contact or have engaged in criminal activity; they simply need a data link to the central person of interest.

Returning to the field interview cards (FIs), in addition to recording information on individuals with high point values, FIs record the names, addresses, and geocoded information on "Persons with Suspect" via an open-ended narrative section. That data makes it into Palantir, so relationships codified on FIs can thus look to the system like evidence of criminality. If law enforcement can FI an individual multiple times and record that they had contact with a person on multiple occasions in the company of another individual who is a known gang member, for example, they can classify the person as a documented gang affiliate and put them into the gang database. In that sense, data begets more data and classifications.

Secondary surveillance has implications for inequality, as minority individuals and individuals in poor neighborhoods have a higher probability of being in this secondary surveillance net than those in higher-income neighborhoods where the police are not conducting points-driven surveillance. Recall the network diagram presented in detail in Figure 3.3. The person of interest in the center of the network has had direct police contact. However, the people and phone numbers and addresses and cars radiating out from that person need only have a link to the central person of interest. New "trigger mechanisms" mean that dragnet and directed surveillance tools have lowered the criteria for inclusion in criminal justice databases.[28]

The incentive to "get people in the system"—a trend I witnessed time and time again in my fieldwork—makes sense if you take the perspective of the police and their organizational imperative. As one software engineer explained it, little pieces of data that might seem unsuspicious at the time of collection can eventually be pulled together to create useful intelligence— "the sum of all information can build out what is needed to identify where a suspect is located." On ride-alongs, I repeatedly heard officers say that even if they can't arrest someone, they want to "get them in the system." This could mean all kinds of things, including filling out an FI or asking to take a consensual fingerprint with BlueCheck (a digital fingerprint system). One sergeant explained, "you wanna fingerprint these cats out here," telling me that gang affiliates often give a fake name or claim to not have ID when they are stopped. Where a casual chat with a beat cop in decades past might become data that that specific cop remembers the next time he sees you on his patrol, the exponential capture and cataloging of personal data is a strategic means of populating a database and channeling more individuals into a wider system, thus facilitating future tracking of more people in more ways by more law enforcement representatives. Once entered into the system, you can be autotracked, meaning an officer can receive notification if you are "touched" (come into contact with) by the police or other government agencies again. If you're in an area where, say, a points system is used, your tally just went up.

Net Widening

New digitized surveillance practices broaden the scope of people law enforcement can track. This can be understood as a new form of "net widening,"[29] though even this is happening unequally. The ALPRs mentioned above are now one of the primary means of tracking people without police contact. Even though ALPRs are dragnet surveillance tools that collect information on everyone, rather than merely those under suspicion, the likelihood of being input into the system is not randomly distributed. Crime and enforcement patterns lead to unequal data capture across individuals, groups, and geographic areas. In the LAPD, ALPRs are deployed based on department crime statistics (i.e., they are placed in higher-crime areas), and they, too, raise questions about unequal enforcement, detection, and reporting practices along lines of race, class, and neighborhood. In that sense, ALPR datasets are investigatory tools disproportionately "populated by the movements of particular groups."[30] Similarly, the ability to build out secondary surveillance networks in Palantir has implications for inequality, as racial minorities and people living in low-income neighborhoods have a higher probability of being in the primary (and thus secondary) surveillance net than people in neighborhoods where the police are not conducting data-intensive forms of policing.

Once again, the simple argument might be that if you have nothing to hide, you have nothing to fear from being included in law enforcement's big data systems. However, the legitimacy of using a series of data points to reconstruct an individual's intentions and behaviors—whether incriminating or exculpatory—and using that data to predict future behaviors, relies on the infallibility of both the state and the state actors who enter data. It is to assume the system is free from bias, error, or prejudice. That is a big assumption, and one that the findings on the previous pages of this book suggest is unsupportable.

Although you may just be going about your daily life, having no law enforcement encounters, particular *configurations* of data points may be flagged as suspicious. In Chapter 1, you saw that our digital traces are so broad as to make it impossible that you could consent to your data being collected at each time point. When those streams of information flow together, they form a "data double,"[31] or an incomplete picture of you that can nonetheless be a powerful tool in the hands of law enforcement. Once you are gathered up in a primary or secondary surveillance net, you can become an intelligence target. You can be linked to future data points. And by virtue of being in the surveillance system, you are more likely—correctly or incorrectly—to be identified as worthy of surveillance.

How are unequal mechanisms for inclusion in the surveillance net consequential for social inequality? Recall the detective's theory, recounted in Chapter 3, that if people are not doing anything wrong, the cops shouldn't be looking them up many times over the course of their lives. Yet racial disparities in police stop rates are well documented,[32] as are disparities in rates of release without charge. Empirical research consistently demonstrates that stop-and-query patterns are unequally distributed by race, class, and neighborhood.[33] In short, queries are not raw data but, at least in part, a product of enforcement practices. Not everyone is equally likely to come under police scrutiny, but once they do, the person who has more FIs filled out on them—even if they were never arrested or convicted—is less likely to be given the benefit of the doubt than the person who has none by virtue of living in a neighborhood with lower police presence or where they aren't conducting points-based predictive policing.

Moreover, much like in DNA databases,[34] in order to be a hit, one has to be in the database in the first place. Unequal rates of database inclusion can have real consequences, including false discovery[35] and wrongful conviction. It should not surprise that the risk of such outcomes is unequally distributed—for example, Black people are seven times more likely than white people to be wrongly convicted of murder.[36]

Analyzing the feeder mechanisms by which individuals are channeled into criminal justice databases helps us better understand how inequalities produced by differential surveillance may be magnified as individuals and their data are processed by the criminal justice system.

System Avoidance

Integrating external, nonpolice data into the law enforcement corpus may have unintended consequences. Although integrated systems create new opportunities for service delivery, they also make surveillance possible across formerly discrete institutional boundaries. Recent research suggests institutions such as hospitals, schools, workplaces, and banks have increasingly been "drawn into the harder edge of social control"[37] and oriented toward surveillance.[38]

At the same time, the rise in surveillance—and, more importantly, individuals' *perceptions* of pervasive surveillance—may be met with a concomitant increase in individuals' efforts to evade it. I used nationally representative data from the National Longitudinal Study of Adolescent Health and the National Longitudinal Survey of Youth to test the hypothesis that individuals wary of police surveillance engage in what I have termed "system avoidance,"[39] or deliberately and systematically avoiding institutions that keep formal records, such as hospitals, banks, schools, and employment, to avoid coming under heightened police surveillance. Results from a range of cross-sectional and longitudinal models suggest that individuals with criminal justice contact systematically avoid interacting with important institutions where they would leave a digital trace. More specifically, individuals who have been stopped by police, arrested, convicted, or incarcerated are more likely to avoid surveilling institutions such as medical, financial, educational, and labor market institutions that keep formal records (i.e., put them "in the system"). For example, net of sociodemographic and behavioral characteristics, individuals with criminal justice contact have 31 percent higher odds of reporting not obtaining medical care when they thought they needed it, compared to those without criminal justice contact (see Appendix C for full results).

However, perhaps it is individuals' preexisting characteristics that lead them to both have contact with the criminal justice system and have lower levels of institutional involvement, and it is those underlying differences—rather than criminal justice contact itself—that are driving different levels of institutional attachment. If selection into the criminal justice system also influences institutional attachment, we would expect to find reduced attachment across both surveilling and non-surveilling institutions, including volunteer and religious groups. Yet criminal justice contact does *not* reduce the odds that individuals will interact with these sorts of non-surveilling institutions (i.e., ones where you can opt out of record keeping or participate without showing ID). I also analyzed change over time, finding that individuals who transitioned from no contact to contact with the criminal justice system between waves of the survey had higher odds of, in the same pe-riod, stopping obtaining necessary medical care, closing a bank account, and going from having a job to not having a job. By contrast, none of the results from the models predicting change in involvement with non-surveilling institutions are statistically significant, providing further support for the original hypothesis that criminal justice contact, net of individual-level char-acteristics, is associated only with avoidance of surveilling institutions. I also used a number of other techniques to mitigate the possibility that it was not that individuals were avoiding institutions, but rather that institutions were excluding them.[40] Because involvement in the criminal justice system is the cause *and* consequence of complex social processes, multiple mechanisms are likely at work in conjunction. System avoidance is an important, previ-ously ignored, part of the story.

This research shows that because they are built, in part, by incorporating other institutions' data, criminal justice surveillance practices likely have a chilling effect, deterring people from using such institutions and thereby subverting their original mandates. And system avoidance and unequal insti-tutional involvement may have real consequences for inequality. Given that involvement with the criminal justice system is highly stratified by race and class, the negative consequences of system avoidance will be similarly dis-proportionately distributed, thus exacerbating preexisting inequalities for an expanding group of already disadvantaged individuals. Lack of attachment to medical care, banks, schools, and employment is associated with poorer outcomes for health, financial security, upward mobility, and desistance from crime, respectively. As the surveillance scholars Kevin Haggerty and Richard Ericson suggest, "efforts to evade the gaze of different systems involves an attendant trade-off."[41] That trade-off is full participation in society.

System avoidance is but one unintended consequence of the mass digi-tization of information and the consequent surveillance it makes possible. The sociologist Sarah Lageson conducts research on a different kind of avoidance—digital avoidance. In her work on the proliferation of criminal records online, Lageson finds the availability of online criminal records leads people to avoid situations that might induce an Internet search for their name, like volunteering at their child's school. This avoidance means that people—even some whose only criminal justice contact was the recording of a mugshot, without formal charges—get stuck in undesirable employ-ment, housing, and relationships (and digital avoidance is further stratified along class lines).[42] Much like the police increasingly use data aggregated by private data brokers, criminal record data are routinely bought and sold by data brokers and background check vendors. While expungement might seal someone's governmental record, privately sourced records remain on-line unless the record subject identifies each source, one by one, serving their expungement order to the website publisher or paying a fee to have their record removed. Much like the digital trails we leave, the digital trails the police leave are increasingly indelible. Lageson cautions that this is not a small group of people we are talking about here—about one in three, or 100 million US residents, have some type of criminal record, and almost half of American males (49 percent) have been arrested by age 23.[43]

The sum of this research is an unavoidable conclusion: that the mass dig-itization, integration, and availability of records may effectively extend the "mark" of a criminal record, and even a criminal justice *contact*,[44] into other institutions, and vice versa. This creep of data across institutional contexts can lead to "cascading disadvantages."[45] As individuals leave more digital traces, a "new economy of moral judgement"[46] becomes possible. Institutions of all kinds use actuarial techniques to track, sort, and categorize individuals into "classification situations" with different rewards and punishments at-tached.[47] These classification situations differentially shape life chances.[48] For example, classifying individuals as low or high risk for crime, terrorist activity, loan default, or medical conditions structures not only whether and how they will be surveilled, but also their life chances more generally. This book only begins to account for how the marking process may be changing in the age of digitized policing, let alone the ways the big data environment creates potentially farther-reaching digitized collateral consequences of in-volvement in the criminal justice system.

———

The use of big data has the potential to ameliorate discriminatory practices, yet as currently employed, simultaneously amplifies and obscures ine-quality, particularly for those who are already structurally disadvantaged. If not implemented with mechanisms for transparency, accountability, and on-going assessment, it will ultimately serve to entrench existing inequalities under the veneer of objectivity.

Indeed, organizational theory and literature from science and technology studies suggests that when new technology is overlaid onto an old organiza-tional structure, long-standing problems shape themselves to the contours of the new technology. The process of transforming individual actions into "objective" data raises fundamentally sociological questions that this book only begins to address. In many ways, it transposes classic concerns from the sociology of quantification about simplification, decontextualization, and the privileging of measurable complex social phenomena onto the big data landscape.

If we look at how systems can exacerbate inequalities now, we will be better positioned to design tools that are fairer later. So as police departments—and organizations more broadly—invest in new predictive tools and surveillance technologies, they need to commit to fairness and due process. This will require accountability from tech companies. Data-intensive surveillance is less visible than traditional street policing methods,[49] and the companies that develop predictive policing algorithms often keep their formulas secret, citing trade secrecy. Like all technologies before them, predictive policing algorithms reflect the values of their creators, but absent transparency, we cannot correct for such biases. Therefore, as Kate Crawford, a principal researcher at Microsoft Research and co-founder of the AI Now Institute, states, "inclusivity matters—from who designs it to who sits on the company boards and which ethical perspectives are included. Otherwise, we risk constructing machine intelligence that mirrors a narrow and privileged vision of society, with its old, familiar biases and stereotypes."[50]

It is easy to view "data-driven" policing as either a panacea or an irreparably flawed technique by which automated systems entrench social and economic inequality by design. The reality is that the implications for inequality ultimately depend on recognizing bias in data, privileging transparency and community engagement, solving for the right problems, implementing the correct interventions, and constantly reevaluating our data systems. We should think big. How can we use big data to predict not only offenders but also victims, to target not only punitive interventions but also services, to track not only civilians but also police? How can we use it to analyze the underlying factors that contribute to crime in the first place, and to evaluate which interventions are most effective in remedying them?

CHAPTER 7 | Algorithmic Suspicion and Big
Data Searches

The Inadequacy of Law in the Digital Age

The progress of science in furnishing the government with means of
espionage is not likely to stop with wire tapping. Ways may someday
be developed by which the government, without removing papers from
secret drawers can reproduce them in court, and by which it will be
enabled to expose to a jury the most intimate occurrences of the home.
Advances in the psychic and related sciences may bring means of
exploring unexpressed beliefs, thoughts and emotions.

—Justice Louis Brandeis, *dissenting*
Olmstead v. United States 277 U.S. 438 (1928)

. . . if such dragnet-type law enforcement practices as respondent
envisions should eventually occur, there will be time enough then to
determine whether different constitutional principles may be applicable.

—*United States v. Knotts* 460 U.S. 276 (1983)

A COUPLE OF YEARS ago, a group of criminal defense lawyers reached out
to me. They suspected policing had undergone important changes in the
digital age, with implications for how their clients were being investigated,
charged, and prosecuted. As I shared what I had learned within the LAPD—
how Palantir is used to merge disparate data sources, how person- and
place-based predictive policing shaped patrol activities and informed the reasonable suspicion calculus, and how secondary surveillance networks could
be built out to include individuals with no direct law enforcement contact—
the lawyers seemed dismayed. All of this was basically invisible to them,
because it all happened in investigations *before* the case. Indeed, as we have

seen in this book, data does not eliminate discretion, but rather displaces it to earlier, less visible (and therefore potentially less accountable) phases of the criminal justice process. Predictive policing and algorithmic control are at work well before any officer handcuffs a suspect and lawyers get involved.

Thus far we have looked at the data police are using and how they are using it in the name of the law. Now we turn to how the law regards these swiftly changing policing practices. For example, does aggregating, accessing, and analyzing your digital traces count as a search, and should it require a warrant? Are data being mustered to justify discriminatory policing? Do laws about proprietary information prevent defense teams from knowing information about the basis for their clients' arrests? Criminal procedure is still largely informed by case law from the 1970s. But it should be clear by now that policing looks very different on the ground today than it did half a century ago. Police-civilian interactions are no longer one-off, in-person encounters. Much of contemporary policing is programmatic, suspicionless, cumulative, probabilistic, and technologically mediated. It involves not only police-civilian interactions, but also police–dataset interactions, in which the data are often collected by nonpolice actors, before legal protections guarding against police overreach come into play. Consequently, existing legal frameworks are anachronistic and inadequate for governing police work in the age of big data.

In some ways, this research surfaces classic questions about government overreach. There is now a burgeoning body of legal scholarship analyzing the legal implications of big data policing, yet it is largely theoretical. Few law professors undertake fieldwork, conducting empirical research and watching how the police interpret and enact law in their everyday work.[1] Rather than intervening in ongoing doctrinal debates about how legal constructs can or cannot adapt in the digital age, my scholarship is better suited to allow me to stand back and ask, What are the legal implications of ignoring the fact that big data is social?

By grounding legal debates about police use of data in empirical detail, this chapter makes the case that basic legal principles are inadequate not simply because they are anachronistic, but also because the legal debates are too narrow. By not attending to the sociological processes that underpin basic legal principles, they take existing legal categories for granted. Put differently, big data—and the legal implications of its use—are not being considered in a sufficiently *sociological* way. As a result, as social life and its attendant data evolve, legal scholars are developing theories to explain the increasing gulf between the way the modern courts understand data and the central concerns of foundational legal concepts such as reasonable suspicion, the Fourth Amendment, and the third-party doctrine. However, these theories are insufficiently sociological. In addition to considering how legal constructs *should* adapt, we must be sure that constitutional modes of police regulation are constructed in such a way that they *can* adapt.

There are a number of ways legal frameworks are overlooking the social side of big data. In this chapter, I will look at four. First, the way the conceptual categories that underpin legal doctrine—like individualized suspicion—are deployed and organized to make normative assessments do not reflect how decision-making plays out on the ground. Second, police are not simply scaling up data collection in the digital age; rather, different kinds of data are being produced. Despite the fact that there is a difference in kind—rather than just degree—old legal doctrine is still being laid on top of these data. Third, relying on extant legal mechanisms like the exclusionary rule means using what is meant to be a check on state power at one point in time and space, whereas data is fundamentally social and, as such, has a life course. Fourth, unfettered big data policing creates new opportunities for information asymmetries and can threaten due process through a long-standing practice called "parallel construction."

Before big data analytics became one more tool in the law enforcement arsenal, there were flaws in the criminal justice system. So too are there cracks in our laws governing police activity. Police use of big data is the dye injected to illuminate those cracks and bring the fault lines into stark relief.

Unsettling Underlying Legal Categories

Big data policing is shifting the ground under the foundational legal concepts that govern police activity. The use of algorithms to predict criminal risk, for example, lays bare internal inconsistencies in basic legal principles such as individualized suspicion.

In principle, different police activities must meet different standards of suspicion. Legally, the police cannot undertake a full-blown search, arrest someone, or get a warrant for personal information without probable cause. By contrast, they can briefly stop and conduct a limited pat down of a person with only reasonable suspicion, a lower standard of certainty. Reasonable suspicion is predicated on "specific" and "articulable" facts "taken together with rational inferences from those facts."[2] However, police do not have to rely exclusively on their personal observations in their reasonable suspicion calculus. The Supreme Court held, for instance, that police observation in a "high crime area" can be a deciding factor with regard to reasonable suspicion or probable cause.[3] The Court never precisely defined what constituted a high crime area, and so it is reasonable to assume that the area inside a predictive policing box might qualify. When big data—such as a predictive policing forecast—is combined with small data—such as traditional individualized suspicion based on particularized facts about a person observed at a given time and place—it effectively makes it easier for law enforcement to meet the reasonable suspicion standard.

The more circumspect of the LAPD captains I interviewed knew it was plausible that their officers might assess that a person walking inside a 500-square-foot predictive box was more suspicious than the same person walking outside the box. One captain who used PredPol in his division expressed his concern:

> But at some point, a case is going to go to court where . . . an officer's going to write in a report "I arrested this guy because he was in the box." The predictive box. And that's not why you should be arresting someone. I mean we need independent reasonable suspicion that then leads to probable cause that then leads to an arrest, right?

When predictive policing is not used in conjunction with traditional, individualized suspicion, it can create "categorical suspicion," which is not legally defensible.

Think back to Chapter 4 and my description of Operation LASER, the program that gives a top-tier list of "chronic offenders" based on risk scores for committing future crimes. Someone labeled a "chronic offender" in this person-based predictive policing system gains that label based on past data. So when cops observe someone with a high risk score walking back and forth in front of a store, they might perceive that as "casing," but if they see someone who is not on Operation LASER's Chronic Offender List doing the same thing, they might perceive it as window shopping or waiting for a ride.

Some legal scholars have, however, analyzed whether it is legally defensible for algorithmic predictions to play a role in law enforcement's suspicion calculus.[4] One expert on the legal implications of big data policing, Andrew Ferguson, writes, "If walking through a predicted red box changes my constitutional rights to be free from unreasonable searches and seizures, then a higher level of scrutiny might need to be brought to bear on the use of technology."[5] He further argues that the "courts should require a higher level of detail and correlation using the insights and capabilities of big data."[6] Although predictive models may be a preliminary factor in establishing reasonable suspicion, Ferguson contends that predictive policing forecasts are not, in and of themselves, sufficient to justify reasonable suspicion or probable cause. The data used in predictive policing forecasts is culled from previously observed circumstances with no direct relationship to the specific situation on the street at the moment of the reasonable suspicion calculus.[7] In other words, individualized suspicion is, by definition, incongruous with probabilities, because probability is not individualized. Individualized suspicion is supposed to be observable at a particular time and place.

But that takes for granted the category of individualized suspicion. I argue that the individualized/probabilistic distinction is a false binary. In most cases of individualized suspicion, the police officer does not actually observe someone committing a crime. Rather, they usually observe probabilistic indicia that they infer are associated with criminal activity. In that sense, what we might label *individualized suspicion* is actually a probabilistic assessment that criminal activity is afoot.

Consider this example: A person has a visible bulge, which is a common factor in establishing reasonable suspicion, because a bulge could be a gun. The police stop and search this individual. Is the stop defensible? Typically, an officer would not *know* that the person has a gun; rather, they see a bulge and are acting under a condition of uncertainty—is it a gun, is it a snack, is it an ostomy bag? A bulge becomes simply another way of articulating a probabilistic assessment that Person X has a higher probability of being involved in criminal activity than Person Y. It starts with a statistical claim—at the population level, people with bulges are more likely than people without bulges to have guns, and guns are associated with criminal activity. Then comes the normative claim—because people with bulges are more likely than people without bulges to be involved in criminal activity, observing a bulge on a person contributes to a certain risk threshold, and it becomes legally defensible to stop them.

Legal doctrines can be thought of as routinized ways of accepting uncertainty and legitimating state power under those conditions. Acceptable police actions under uncertain conditions are then institutionalized in common law doctrine. From an organizational theory perspective, individualized suspicion—and the Fourth Amendment more broadly—is an institutionalized covering practice that does not reduce uncertainty, but does render it more acceptable.[8] Predictive policing is upsetting these settled ways of dealing with uncertainty and forcing us to articulate the normative logic of past practice.

Officers' probabilistic assessments of a bulge may be informed by a whole host of factors, ranging from predictive algorithms to implicit bias.

For example, the same bulge might be interpreted as suspicious and more likely to be a gun inside a predictive box. It might also be interpreted as suspicious on a Black person, but not a white person. And the former justification for reasonable suspicion may legally cover the fact that the second was the real reason for the stop. L. Song Richardson, who studies implicit bias in decision-making, argues as much: that probabilistic assessments of suspicion are fundamentally racialized, and so the courts should take each individual officer's hit rate (the percent of time they successfully detect criminal activity during a stop) into account when testing the constitutionality of a stop.[9]

So at first it might seem like the challenge with predictive policing and reasonable suspicion is that predictive policing involves probabilities, whereas reasonable suspicion is individualized and particularized. But, actually, individualized suspicion is often a probabilistic assessment, too. Just because somebody—such as a "chronic offender" with a high point value—has committed crimes in the past, that does not give officers individualized suspicion in the present. Predictive policing does not simply erode the individualized suspicion versus probabilistic assessment binary, but also sheds light on the fact that it was a false binary to begin with. Algorithmic suspicion forces us to rethink legal categories. Should the courts, as Ferguson argues, require a higher level of individualization because the source of the probabilistic determination is an algorithm, as opposed to a police officer's judgment? Humans were running such probabilistic assessments in their minds long before cops used computers. There is nothing different about the logic involved in an officer seeing a bulge and conducting a quick mental probabilistic determination that criminal activity is likely afoot and a predictive algorithm saying Person X is more likely than Person Y to be involved in criminal activity. But you can argue about a suspicious bulge in court. A nonexpert can argue about the reasonable inferences a reasonable person can draw from seeing a bulge. It's an argument about cognitive shortcuts[10] and whether or not it is reasonable to think that a person has a gun on them—and whether it matters if they are walking in a particular neighborhood at night or what race the officer attributes to the suspect. But if the *algorithm* is uninterpretable, we cannot say whether its prediction is a fair or unfair basis for a stop. As previous chapters have shown, algorithms are often proprietary and protected from scrutiny. Judges, juries, and legal counsel cannot determine whether the predictive algorithm is reasonable and cannot put their fingers on specific points of bias if they do not have access to and understand its code, the ways it weights different types of data, the training data it uses, and the ways officers are trained to use the data it produces.

In assessing fairness, we need to also consider the costs of false positives versus false negatives, a calculus that varies according to context. The philosopher Renée Bolinger argues that humans make a flawed assumption: that the more statistically likely something is, the more we believe we are justified in treating it as true.[11] But, she argues, even for probabilities that clear a threshold for reasonable belief, if the error costs are high enough, we should not accept it as true. To do so would be to risk mistreating a particular person. Is it worse to stop and frisk an innocent person or miss interdicting a shoplifter? Does that calculus change if it is an armed robber or a murderer? She argues that, in statistical inference cases, the cost of false positives (treating something as if it's true when it isn't) are actually quite high, and therefore we should raise the evidentiary bar.

The risk of false positives is of particular concern when the risk concentrates among particular groups. And, as Bolinger points out, that is precisely what statistical prediction does—it reinforces concentrations.[12] In that sense, it is possible for statistical generalizations to be both accurate and unjust. For example, say there were different baseline rates of crime commission by gender, such that 90 percent of people committing crimes are men. You would be statistically justified in treating all men as criminals, but you would also constantly treat innocent men as criminals and subject them to ongoing mistreatment. Ironically, then, the more accurate a prediction, the more unjust it can be in implementation: the more accurate, the more likely police are to act on the prediction and treat people unjustly (with, as we saw in Chapter 6, a host of negative knock-on consequences). So, from a policy perspective, we need to consider not just the *efficacy* of predictive algorithms, but also the *chilling effects* of unevenly applied police contact.

It remains an open question whether predictive policing will lead to revolutionary change in standards of reasonable suspicion. Yet the courts will likely accept the outputs of predictive models as one of the many defensible factors that can be taken into consideration for suspicion in the age of big data—*that is, if the cases even make it to court.* As the sociolegal scholar Issa Kohler-Hausmann points out, "trials have gone the way of the dodo bird." Many people accept plea deals, for instance, for a raft of reasons: they can't afford to take time off work for a trial, they can't risk getting a longer sentence than the one offered by the plea (even if they insist on their innocence), and so on. But if they don't go to trial, the basis for their arrest will not be examined in a court of law. It is functionally impossible to consider how often courts might rule against the legality of algorithm-informed police contact, because they so rarely have the chance to do so. As Kohler-Hausmann explains, "Fourth Amendment jurisprudence is built on the premise that substantive rights . . . are secured by the mechanism of excluding unlawfully seized evidence and arrests . . . [but] [t]he overwhelming amount of police work is low-level enforcement activity, not serious violent felony arrests."[13] In other words, we can't simply rely on the exclusionary rule, which says that the police cannot use particular pieces of information in trial, as *the* opportunity for defendants to invoke their procedural rights; challenge the legality of a police stop, search, or seizure; or establish and exclude evidence as inadmissible, because law enforcement use of big data is so infrequently scrutinized in an adversarial trial context.

That is why it is important to structure the police's use of data and power in a way that protects the underlying interests that we thought were at issue in the Fourth Amendment to begin with: protection from arbitrary, unjustified state intrusions into people's lives.[14] In Kohler-Hausmann's words, "If we are serious about bringing police activity in line with substantive legal principles governing stops, searches, and seizures, then we must innovate other political and organizational mechanisms to do so."[15] We should look not only to law, but also to political incentives and more mundane organizational practices to protect individual rights.

In more sociological terms, cut-offs do not make sense because that is not the way the world works. Data is social and relational, and it has what we can call a "life course."[16] So although the law is better equipped to look at specific cut-off points, we have to look at the whole sequence of events in determining reasonable suspicion. For example, the exclusionary rule says you cannot admit illegally obtained evidence in court. But law is only thinking about the data in its mature life-course stage. We need to think about the nascent data, produced in social contexts and connected to other data points across time and space.[17] If the underlying data is flawed, one might argue, the visible data—the predictive box or the Operation LASER score—may lose its defensibility.

Data Are Different in Kind, Not Just Degree

This book has detailed a wide range of dragnet and directed surveillance techniques, data sources, algorithms, and risk scores routinely used in law enforcement's patrol, investigative, and crime analysis activities. Some of the data is collected by law enforcement themselves, some of it is collected by third parties, including data brokers. However, what is sociologically important and legally consequential is not simply that law enforcement is scaling up data collection; rather, it is that different kinds of data are being produced and policed. In particular, big data policing is programmatic, often suspicionless, and primarily operates below legal thresholds of reasonable suspicion and probable cause.

Take the automatic license plate reader, or ALPR, a dragnet surveillance tool that collects data on everyone, not only those under suspicion. Some ALPR data is collected by the police and some by third parties, such as vehicle repossession agencies. Police access to aggregated ALPR data means that police have access to locational and temporal information on individuals who have never had any police contact. In that sense, the ongoing nature of license plate readings represents a proliferation of pre-warrant surveillance. Information is routinely accumulated, and files are lying in wait. Individuals' movements are codified as data, and once in a database, data points—such as the dates, times, and locations an individuals' vehicle is picked up at by an ALPR—can be marshaled as evidence *retroactively*, once that individual comes under suspicion.

Further, police can query datasets either deductively or inductively. Thus, if they are interested in knowing which individuals' cars were located near the scene of a crime, they can look up all license plates captured within a specified radius within particular time bounds. Conversely, if the police have a specific person of interest, they can search Palantir for all of the places and times an ALPR picked up that person's car. Once they are in a database, individuals can be surveilled repeatedly—and that raises a question: Should new surveillance technologies facilitating the constant analysis and reanalysis of data be treated as "searches" subject to the Fourth Amendment?

The Fourth Amendment reads: "The right of the people to be secure in their persons, houses, papers, and effects, against unreasonable searches and seizures, shall not be violated, and no Warrants shall issue, but upon probable cause, supported by oath or affirmation, and particularly describing the place to be searched, and the persons or things to be seized."[18] In simpler terms, it prohibits unreasonable searches and seizures, such as the police entering an individual's house without a warrant and rummaging through their drawers. But what is the big data equivalent of rummaging through someone's drawers? There are both qualitative and quantitative differences between pieces of paper in a drawer and the digital traces we leave in the course of our everyday lives. These differences do not map easily onto existing legal frameworks.

Previous practical constraints, which placed natural limits on the scope of law enforcement surveillance, are becoming less relevant as new surveillance tools and data sources proliferate. Justice Alito's concurring opinion in the Supreme Court's decision in *United States v. Jones* (2012), a case regarding the GPS tracking of a single suspect over 28 days, is pointed: "In the pre-computer age, the greatest protections of privacy were neither constitutional nor statutory, but practical. Traditional surveillance for any extended period of time was difficult and costly and therefore rarely undertaken."[19] Indeed, officers more commonly cited resource constraints than legal barriers to surveillance. In the words of one detective I met, "It's not illegal for anyone to watch anybody." However, long-term surveillance is becoming cheaper and easier. So should laws introduce friction to the increasingly easy surveillance process? And does long-term police surveillance of an individual, even in public, constitute a Fourth Amendment search?

Legal scholars have come up with various theories to answer this question. In response to *Jones*, Orin Kerr, a legal scholar who specializes in criminal procedure and computer crime law, described the "mosaic theory" of the Fourth Amendment. Mosaic theory maintains that large-scale or longitudinal data collection made possible by new surveillance technologies and big data reveal information about individuals that is qualitatively different from individual observations.[20] As the policing, technology, and surveillance scholar Elizabeth Joh summarizes, according to mosaic theory, "[t]he threat to Fourth Amendment privacy lies in the *aggregation* of discrete bits of data, even if each piece standing alone would not be subjected to constitutional protections."[21] According to this perspective, the combinatorial power of using, for example, predictive policing scores in conjunction with ALPR readings in conjunction with network diagrams may grant authorities a level of insight into an individual's life that might constitute a search and thus should require a warrant. Instead of the traditional approach of the courts evaluating each step of an investigation individually, the mosaic approach involves evaluating a collective sequence of government activity as an aggregated whole. Although Kerr actually thought the courts should reject the mosaic approach and stick to the traditional parameters of the sequential approach to Fourth Amendment analysis, Fourth Amendment scholars are far from consensus.

A related but distinct concept is the right to "quantitative privacy," as articulated by David Gray and Danielle Citron.[22] In *Jones*, law enforcement's GPS tracking yielded over 2,000 pages of data on Jones. Five justices insisted that citizens possess a Fourth Amendment right to expect that certain *quantities* of information about them will remain private, even if they have no such expectations with respect to any one piece of information. So short-term monitoring of someone's movements on public streets might be fine, but long-term GPS monitoring might impinge on their expectations of privacy.

Trying to identify consistent principles in Fourth Amendment case law is challenging, to say the least. For example, *Terry v. Ohio* (1968) created a new category of searches and seizures—the limited pat down—that doesn't require a warrant or probable cause.[23] The particularities of each case vary widely, and the rules that outline the Fourth Amendment protections sometimes contradict one another. On the positive side, the Fourth Amendment is remarkably flexible, but on the negative, judicial interpretations have developed into a "byzantine patchwork of protections."[24] Consequently, it is difficult for judges and lawyers—let alone police officers and civilians—to put their finger on what exactly the Fourth Amendment protects against.

The abundance of technologies and big data sources that enhance law enforcement's surveillant capacity by the day has only added to this confusion. *Riley v. California* (2014),[25] a landmark US Supreme Court case regarding the warrantless search and seizure of the digital contents of a cell phone during arrest, brings the legal challenges of technological advances into further relief. The Court unanimously held that absent exigent circumstances, the police cannot search cell phones incident to the arrest. The case highlights some of the ways that smart phones are qualitatively and quantitatively different from flip phones or other objects in an individual's pocket. In the opinion, Chief Justice Roberts wrote:

> Modern cell phones are not just another technological convenience. With all they contain and all they may reveal, they hold for many Americans "the privacies of life." The fact that technology now allows an individual to carry such information in his hand does not make the information any less worthy of the protection for which the Founders fought. Our answer to the question of what police must do before searching a cell phone seized incident to an arrest is accordingly simple—get a warrant.

A variety of other cases on government data collection, involving issues ranging from aerial surveillance to thermal imaging to beeper records, have come down with different decisions, making it difficult to identify consistent theoretical underlying principles.[26] For example, despite more intrusive practices being found constitutional, a recent decision in the US Court of Appeals for the Sixth Circuit unanimously found that tire chalking—when parking enforcement draws a line of chalk on a parked tire to keep track of how long cars have been parked in the same spot and detect "meter feeders"—constitutes a search under the Fourth Amendment.[27]

There have been thousands of judicial decisions interpreting the Fourth Amendment, to the extent that some claim the Fourth has crumbled under its own logic and others laud its adaptability. Kerr, for example, argues Fourth Amendment case law is not an inconsistent mess, but the product of hundreds of systematic recalibrations made over time—an "equilibrium-adjustment" that is the natural "judicial response to changing technology and social practice."[28]

Among those who are less sanguine about Fourth's flexibility, some scholars argue that an entirely different branch of law—administrative law—may be better suited to govern police activity in the big data age. For example, the law professor Daphna Renan argues that the traditional paradigm of Fourth Amendment law is *transactional*, focusing on the one-off interaction between law enforcement and a suspect. However, police surveillance in the age of big data is *programmatic*: it involves ongoing, cumulative, and sometimes suspicionless data collection and use.[29] In the context of ALPRs, Renan writes, "[W]hat begins as more generalized collection can morph into something quite different when the government runs individuated searches in its datasets."[30] Therefore, Renan suggests, administrative law may be a more appropriate legal framework than criminal procedure for governing cumulative surveillance.[31] The Fourth Amendment and technology expert Christopher Slobogin agrees that administrative law—in conjunction with the "minimal" restrictions imposed by the Fourth Amendment—may provide a useful framework for governing data-based surveillance by law enforcement and other government agencies.[32]

Up until this point, we have been discussing data collected by law enforcement for law enforcement purposes. But as previous chapters of this book have demonstrated, police are gaining access to data collected by other public and private institutions for purposes hardly related to law enforcement. Function creep—the repurposing of data—is not well addressed by the Fourth Amendment.

Data is repurposed all the time. However, the privacy scholar Helen Nissenbaum argues that the sharing of information is *contextual*: we talk to our accountant about personal financial information and to our doctor about medical issues, but we don't want either to share our information with each other. Law, Nissenbaum argues, should correspondingly maintain the "contextual integrity" of information. However, existing privacy laws—such as the Privacy Act of 1974—largely relate to data's custodians and collection contexts, not the data themselves. In fact, the United States lacks a comprehensive privacy law to protect data; instead, such protections are sectoral and context-based.[33] For example, if you tell your doctor medical information, that is protected by what is arguably the country's most comprehensive privacy regime, HIPAA (the Health Insurance Portability and Accountability Act of

1996). However, if you share that same information with your employer as part of an employee wellness program, HIPAA protections are not in place. Likewise, the Fourth Amendment is primarily interested in the legitimacy of information acquisition, not use and repurposing. Some scholars argue that courts could upend the focus of the Fourth Amendment from data *collection* to its intended *uses* by the government.[34]

Function creep is not an entirely new concern. Over twenty years ago, the law professor Harold Krent suggested that government repurposing of information collected earlier could be deemed unreasonable and that courts might consider whether "the original seizure . . . would have been reasonable had the additional governmental objective been known" at the time.[35] What is new about the digital age is that individuals leave so many more seemingly innocuous digital traces in the course of their everyday lives that can now be linked together using big data systems, and thus grant law enforcement a level of insight that almost certainly would have been considered an intrusive investigation in years past. Our digital traces make it possible for law enforcement to start to build a case against us at any point in time, rather than only after suspicion has been determined. The case for use restrictions lies in the simple fact that we cannot prevent individuals from leaving digital traces with every financial transaction, commute, or Internet search, but perhaps we can govern the use of those traces by law enforcement or other government entities. Secondary uses of data thus challenge conventional consent practices and undermine the current patchwork of federal privacy laws that regulate the governmental collection of personal identifiable information.

Others believe use restrictions offer nothing but false promise. The Fourth Amendment and technology scholar Ric Simmons[36] argues that the doctrinal bases used to justify use restrictions, such as making the purpose of the data collection a factor in determining whether collecting the data constitutes a search, are usually insufficient to justify imposing use restrictions. Moreover, Simmons suggests, adopting use restrictions would be bad policy, since what constitutes "use" is ambiguous, as is the level of detail that would constitute an infringement upon reasonable expectations of privacy. Use restrictions may also import unintended consequences, such as effectively discouraging the creation of tighter collection restrictions and hindering important law enforcement functions.

Currently, a patchwork of statutory use restriction precedents and law enforcement exemptions affect privacy and policing. Some 20 separate statues restrict police access to driver's licenses, educational records, health records, and e-mail messages, for instance.[37] Outside the criminal law context, examples include the policy that the Internal Revenue Service does not share data with Immigration and Customs Enforcement, so as not to penalize positive civic behavior such as paying taxes, and that foreign surveillance for intelligence purposes is governed by rules under the Foreign Intelligence Service Act (FISA). On the flipside, statutory exemptions enable, for instance, warrantless access to certain data for certain law enforcement purposes.

One of the most common ways of circumventing Fourth Amendment protections is through the third-party doctrine. The third-party doctrine maintains that "when an individual voluntarily shares information with third parties, like telephone companies, banks, or even other individuals, the government can acquire that information from the third-party absent a warrant without violating the individual's Fourth Amendment rights."[38] Barry Friedman, the founding director of NYU Law's Policing Project, describes the third-party rule as a "serious chink in the Fourth Amendment's armor."[39] As we leave a growing number of digital traces with cell phone companies, Internet service providers, and online retailers, more and more of our information is sitting in third-parties' hands. If law enforcement wants access to that data, Friedman explains, "it need only subpoena it from whoever happens to be holding it. No warrant is needed and no probable cause required, thank you very much."[40] The legal threshold for issuing a subpoena is much lower than what is needed to get a warrant, because a lot of investigations would not get off the ground if probable cause was required.

However, I suggest there is an even more fundamental critique. Legal constructs like the third-party doctrine are set up in a way that is basically inapplicable to modern life. Today, communication is so technologically mediated that we simply cannot communicate without exposing data to a third party. Whereas the third-party exception made intuitive sense when, if I showed John Mary's handwritten letter to me, John could then tell the police what Mary wrote, it makes a lot less sense when I'm "showing" Gmail, not John, the communication[41]. Because inevitably our transactions and communications generate data, the third-party exception has become the exception that swallows the rule. We are no longer entrusting John, but rather Apple or Google, to protect our data[42].

As I worked on this book, the landmark Supreme Court decision in *Carpenter v. United States* came down.[43] This ruling essentially sidestepped the third-party doctrine.[44] The case concerned whether the police needed a probable cause warrant to obtain cell-site location information (CSLI) from private cell phone company providers.[45] The majority opinion held that police acquisition of more than six days of CSLI constituted a "search" for Fourth Amendment purposes and violated reasonable expectations of privacy. In his majority opinion, Chief Justice Roberts cited the "depth, breath, and comprehensive reach, and the inescapable and automatic nature of its collection," as relevant features of the data. The court reasoned that "the fact that the information is held by a third party does not by itself overcome the user's claim to Fourth Amendment protection." The Court described the danger inherent in the government's ability to conduct "near perfect surveillance," with digital data giving police the power to "travel back in time to retrace a person's whereabouts" and create a "detailed chronicle of a person's physical presence compiled every day, every movement, over several years."

As I argued in Chapter 3, the data traces we leave—and surveillance opportunities they afford—mean that *individuals lead incriminating lives.* Importantly, the implications of *Carpenter* extend beyond the specific context of CSLI—it may protect our personal digital trails with all kinds of third parties, ranging from ALPR data to social media posts (although it remains to be seen how lower courts will deal with the third-party doctrine moving forward). The *Carpenter* case rested, in part, on the fact that cell signals are not voluntarily provided and cell phones are a growing necessity in daily life.[46] It did not address data from devices that might be deemed "voluntary."

A further complication is that the Fourth Amendment understands all kinds of data, including communicative data, transactional data, and even bodily data,[47] as being fundamentally the same. But they are not, because of the distinct social significance of different kinds of data. Just as economic sociology teaches us that different types of money are not all fungible,[48] neither are data interchangeable. It also remains to be seen how laws will govern the combinatorial power of aggregated data, like the police using ALPRs in conjunction with predictive policing scores and network diagrams. The rub is that it is both the types of data themselves—which are sociologically different in that they are suspicionless and relational—and the *combination* of those data that are changing in ways that challenge extant legal frameworks.

New Opportunities for Parallel Construction

Parallel construction is another Pandora's box when it comes to data and the law. Parallel construction is defined in a training slide from the Drug Enforcement Administration (DEA) as "the use of normal investigative techniques to recreate the information provided by the SOD" (Special Operations Division of the DEA).[49] It is the process of building a separate evidentiary base to conceal how an investigation began because it involved informants, warrantless surveillance, or other inadmissible evidence.

Or, as Nancy Gertner, a law professor and former federal judge puts it, parallel construction is "a fancy word for phonying up the course of the investigation."[50]

For example, say law enforcement learned about a crime through an intelligence surveillance program or platform it wishes to keep secret. Law enforcement could claim the information came from a confidential informant, or follow the individual of interest until they neglect to use their turn signal, at which point they can conduct a pretextual stop and recreate the investigative trail such that it appears the traffic stop was the point at which the investigation began. If they end up arresting the individual, nothing admitted as evidence would say anything about the surveillance strategy. "It's just like laundering money—you work backwards to make it clean," said one former DEA agent.[51]

The use of big data for parallel construction can increase information asymmetries—and therefore power asymmetries—in the criminal justice system. In essence, parallel construction helps law enforcement to circumvent Fourth Amendment protections, ultimately violating defendants' constitutional right to a fair trial by obscuring the means by which they came under law enforcement surveillance. By misleading the court about what happened, the court, too, is disempowered by parallel construction. It cannot determine what really happened and whether or not it was legal.

Moreover, if surveillance strategies are not disclosed, we may underestimate the extent of privacy and civil liberties violations occurring, judges will not have the opportunity to evaluate the constitutionality of law enforcement activities, and defendants may be denied the opportunity to know about and access exculpatory evidence in violation of pretrial discovery rules.[52] As stated in the landmark Supreme Court decision in *Brady v. Maryland* (1963):

> We now hold that the suppression by the prosecution of evidence favorable to an accused upon request violates due process where the evidence is material either to guilt or to punishment, irrespective of the good faith or bad faith of the prosecution. . . . Society wins not only when the guilty are convicted, but when criminal trials are fair.[53]

Checks on police data collection can be traced back at least to *Nardone v. United States* (1939), in which the "fruit of the poisonous tree" doctrine was first articulated. According to the doctrine, which is an extension of the exclusionary rule, if evidence is obtained illegally (e.g., through an unconstitutional search), anything gained from that tainted evidence will also be tainted and is inadmissible in court.[54]

Even though the concept itself is not new, as the number of ways police use surveillance technologies and new sources of data increases, so too do the possibilities for parallel construction. Recall from Chapter 3, at a surveillance industry conference, a member of Palantir's legal counsel explained how the platform could be used to knit together circumstantial evidence into a comprehensive picture. Whereas it is relatively rare to find a smoking gun, he explained, Palantir users might be able to build up a sequence of events that could have been impossible for prosecutors to construct in the past. By integrating data into a single ontology, he pointed out, you can draw connections between actors and depict a coherent scheme. On the one hand, this could be incredibly useful to investigators who previously operated in siloed jurisdictions with limited access to historical information on potential suspects. But on the other hand, officer hunches that would be insufficient grounds for obtaining a warrant can now be retroactively backed up using existing data, and queries can be justified *after* data confirm officer suspicions.

Palantir has actually tried to address concerns about abusive uses of their platform. It has a number of built-in protections, and the company has a Privacy and Civil Liberties team dedicated to thinking about and working on such issues. Interviewees at the company explained how they are CJIS-compliant (Criminal Justice Information Services Division, a division of the FBI) and that they use GFIPM (Global Federated Identity Privilege Management), advanced authentication, and variegated access controls depending on the platform's user. The main Palantir protection against abuse that came up in my interviews was the "immutable audit log" (see Chapter 6). However, just because Palantir's system has a built-in audit capacity does not mean that their clients use it. I was unable to find a single instance, for example, in which the LAPD conducted an audit of their logs in Palantir.

To be sure, I did not observe parallel construction occurring during my fieldwork with the LAPD. The point here is simply to suggest that big data increases the *opportunities* for parallel construction to take place. Future research can investigate the extent to which this does or does not occur.

The constitutionality of new surveillance technologies used by the police is an open legal question, and one that is difficult to address because we do not even know how much or how little prosecutors cite software like PredPol or Palantir in evidentiary documents. To reiterate, whatever is not admitted as evidence puts criminal defense teams at a fundamental disadvantage, cuts judges out of the process of discerning whether evidence was legally obtained, and impedes the right to a fair trial.[55] What we *do* know is that new technologies and integrated databases have shifted the locus of discretion about what constitutes admissible evidence from judges to the police.

––––––––––

Laws regulating organizations always include some degree of legal ambiguity.[56] The police are interpreting and enacting the law in these ambiguous contexts every day.[57] But the ambiguity has been and will continue to be magnified by advances in technology. What is distinctive in the age of big data is not simply information collection outside the Fourth Amendment (and other relevant legal frameworks); rather, it is the scale and connectivity of the resulting informational yield.

Police use of big data thus forces us to question the taken-for-granted assumptions of how the world works that are embedded in the law. What made us think these frameworks were fair in the first place, and does that logic hold in a new data-intensive context?

The law is insufficiently sociological. For example, Fourth Amendment doctrine is at the forefront of many of the debates in this chapter. However, despite recurring themes of bias, racism, and discretion in challenges to what, exactly, constitutes a legal search, the Fourth Amendment doctrine is remarkably divorced from race. For example, in the foundational *Terry v. Ohio* case, not once is it mentioned that Terry was Black and the officer was white, even though, given the substantive features of the case and what we know about patterns of police stops by race, this would seem to be a central fact. No matter how much we would like to believe that data is color-blind—a trap that has ensnared so many legal academics—*data is not color-blind.*

Finally, the fact that many of the new technologies and databases used by the police today are created and maintained by private companies makes it more difficult to legally contest civil liberties violations and algorithmic opacity. Developers often claim that their tools are proprietary and that the details of how their tools work are trade secrets. They refuse to disclose that information to the public (or to criminal defendants and their attorneys.)[58] But if the police are increasingly using tools whose inner workings are privileged trade secrets, trade law is making it impossible for defendants and counsel to access potentially crucial evidence in criminal law contexts.[59] We must seriously and comprehensively consider the practice of policing on the ground—the organizational practice of law enforcement—if we are to truly undertake a review of the interests we thought were at issue in the Fourth Amendment, like freedom from arbitrary and overreaching state power. Big data policing is the dye injected into the system, revealing its myriad intersecting flaws and inconsistencies.

CHAPTER 8

Conclusion

Big Data as Social

ON JULY 24, 2018, the Board of Police Commissioners—the civilian panel that oversees the LAPD—met with the chief of police, the inspector general, and community members, as they do every Tuesday, at City Hall in downtown Los Angeles. But this was a special hearing, dedicated to data-driven policing. Protesters from the Stop LAPD Spying Coalition chanted and held up signs reading, "Data Driven Evidence Based Policing = Pseudoscience," "Data Driven Evidence Based Policing = Racism," "Dismantle PredPol & Operation LASER," and "Crime Data Is Racist." In turn, representatives from the LAPD, Office of the Inspector General (OIG), American Civil Liberties Union of Southern California, and Stop LAPD Spying Coalition presented their takes on the LAPD's use of predictive policing tools. Once the meeting was opened up for public comment, local community members emphatically critiqued PredPol, Operation LASER, and the department's data-driven tactics more generally. Amid shouts from the audience, the commissioner adjourned the meeting after three hours.

Less than a month later, in response to requests for an audit from the Stop LAPD Spying Coalition, the Board of Police Commissioners unanimously approved a motion directing the OIG to review the costs and benefits of Operation LASER and PredPol. The OIG's 52-page audit summary was released the following March.[1] In it, the OIG focused on the programs' effectiveness and impact on communities of color, while "caution[ing] against drawing strong conclusions on whether any of the new approaches lessened crime." Put simply, the report said there was not strong evidence that predictive policing reduced crime rates and that there were significant civil rights concerns with inconsistent enforcement, opacity, and lack of accountability.

It stopped short of calling for an end to the programs, but did recommend greater transparency, and oversight.

Chief Michel Moore responded to the critical report in writing by stating that the department would evaluate its location-based predictive policing programs and stop issuing Chronic Offender Bulletins.[2] At a subsequent press briefing, he clarified that the entire LASER program had been cancelled.[3] During an oral report to the Board of Police Commissioners, Moore said the Chronic Offender program "did not bear the types of results that in the face of its criticism and the face of concerns relative to whether or not the underlying algorithm truly was fair and unbiased for us to continue going forward."[4]

Chief Moore's response memo indicated that "the Department will transition its efforts into developing a Precision Policing model."[5] So, what exactly is "precision policing?" Moore said a formal precision policing manual and procedures would be issued in summer 2019, but as this book goes to press, we still have little idea. The LAPD stated it will include both offender- and location-based strategies.[6] Is precision policing simply predictive policing by another name? In a 2018 report by the Heritage Foundation, a conservative think tank, William Bratton—former LAPD chief of police and driving force behind CompStat and many of the department's predictive policing programs—described precision policing as "something we initially called 'intelligence-led policing' and 'predictive policing' and now, assisted greatly by algorithms, advanced data mining techniques, we call 'precision policing.' Effectively, it's the CompStat of the '90s on steroids in the 21st century."[7]

While the LAPD continues to use many of the other forms of big data policing described in this book, the report and subsequent suspension of the Chronic Offender Bulletins illustrate the potential to disrupt, review, and carefully consider big data policing. Nothing about it is inevitable, and academic studies and local democratic accountability can be brought to bear in a public and transparent forum. Crucially, it wasn't technical problems or glitches in the algorithms that ended the program, but direct social organizing and action.

The LAPD's continued use of big data policing underscores the primary argument running through this book—that big data is *fundamentally* social. At every phase—from big data's adoption to collection and analysis, institutional intervention, and reception—there is a social patterning to how data is used. Recognizing that data both shapes and is shaped by the social world helps us understand that despite the argument made by proponents that big data policing is more objective and less discretionary than "human" decision-making, databases are populated by information collected as a result of human decisions, analyzed by algorithms created by human programmers, and implemented and deployed on the street by human officers following supervisors' orders and their own intuition. As such, big data may work to simultaneously obscure and amplify existing inequalities.

But just as the social side of big data can make it perilous, it is also what gives it real promise. The question is how we get there. How do we fulfill that promise? How do we approach and apply big data to make policing fairer and more accountable? And as big data pervades more and more of our everyday lives, what might the lessons learned in the realm of policing teach us about how big data surveillance structures life chances in the digital age?

Beginning around 2010, we have seen a mass deployment of publicly and privately collected data, sorted, weighted, geotagged, and cross-referenced. Much of predictive policing's rise reflects the hope that big data and predictive analytics represent a silver bullet, an answer to any number of organizational problems. Scarce resources? Data can help allocate them more efficiently. Need to reduce bias in decision-making? Automate it. Want to increase the accuracy with which you can predict risk in times of uncertainty? Try predictive algorithms.

Law enforcement agencies have placed great hope into programs like PredPol. In light of serious public concerns regarding racial bias, police use of force, legitimacy, and costs, these agencies have turned to big data as an antidote. Its promise of both *efficiency* and *accountability* is almost irresistible for departments trying to adopt a managerialist approach and "do more with less."[8] Its presumption, however, is that big data will help law enforcement more *fairly* enforce the law *with less bias*. The very mission of the now defunct White House Police Data Initiative was "improving the relationship between citizens and police through uses of data that increase transparency, build community trust, and strengthen accountability."[9]

Owing to a range of corruption cases, training deficiencies, and civil rights abuses, the LAPD was under a federal consent decree from 2001 to 2013. More formalized, quantified, and data-driven decision-making was a key part of its approach to this crisis of legitimacy. Crime rates had declined, but the LAPD was being pressured to push them even lower. PredPol and the other predictive tools offered a relatively cheap way to meet the mandate to do more with less, and in a more transparent way. Decisions about the path forward, made around balance sheets and supposedly neutral algorithms, came down to the question: *Who could argue with numbers?*

In theory, big data *can* be used to improve the administration and accountability of justice. There is simply little evidence, thus far, that it *does*.

Sanguine rhetoric and piles of federal funding have attended the arrival of "evidence-based policing," allowing departments to implement algorithmic control broadly—and before it's been proven effective.

Big data is a form of capital, both a social product and a social resource used by actors within organizations. It can be differentially exchanged, leveraged, accumulated, and taken away. Thinking of data as capital allows us to consider how police departments, like other organizations, are situated within what the foundational sociologist Pierre Bourdieu called a *field*.[10] The field is the whole constellation of organizations and actors involved not only in patrol, investigations, and crime analysis, but also incarceration, and even national defense, all vying for funding and seeking legal compliance, organizational legitimacy, and longevity. They all have their relative hierarchies and prevailing norms (the rules of the game, so to speak). If the actors in the criminal justice field largely agree that organizations within it should be enforcing the law, chipping away at already historically low crime rates, and doing all of that in a way that's transparent and unbiased, their departments may start using big data in response to those wider beliefs about what actors within the field are *meant* to do.[11]

In these ways, we can see that the motivations for adopting big data are social. Decisions about what data to collect, on whom, and for what purpose are all made by humans embedded in social, organizational, and institutional contexts rife with preexisting priorities, preferences, imperatives, and constraints. Humans embedded in organizations operationalize socially significant concepts and categories like "crime," "criminal," and "risk" in automated, algorithmic infrastructures. Furthermore, the ability to collect data, make decisions, construct policies, and intervene in others' lives based on data is not evenly distributed.

Data does not and cannot eliminate discretion. Rather, its use *displaces* discretionary power to earlier, less visible (and therefore potentially less accountable) parts of the policing process. Big data policing starts well before there's any police contact. It even starts before a department implements a given program. It starts way back with third-party, private firms designing analytic platforms, deciding which data to collect on whom (and which data to buy from even more private, third-party vendors), and how that data should inform predictions. The whole chain is mired in discretionary choices. As the anthropologist Nick Seaver puts it, "algorithms are not autonomous technical objects, but complex sociotechnical systems . . . While discourses about algorithms sometimes describe them as 'unsupervised,' working without a human in the loop, in practice there are no unsupervised algorithms. If you cannot see a human in the loop, you just need to look for a bigger loop."[12]

In other words, big data and associated algorithms are not detached from human activity, but rather are fundamentally shaped by it (even if the human side of algorithmic decision-making is often invisible at first glance).

Although police use of big data is a relatively recent phenomenon, it sheds new light on old problems. Models are codifications of social processes, quantified instantiations of laws and policy decisions. They encode all kinds of very human decisions and all kinds of institutional policies and priorities. They encode discriminatory laws and past precedents and legacies of segregation and inequality. All these cracks were already present in the criminal justice system and the exercise of state power, but big data policing practices have made them more readily visible. In this way, predictive policing may be an unintended boost to those who hope to reform law enforcement: it's acting as a dye, illuminating the fault lines in a long-flawed system.

Understanding big data policing thus requires rethinking both the practice of *policing* and the institution of *the police*. Data has a long history as a tool of governance,[13] and surveillance is a tacit right of the state. Yet the present moment is an unprecedented one: we leave untold digital traces in every moment of our smartphone, smartwatch, smart-home lives. Big data surveillance involves extracting information from all of these digital traces and information flows[14] and reassembling them into "data doubles,"[15] or digital approximations of individuals based on the electronic traces we leave. Private companies store that data on private platforms and analyze it using proprietary algorithms. This privatization is part of a broader shift, in which we have seen the introduction of market logic into state services including welfare,[16] education,[17] and punishment.[18] The result is that big data policing is harder to challenge.[19] Private vendors can hide behind trade secrecy and nondisclosure agreements, ultimately circumventing typical public-sector transparency requirements and lowering police accountability by making it harder for scholars to study, regulators to regulate, and activists to mobilize for or against specific practices. And existing legal frameworks are inadequate for governing police work reshaped by private partnerships.

"Techwashing" has allowed many of us to feel satisfied about "objective," "neutral," and "color-blind" data. But techwashing inequality means appearing to replace subjectivity and legally contestable bias with quantification, computation, and automation. That bears repeating: big data has the potential to reduce inequality and discrimination, yet, as currently used, it increases inequality while *appearing* objective. Characterizing predictive models as "just math" and fetishizing computation as an objective process obscures the social side of algorithmic decision-making. It allows us to ignore how big data can simultaneously work to obscure and amplify biases. It comforts us that data can be used to "police the police" and re-place unparticularized suspicion of racial minorities and human exagger-ation of patterns with less-biased predictions of risk. On the other hand, data-intensive police surveillance practices are implicated in the reproduc-tion of inequality by deepening the surveillance of individuals already under suspicion, widening the criminal justice dragnet to include individuals who have no direct police contact (and doing so in socially patterned ways),[20] and leading people to avoid important institutions,[21] all while appearing to be neutral, impartial, and objective.[22]

Additionally, a strong body of scholarship demonstrates that marking someone in the criminal justice system is consequential for life outcomes and patterns of inequality.[23] Scholars are only starting to bring labeling theory into the digital age and trace out how the integration of records and data across platforms may effectively make the mark of a criminal record or criminal justice contact indelible, and cascade across previously discrete institutional boundaries.[24] Existing research underestimates the effects of involvement in the criminal justice system when that involvement is tied to impenetrable, interwoven, and proprietary data systems. We literally don't know where all the data *goes*.

Crafting Change

The fact that big data is social is both a problem and a saving grace. That it is social means that social movements and activists, law enforcement agencies, scholars, and policymakers all have the power to recraft it. Big data is neither a panacea nor the root cause of many of the problems associated with its use. Having mapped data's social dimensions throughout this book is one step in identifying key points of leverage. Reforms that don't take the social into ac-count will inevitably fail; those that understand big data analytics, usage, and administration as a social as well as a technical project are well positioned to insist upon change.

At this critical inflection point, I have worked to articulate changes and continuities in the practice of policing and the institution of the police. Police contact is the feeder mechanism into the criminal justice system. If we can restructure the law enforcement field in the digital age, the whole system may become a bit less closed, unfair, and unequal. To that end, I offer six provocations meant to send readers into the world ready to seek change.

Slow down. Organizations today have a seemingly insatiable appetite for digital troves.[25] I am not calling for wholesale rejection of data analytics or new surveillance technologies. Rather, instead of continuing with the current pattern of data collection and law enforcement intervention first, assessment and evaluation later, we need to invert the order of operations. Despite the rhetoric, the evidence is still weak. We don't actually know whether and how algorithms "outperform" humans and what harms may come with their implementation. The onus should fall on law enforcement to justify the use of big data and new surveillance tools *prior* to mass deployment. Moreover, such evaluation needs to be *independent*. The only peer-reviewed study evaluating PredPol[26] in LA, for example, was conducted by cofounders of and stockholders in PredPol, and the only peer-reviewed study of Operation LASER[27] was conducted by the CEO and a research associate at Justice and Security Strategies Inc., the company that designed Operation LASER.

The fact that algorithmic systems currently reflect and reiterate biases and inequalities more than they reduce them is not a problem unique to big data policing, but a feature of prediction itself.[28] Front-ending accountability will mean interdisciplinary work—whereas computer scientists are trained to see what insights they can glean from an existing corpus of data, social scientists are trained to pay particular attention to sampling. It will mean starting with a fundamental question: What do we want out of big data policing? If we hope to optimize crime reduction, that will require something different than, say, optimizing equal protection under the law, chiseled departmental budgets, cases cleared by arrest, or dragnet comprehensiveness. Relatedly, it is crucial to recognize that not all data are created equal. For example, data on officer-initiated interactions have different patterns of bias than data on citizen-initiated interactions.

In considering disparate impact, we should ask a number of questions: Who benefits and who is harmed by the deployment of the new technology? Who bears the cost when machine-learned predictions are wrong? In its current form, the burden of new surveillance practices is not borne equally, nor are the errors they produce. The criminal justice system is historically implicated in the reproduction of inequality; therefore, understanding the intended and unintended consequences of machine-learned decisions and new surveillant technologies in the criminal justice system is of paramount importance. When big data analytics are adopted into an organization and field with preexisting organizational logics and power dynamics, the unintended consequences of algorithmic systems is that they may reflect biases and inequalities in society more than they reduce them. What algorithmic prediction does is reveal, formalize, and quantify this process.

An interdisciplinary design, deployment, and audit approach will also help craft the how new surveillance tools will be received. As this book has shown, when you introduce new data analytic rationalities into older organizational cultures, there is friction. In simple terms, if cops aren't going to use it,[29] if the public and lawmakers won't accept it, and if there aren't ways to improve it iteratively, an algorithm's *accuracy* is moot.

Use big data to police the police. A byproduct of many data-intensive policing practices is the creation of more data on police activities. By leveraging data on who, how, and where officers police, we can bring data to bear on instances of officer misconduct, police killings, and systematic patterns and institutional practices that may previously have been dismissed as symptoms of individual-level bias. Digital trails also afford us the opportunity to measure the "costs" of policing. For example, as Mark Moore, an expert in the field of public management, argues, "[i]f we reduced crime, but did so by relying on more intrusive investigative techniques, or patrol techniques that were both more assertive and viewed as biased, then the increased use of authority would have to be viewed as a loss to be put against the gain."[30] Historically, we have had more ways of measuring the gains than the losses. But now that each police stop leaves a digital trace, we can measure the "coercion costs" of policing, such as, for example, the average number of times residents in a given community are stopped and searched by the police.[31] If the surveillant gaze is inverted, data can be used to fill holes in police activity, shed light on existing problems in police practices, monitor police performance and hit rates, and even estimate and potentially reduce bias in police stops. We need to harness the potential for algorithms to formalize the problems in a way that can help us fix them. Indeed, interdisciplinary research is starting to show that big data can be leveraged to make policing more just and equitable, such as by improving officer hit rates, without compromising public safety.[32]

Use data to identify and remediate errors. Relatedly, big data may also afford us new opportunities to understand patterns of error in the legal system in similar ways to how many companies use data in other contexts. The stakes for being wrongly arrested are very different from receiving a bad Netflix recommendation, but data can make both plain—and help us avoid those errors in the future. This means policing data must become more transparent. Just as you can see and correct errors in your credit score, people should be able to argue and even change information about themselves populating the machine learning models used by the police.[33] There is not, however, any sort of FACTA (Fair and Accurate Credit Transactions Act) equivalent for criminal history reports, and few of us have any idea what data the police have about us. In her research on online criminal records, for example, the sociologist Sarah Lageson met overwhelmed individuals who did not know how to find out what police and third-party criminal record distributors "knew" about them, where that data and its errors came from, or how to fix mistakes. In one case, Lageson spoke with a man who had spent countless hours fighting against a record populated by crimes committed by someone with a similar name. He only learned there was a problem when he was denied housing, and he learned some of the crimes on his record had been committed before he was born.[34] FOIA clinics, in which individuals experienced at filing public records requests assist individuals and organizations as they request documents, files, and records from government agencies, are a start, but they are slapdash and scattershot, limited to those individuals who know there is a problem and are able to seek out help.[35] The people most at risk of harm from big data systems are often those least able to contest the outcomes. We must increase support for robust mechanisms of legal redress.

Use data to direct nonpunitive interventions. Law enforcement over-polices minor offenses, and police are frequently called upon to respond to situations that might better be handled by medical or social service professionals.[36] What does this have to do with big data? Police use data to allocate resources. If the only resources deployed are punitive, any bias in the data—and there is almost always bias in the data—will inevitably exacerbate existing inequalities. A word of caution however: even "benevolent" interventions can problematize behaviors and lead to increased surveillance and its negative knock-on effects in systematically disadvantageous ways. Tools deployed under a "welfarist ideology of service delivery" can be "drawn into the harder edge of social control."[37] Electronic medical records, for example, were created to improve prescription drug and care coordination, but they are increasingly used by law enforcement agencies to police the illicit use and sale of prescription drugs.[38] Big data's preventive potential is dampened, as well, when programs are underfunded such that there is insufficient training and long-term commitment to their ongoing improvement.

Leverage data to help clear cases and solve cold ones. Law enforcement under-polices serious offenses. By "under-police," I do not mean that cops are insufficiently punitive, but that they are missing a lot of serious crimes and failing to solve many more. For example, despite all the advances in technologies and increases in data sources at investigators' fingertips, approximately 40 percent of murders go unsolved each year in the United States. Given the connection between rapes and murders, for instance, testing the enormous nationwide backlog of "rape kits" for DNA evidence would improve data systems and help identify repeat offenders. Yet rape is deprioritized as a crime, and the potential data represented in untested rape kits is frequently incinerated. By contrast, the LAPD improved its homicide clearance rate three years running (2015–2017), which make its clearance rate higher than the national average, at just over 73 percent.[39] One of the benefits of large datasets is that they can be leveraged to identify *emergent* patterns, things humans might have missed or been unable to detect when they span jurisdictions (as is often the case with weapons and sex trafficking). Recent developments in data science may offer tools to help law enforcement agencies address seemingly intractable problems.

Redefine successful policing. Success, in the policing context, is typically measured by whether crime rates go up or down. Because police are overwhelmingly concerned with year-to-dates, the companies that design predictive policing software are predominantly concerned with the association between the use of their program and crime rates.[40] Yet individual officers told me about all kinds of frameworks they used for analyzing "what works." An officer who was an enthusiastic advocate of Operation LASER said that the "proof" that it works is that the majority of people listed as chronic offenders are rearrested. What he might define as success, another might define as evidence of a problematic self-fulfilling prophecy.

Communities that benefit most from violence and homicide reductions are minority communities and those in positions of structural disadvantage. What does successful policing look like for these communities? There is basically no evidence that big data analytics has led to higher clearance rates, fewer stops without arrest, or a reduction in racial disparities in false arrests. It reminds us that what defines "fairness" is not only a measurement question, but also a normative one. Does fairness mean that errors need to be symmetrically distributed along racial lines?[41] Or that everyone who commits a crime has an equal likelihood of getting caught? Or that data systems reflect different baseline offending rates across race/class/gendered lines or reject them prima facie as products of biased policing practices? All data-driven models require fairness trade-offs, and there is no one method that can satisfy all conditions simultaneously.[42] The *presumption* of fairness in algorithms is what undermines the promise of big data for reforming the actual practice of policing.

The Private Impediment

A key impediment to effective reform is the role of private companies in the big data policing space. We are not merely witnessing a transformation of policing, but rather, as scholars such as Loïc Wacquant, Joe Soss, Richard Fording, and Sanford Schram have pointed out,[43] a neoliberal transformation of the state that has shifted any number of public provisions to private, for-profit providers who typically give very little documentation to government. Corporate secrecy laws are a barrier to due process, in that they make it hard to assess bias, contest decisions, or remedy errors. And, crucially, much of the secrecy is unnecessary.

Research on algorithmic transparency suggests that algorithmic opacity is not an insurmountable obstacle. Most algorithms are simple, and the value added of a complex algorithm is rarely enough to justify using it over a simpler one.[44] In fact, algorithmic transparency is one point where the interests of the reformers and the police align. The secrecy is driven by profit imperatives and exacerbated by corporate consolidation. For instance, ShotSpotter, a gunshot detection system, acquired HunchLab, the second-biggest predictive policing company in the world, in 2018, while Axon—formerly Taser International—began using footage from their body cameras to build out facial recognition AI to sell to other agencies, and Vigilant Solutions, a license plate surveillance company, entered the body camera market. None of this should be acceptable in the public sector. Modern governance should not be shrouded behind impenetrable computer code and redundancy. If a tool is procured by a public agency, it should require ongoing documentation and have clear data and records ownership practices. Police—and other public agencies—need a framework for assessing automated decision-making systems and facilitating transparency and accountability. Detangling these webs and analyzing law enforcement's procurement process for predictive tools, datasets, and analytic platforms will likely require massive public records requests to obtain public contracts, documents, grants, and e-mails. Still, it is required if we hope to assess questions like whether departments continue using platforms because they are effective or because of behavior patterns around path dependence and sunk costs, which prioritize the known over the unknown. Of course, accountability does not flow automatically from transparency. For example, consider the immutable audit logs in Palantir. An accountability mechanism was built into the platform but was never used by the police. Nonetheless, accountability cannot happen without a greater degree of transparency.

Scholars and activists have also suggested a number of ways of assessing the risks and benefits prior to a new technology's implementation. One is algorithmic impact assessments. The legal scholar Andrew Selbst explains:

> Modeled on the environmental impact statements of the National Environmental Policy Act, algorithmic impact statements would require police departments to evaluate the efficacy and potential discriminatory effects of

all available choices for predictive policing technologies. The regulation would also allow the public to weigh in through a notice-and-comment process. Such a regulation would fill the knowledge gap that makes future policy discussions about the costs and benefits of predictive policing all but impossible.[45]

City surveillance ordinances are another way to subject new technologies to citizen oversight. Local ordinances such as those passed in Seattle, Oakland, Berkeley, and Davis require that police departments and other government agencies demonstrate that the benefits of new surveillance technologies outweigh possible harms to privacy and civil liberties *before* they purchase the tools. For any algorithm to be used by the police and gain public legitimacy, the public needs to know what the training data is; how the data is collected, culled, and analyzed; how the final model was selected (and what alternatives were tried prior); how risk is defined; what the ongoing validation process is; how the model is implemented; and how outputs are interpreted and acted upon.

Right now, all of this is being done piecemeal. We lack a comprehensive legal and regulatory regime governing police use of data. To take a simple example, there is no federal legislation regulating the retention of ALPR data.[46] As machines play a greater role in criminal justice, third-party auditing and oversight is essential. The individual efforts undertaken by citizen groups and city ordinances are a step in the right direction, but comprehensive, top-down legislation would involve a much more in-depth process of questioning the purposes, design, and effects of predictive policing.

The one thing that almost everyone agrees on is that successful police reform requires community engagement. Sure, community members, law enforcement, technologists, lawyers, and researchers all need to work together. But how? Algorithmic control is largely invisible, and few community members know about the programs in place. You can't comment on practices you don't know are happening. The political scientist Virginia Eubanks writes,

> That's the thing about being targeted by an algorithm: you get a sense of a pattern in the digital noise, an electronic eye turned toward *you*, but you can't put your finger on exactly what's amiss. There is no requirement that you be notified when you are red-flagged. There is no sunshine law that compels companies to release the inner details of their . . . systems. With the notable exception of credit reporting, we have remarkably limited access to the equations, algorithms, and models that shape our life chances.[47]

What data we have shapes how we see the social world. It shapes how the police see the social world, but goes far beyond policing. It shapes how the state engages with its citizens, and how private institutions classify and sort people. Simply put, big data surveillance is a routine organizational practice that is central to the structuring of life chances[48] in the digital age. Although big data surveillance is growing in fields ranging from healthcare to finance, immigration, education, and insurance,[49] its penetration is unevenly distributed.[50] Different individuals, groups, areas, and institutions are surveilled by different institutions, some are surveilled more than others, and they are surveilled for different purposes.[51] On the one hand, there is a deepening of surveillance of "at-risk" groups[52] who can increasingly be tracked across institutional boundaries. On the other hand, emerging dragnet surveillance practices result in increased monitoring of groups "previously exempt from routine surveillance."[53]

Future work should examine the precise mechanisms through which big data surveillance and its associated scoring, sorting,[54] and classification schemes[55] reinforce or reduce social inequalities. The extent to which big data surveillance differentially shapes life chances and patterns of inequality varies along two axes: the composition of individuals under surveillance (often a direct function of their levels of institutional involvement) and the form of the institutional interventions. In general terms, big data surveillance stratifies if individuals in positions of structural disadvantage are more likely to be subject to surveillance by organizations with punitive interventions while those in positions of structural advantage are subject to more advantageous surveillance and classification schemes.[56] However, there is still so much we do not know about how the data that make up our digital doubles structures the types of communications, opportunities, constraints, and care we receive.

As we move through the world, we slough off a trail of data, large and small, important and inconsequential, and institutions are all too happy to sweep it up. Their algorithms weight and sort the data, placing it in conversation with seemingly unrelated data sources so that photographs of our license plates taken by automatic plate readers are suddenly mixed in with criminal risk scores, social networks, and data from millions of people we've never met and millions of lives whose unequal outcomes have been enshrined in predictive scores. When the system is this far-reaching and this opaque, earning a spot on the Chronic Offender List can feel like alchemy. But the data is social, and its effects are social. That means we have the power to interrogate and change the social life of big data, in policing and beyond.

APPENDIX A | LAPD Ranks

Chief of Police
Police Deputy Chief
Police Commander
Police Captain I, II, III
Police Lieutenant I, II
Police Sergeant I, II
Police Detective I, II, III
Police Officer I, II, III

Source: Adapted from "Sworn Police Officer Class Titles and Job Descriptions," Los
Angeles Police Department, accessed January 15, 2020, http://www.lapdonline.org/
join_the_team/content_basic_view/9127.

APPENDIX B | LAPD Bureaus and Areas

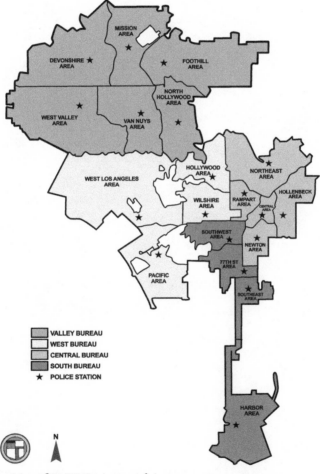

FIGURE B.1 Map of LAPD Bureaus and Areas

SOURCE: "Community Station Location," Los Angeles Police Department, accessed January 15, 2020, http://www.lapdonline.org/inside_the_lapd/content_basic_view/6468. Image by David Hallangen.

APPENDIX C

TABLE C.1 Logistic Regression Predicting Institutional Avoidance

| | AVOIDED SURVEILLING INSTITUTIONS | | | | | | AVOIDED NON-SURVEILLING INSTITUTIONS | | | |
| | MEDICAL CARE | | BANK ACCOUNT | | SCHOOL/WORK | | VOLUNTEER | | RELIGIOUS GROUP | |
	MODEL 6	MODEL 7	MODEL 8	MODEL 9	MODEL 10	MODEL 11	MODEL 12	MODEL 13	MODEL 14	MODEL 15
Any Criminal Justice Contact	1.309*** (.017)		1.186** (.068)		1.314*** (.101)		.906 (.049)		1.084 (.072)	
Stopped		1.332*** (.096)		.939 (.076)		1.198 (.130)		.920 (.064)		.994 (.086)
Arrested		1.293** (.119)		1.294** (.124)		1.302* (.162)		.932 (.089)		1.141 (.135)
Convicted		1.331** (.128)		1.535*** (.153)		1.304* (.169)		.867 (.089)		1.238 (.167)
Incarcerated		1.102 (.195)		1.509* (.273)		2.181*** (.426)		.732 (.149)		1.410 (.369)

(continued)

TABLE C.1 Continued

| | AVOIDED SURVEILLING INSTITUTIONS | | | | | | AVOIDED NON-SURVEILLING INSTITUTIONS | | | |
| | MEDICAL CARE | | BANK ACCOUNT | | SCHOOL/WORK | | VOLUNTEER | | RELIGIOUS GROUP | |
	MODEL 6	MODEL 7	MODEL 8	MODEL 9	MODEL 10	MODEL 11	MODEL 12	MODEL 13	MODEL 14	MODEL 15
Sociodemographic Controls	Yes†	Yes†	Yes	Yes	Yes	Yes	Yes	Yes	Yes‡	Yes‡
Behavioral Controls	Yes	Yes	Yes	Yes	Yes	Yes	Yes	Yes	Yes	Yes
N	14,458	14,411	14,515	14,468	14,167	14,120	14,510	14,463	14,400	14,354
Pseudo R-squared	.071	.071	.207	.209	.089	.090	.095	.095	.283	.284

Note: All coefficients expressed as odds ratios. Standard errors are in parentheses. Sociodemographic controls include sex, race, age, education, parental education, marital status, nativity, household configuration (i.e., number in household and whether individuals live with parents), military service, and whether respondents are in school or have a job. Behavioral controls include whether individuals self-report stealing over or under $50, damaging property, carrying a gun or knife to school or work, stabbing someone, using cocaine or methamphetamine, selling drugs, or being in a gang, and whether respondents are classified as impulsive or candid.

†Includes controls for general health and possession of medical insurance.

‡Includes controls for religiosity and regular church attendance.

* $p < .05$; ** $p < .01$; *** $p < .001$ (two-tailed tests).

Source: Originally published in "Surveillance and System Avoidance: Criminal Justice Contact and Institutional Attachment." *American Sociological Review* 79, no. 3 (2014): 367–91. doi:10.1177/0003122414530398.

TABLE C.2 Effect of Criminal Justice Treatment on Matched Samples

AVOIDANCE	PROPENSITY SCORE MATCHING						DOUBLY ROBUST ESTIMATION			
	TREATED	CONTROLS	DIFFERENCE	SE	T-STAT	SIGNIFICANCE	OR	SE	N	PSEUDO R^2
Surveilling Institutions										
Medical care	.321	.282	.039	.019	2.070	$p < .05$	1.186*	.096	3,148	.057
Bank account	.410	.301	.109	.019	5.620	$p < .001$	1.704***	.146	3,160	.191
School/work	.157	.126	.031	.014	2.170	$p < .05$	1.321*	.144	3,088	.096
Non-surveilling Institutions										
Volunteer	.748	.753	-.005	.018	-.280	n.s.	.951	.083	3,162	.087
Religious groups	.837	.818	.018	.016	1.160	n.s.	1.176	.129	3,134	.249

NOTE: Models include same suite of sociodemographic and behavioral controls as in Models 6 through 15. Sociodemographic controls include sex, race, age, education, parental education, marital status, nativity, household configuration, military service, and whether respondents are in school or have a job. Behavioral controls include whether individuals self-report stealing over or under 50 dollars, damaging property, carrying a gun or knife to school or work, stabbing someone, using coke or meth, selling drugs, or being in a gang, and whether respondents are classified as impulsive or candid. In light of cross-sectional results, criminal justice treatment is defined as arrested, convicted, or incarcerated, although results remain substantially unchanged when stopped is included, with one exception—bank account is only marginally significant at the $p < .1$ level.

*$p < .05$; **$p < .01$; ***$p < .001$ (two-tailed tests).

SOURCE: Originally published in "Surveillance and System Avoidance: Criminal Justice Contact and Institutional Attachment." American Sociological Review 79, no. 3 (2014): 367–91. doi:10.1177/0003122414530398.

TABLE C.3 Individual-Level Fixed-Effects Logistic Regressions Predicting Institutional Avoidance

	AVOIDED SURVEILLING INSTITUTIONS						AVOIDED NON-SURVEILLING INSTITUTIONS			
	MEDICAL CARE[a]		BANK ACCT.		WORK		VOLUNTEER		RELIGIOUS GROUP[b]	
	MODEL 16	MODEL 17	MODEL 18	MODEL 19	MODEL 20	MODEL 21	MODEL 22	MODEL 23	MODEL 24	MODEL 25
Any Criminal Justice Contact	1.478*** (.115)		1.904*** (.417)		1.411*** (.147)		.915 (.178)		1.067 (.093)	
Arrested		1.359** (.14)		1.827*** (.406)		1.287 (.185)		.807 (.216)		1.025 (.121)
Convicted		1.345* (.174)				1.011 (.169)		1.052 (.343)		.841 (.136)
Incarcerated		1.588*** (.160)		1.702 (.842)		1.750*** (.224)		.892 (.226)		1.247 (.144)
Wave fixed effects	Yes	Yes	Yes	Yes	Yes	Yes	Yes	Yes	Yes	Yes
N	7,620	7,574	2,753	2,753	4,422	4,396	16,576	16,426	6,910	6,882
Pseudo R-squared	.069	.069	.092	.092	.137	.137	.87	.869	.106	.108

NOTE: All coefficients expressed as odds ratios. Models 16, 17, and 20 estimated using Add Health; Models 18 and 19 estimated using NLSY97. Standard errors are in parentheses.

[a]Models include controls for general health and possession of health insurance.

[b]Models include controls for religiosity and church attendance.

*p < .05; **p < .01; ***p < .001 (two-tailed tests).

SOURCE: Originally published in "Surveillance and System Avoidance: Criminal Justice Contact and Institutional Attachment." American Sociological Review 79, no. 3 (2014): 367–91. doi:10.1177/0003122414530398.

APPENDIX D | Data Inventory

Databases and platforms

Palantir   Platform with high analytic capacity that is used
                            for merging disparate data sets, visualizing data,
                            measuring dosage, making Chronic Offender
                            Bulletins, and building network graphs. It was ini-
                            tially adopted as a case management tool, but now
                            has spread into patrol and analytics. As of 2018 it
                            integrates the following internal sources: Crime
                            Analysis Mapping System (CAMs), Field Interview
                            cards (FIs), traffic citations, crime alerts bulletins,
                            crime stoppers, LA Automatic License Plate
                            Readings (ALPRs), Long Beach ALPRs, LA County
                            ALPRs, Registered Sex Offenders, VeriTracks
                            (the offender monitoring service, including ankle
                            bracelets), and external sources including Burbank
                            citations, LA County Sheriff incidents, LA County
                            Sheriff citations, LA County Sheriff collisions,
                            LA County warrants for arrest, LA County Sheriff
                            crime stopper alerts, LA County Jail data (in-
                            cluding who is incarcerated with whom and inmate
                            phone data), and California Law Enforcement
                            Telecommunications System (CLETS) data.
                            Previously included other external data sources
                            such as foreclosure data.

PredPol   Predictive policing software that uses data from the
                            department's records management system (RMS)
                            to predict where and when future crime is likely to
                            occur.

Omega Dashboard	Enterprise GIS platform that is used to visualize information in graphs, charts, and speedometer gauges, analyze data, and make deployment decisions about resource allocation to reporting districts. After command approves the resource allocation plan, it is disseminated to the field through NEARme, the mobile application that also collects information on deployment.
California Law Enforcement Telecommunications System (CLETS)	Connects public safety agencies in California to various databases, including Criminal History System (CHS), Department of Motor Vehicles (DMV), Stolen Vehicle System (SVS), Automated Boat System (ABS), Automated Firearms System (AFS), Automated Property System (APS), Wanted Persons System (WPS), Supervised Release File (SRF), Restraining Order System (ROS), Criminal History System (CHS), Missing/Unidentified Persons System (MUPS), and Violent Crime Information Network (VCIN).
Crime Analysis Mapping System (CAMs)	Includes crimes, arrests, calls for service, traffic collisions, and recovered vehicles. Plans to include citations and FIs in the near future. Geocoded data is inputted into the Oracle database hourly.
Consolidated Criminal History Reporting System (CCHRS)	Booking data
NEXT	Criminal report database
Coplink	The old multi-county records management system owned by IBM. Integrates all district databases. Suitable for records management but lacks strong analytic tools. Currently the largest platform. Used predominantly by detectives. There are three entities: persons, locations, and things.
DOJ Cal-Photo	Visual identification of suspects of interest
Department of Motor Vehicles (DMV)	License plates, registered owners' names and addresses, photos
CalGang	Information on documented gang members, including name, monikers or AKAs, tattoos, race, age, affiliates (note: only available to a limited number of officers in the Gang Unit).
National Crime Information Center (NCIC)	FBI clearinghouse of crime data

Property Information Management System	Property information that can be queried with serial number (e.g., for stolen property).
Back Office Server System (BOSS)	Data sharing network for ALPRs across agencies within LA County
Department of Corrections (DOC)	Detention Data
Consolidated Crime Analysis Database (CCAD)	Official department source for statistics
Detective Case Tracking System (DCTS)	Detective's notes, witness statements, case details, final disposition.
TLOxp	TransUnion's skip tracing, investigative search and risk management tool. Includes over 100 billion public and proprietary data points.
CODIS (Combined DNA Index System)	FBI-established national DNA database
Automatic Firearm System (AFS)	Serialized weapons data set
LexisNexis Accurint	Investigative tool aggregating public records. Used to identify people, assets, addresses, relatives, business associates. Accessed via a portal in Palantir.
Foreclosure data	Publicly available by the city on the data.gov portal.
PAgis	GIS data
Esri	GIS mapping software
LA County Warrants System (LACWS)	Warrants data
LAPD Infoweb	Department Intranet site. Includes crime alerts, FI information, warrants information. Also has e-PCD function (electronic probable cause determination).
Department of Justice (DOJ)	Feeder system, processes booking documentation. Includes DABIS, the Automatic Booking Information System.

Sensors

Automated Field Data Reports (AFDRs, formerly DFARs)	Used for tracking employees. As per the consent decree, officers must fill out an AFDR for every self-initiated stop and now radio calls as well. Officers record the incident number, location, gender, ethnicity, whether there was any post-stop activity (e.g., a pat down, pull out of car, etc.). AFDRs used to be much simpler, but they have expanded to include drop-down menus asking questions such as whether the officer perceived the person's ethnicity before stopping them.
Field Interview cards (FIs)	Double-sided index card filled out as record of police-civilian contact; may be used in future investigations.
Digital In-Car Videos (DICVs)	Automatically turns on when someone is in backseat of patrol car. Footage can be useful in investigations.
Automatic Vehicle Locators (AVLs)	Sensors on police units that ping the location of the car every five seconds.
Automatic License Plate Readers (ALPRs)	Cameras mounted on police cruisers and some static cameras at intersections or locations of interest (e.g., tourist attractions).
BlueCheck	In-field fingerprint scanning
Live Scan	Booking system

Chapter 1

1. Kirstie Ball and Frank Webster, eds., *The Intensification of Surveillance: Crime, Terrorism and Warfare in the Information Age* (London: Pluto Press, 2003); Gary T. Marx, *Windows into the Soul: Surveillance and Society in an Age of High Technology* (Chicago: University of Chicago Press, 2016).

2. E. Ann Carson, "Prisoners in 2014" (Washington, DC: Bureau of Justice Statistics, September 2015), https://www.bjs.gov/content/pub/pdf/p14.pdf; David Garland, *The Culture of Control: Crime and Social Order in Contemporary Society* (Chicago: University of Chicago Press, 2002); Sara Wakefield and Christopher Uggen, "Incarceration and Stratification," *Annual Review of Sociology* 36, no. 1 (2010): 387–406, doi:10.1146/annurev.soc.012809.102551; National Research Council, *The Growth of Incarceration in the United States: Exploring Causes and Consequences* (Washington, DC: National Academies Press, 2014), doi:10.17226/18613; Erinn J. Herberman and Thomas P. Bonczar, *Probation and Parole in the United States, 2013*, Probation and Parole Populations Series (Washington, DC: Bureau of Justice Statistics, 2014), https://www.bjs.gov/index.cfm?ty=pbdetail&iid=5135.

3. Jennifer Bronson and E. Ann Carson, "Prisoners in 2017" (Washington, DC: Bureau of Justice Statistics, April 2019), https://www.bjs.gov/content/pub/pdf/p17.pdf.

4. Gary Fields and John R. Emshwiller, "As Arrest Records Rise, Americans Find Consequences Can Last a Lifetime," *Wall Street Journal*, August 18, 2014, https://www.wsj.com/articles/as-arrest-records-rise-americans-find-consequences-can-last-a-lifetime-1408415402.

5. Lynn Langton and Matthew Durose, "Police Behavior during Traffic and Street Stops, 2011" (Washington, DC: Bureau of Justice Statistics, 2013), https://www.bjs.gov/index.cfm?ty=pbdetail&iid=6406.

6. Doug Laney, "3D Data Management: Controlling Data Volume, Velocity, and Variety," Application Delivery Strategies (Stamford, CT: META Group Inc., 2001), https://blogs.gartner.com/doug-laney/files/2012/01/ad949-3D-Data-Management-Controlling-Data-Volume-Velocity-and-Variety.pdf; David Lazer and Jason Radford,

"Data Ex Machina: Introduction to Big Data," *Annual Review of Sociology* 43, no. 1 (2017): 19–39, doi:10.1146/annurev-soc-060116-053457; Viktor Mayer-Schönberger and Kenneth Cukier, *Big Data: A Revolution That Will Transform How We Live, Work, and Think* (Boston: Houghton Mifflin Harcourt, 2013).

7. Sarah Brayne, "Big Data Surveillance: The Case of Policing," *American Sociological Review* 82, no. 5 (2017): 977–1008, doi:10.1177/0003122417725865.

8. Solon Barocas et al., "Data & Civil Rights: Technology Primer," *SSRN Electronic Journal*, 2014, doi:10.2139/ssrn.2536579.

9. Police Executive Research Forum, "Future Trends in Policing" (Washington, DC: Office of Community Oriented Policing Services, 2014). According to a 2014 survey of 200 police departments, 38 percent of responding departments were using predictive policing, and 70 percent of departments indicated they plan to use it by 2017.

10. Clarisse Loughrey, "Minority Report: 6 Predictions That Actually Came True, 15 Years On," *The Independent*, June 25, 2017, http://www.independent.co.uk/arts-entertainment/films/features/minority-report-15th-anniversary-predictive-policing-gesture-based-computing-facial-and-optical-a7807666.html; Natasha Lennard, "Predictive Policing Is Not Like 'Minority Report'—It's Worse," *Vice*, June 26, 2014, https://news.vice.com/en_us/article/gyn3g7/predictive-policing-is-not-like-minority-report-its-worse; Tom Roston, "The Chilling Tech That Brings 'Minority Report' Inches from Reality," *Salon*, May 4, 2017, https://www.salon.com/2017/05/03/pre-crime-movie-documentary/.

11. James C. Scott, *Seeing Like a State: How Certain Schemes to Improve the Human Condition Have Failed* (New Haven, CT: Yale University Press, 1999).

12. Joseph Soss, Richard C. Fording, and Sanford F. Schram, *Disciplining the Poor: Neoliberal Paternalism and the Persistent Power of Race* (Chicago: University of Chicago Press, 2011); Forrest Stuart, *Down, Out, and Under Arrest: Policing and Everyday Life in Skid Row* (Chicago: University of Chicago Press, 2016).

13. Emily Barman, *Caring Capitalism: The Meaning and Measure of Social Value* (New York: Cambridge University Press, 2016); Tressie McMillan Cottom, *Lower Ed* (New York: The New Press, 2018).

14. Loïc Wacquant, *Punishing the Poor: The Neoliberal Government of Social Insecurity* (Durham, NC: Duke University Press, 2009); Reuben Jonathan Miller, "Devolving the Carceral State: Race, Prisoner Reentry, and the Micro-Politics of Urban Poverty Management," *Punishment & Society* 16, no. 3 (2014): 305–35, doi:10.1177/1462474514527487; Ronald Kramer, Valli Rajah, and Hung-En Sung, "Neoliberal Prisons and Cognitive Treatment: Calibrating the Subjectivity of Incarcerated Young Men to Economic Inequalities," *Theoretical Criminology* 17, no. 4 (2013): 535–56, doi:10.1177/1362480613497780; Michelle Alexander, "The Newest Jim Crow," *New York Times*, November 8, 2018, sec. Opinion, https://www.nytimes.com/2018/11/08/opinion/sunday/criminal-justice-reforms-race-technology.html; Reuben Jonathan Miller, "Race, Hyper-Incarceration, and US Poverty Policy in Historic Perspective," *Sociology Compass* 7 (2013): 573–89, doi:10.1111/soc4.12049; Richard V. Ericson and Kevin D. Haggerty, *Policing the Risk Society* (Toronto: University of Toronto Press, 1997).

15. Max Weber, *Economy and Society: An Outline of Interpretive Sociology* (Berkeley: University of California Press, 1978).

16. Paul J. DiMaggio and Walter W. Powell, "The Iron Cage Revisited: Institutional Isomorphism and Collective Rationality in Organizational Fields," *American Sociological Review* 48, no. 2 (1983): 147–60, doi:10.2307/2095101; John W. Meyer and Brian Rowan, "Institutionalized Organizations: Formal Structure as Myth and Ceremony," *American Journal of Sociology* 83, no. 2 (1977): 340–63; Donald J. Black, *The Manners and Customs of the Police* (New York: Academic Press, 1980); Egon Bittner, "The Police on Skid-Row: A Study of Peace Keeping," *American Sociological Review* 32, no. 5 (1967): 699–715, doi:10.2307/2092019; John Van Maanen, "The Asshole," in *Policing: A View from the Street*, ed. Peter K. Manning and John Van Maanen (Santa Monica, CA: Goodyear, 1978), 221–37.

17. Marion Fourcade and Kieran Healy, "Seeing Like a Market," *Socio-Economic Review* 15, no. 1 (2017): 9–29 (see p. 24), doi:10.1093/ser/mww033; Marion Fourcade and Kieran Healy, "Classification Situations: Life-Chances in the Neoliberal Era," *Accounting, Organizations and Society* 38, no. 8 (November 2013): 559–72, doi:10.1016/j.aos.2013.11.002; Angèle Christin, "Counting Clicks: Quantification and Variation in Web Journalism in the United States and France," *American Journal of Sociology* 123, no. 5 (March 1, 2018): 1382–1415, doi:10.1086/696137; Wendy Nelson Espeland and Berit Irene Vannebo, "Accountability, Quantification, and Law," *Annual Review of Law and Social Science* 3, no. 1 (2007): 21–43, doi:10.1146/annurev.lawsocsci.2.081805.105908; Barbara Kiviat, "The Art of Deciding with Data: Evidence from How Employers Translate Credit Reports into Hiring Decisions," *Socio-Economic Review* 17, no. 2 (2019), 283–309, doi:10.1093/ser/mwx030; Wendy Nelson Espeland and Mitchell L. Stevens, "A Sociology of Quantification," *European Journal of Sociology* 49, no. 3 (December 2008): 401–36, doi:10.1017/S0003975609000150; Ian Hacking, "Biopower and the Avalanche of Printed Numbers," *Humanities in Society* 5 (1982): 279–95; Theodore M. Porter, *Trust in Numbers: The Pursuit of Objectivity in Science and Public Life* (Princeton, NJ: Princeton University Press, 1995).

18. Viktor Mayer-Schönberger and Kenneth Cukier, *Big Data: A Revolution That Will Transform How We Live, Work, and Think* (Boston: Houghton Mifflin Harcourt, 2013); Erik Brynjolfsson and Andrew McAfee, *The Second Machine Age: Work, Progress, and Prosperity in a Time of Brilliant Technologies* (London: W. W. Norton, 2014); *Big Data: A Report on Algorithmic Systems, Opportunity, and Civil Rights* (Washington, DC: Executive Office of the President, May 2016), https://obamawhitehouse.archives.gov/sites/default/files/microsites/ostp/2016_0504_data_discrimination.pdf; Alex Pentland, "How Big Data Can Transform Society for the Better," *Scientific American*, October 2013, doi:10.1038/scientificamerican1013-78; Steve Lohr, "The Age of Big Data," *New York Times*, February 11, 2012, sec. Sunday Review, https://www.nytimes.com/2012/02/12/sunday-review/big-datas-impact-in-the-world.html; *Big Data, Big Impact: New Possibilities for International Development* (Geneva, Switzerland: World Economic Forum, 2012), http://reports.weforum.org/big-data-big-impact-new-possibilities-for-international-development-info/; George O. Mohler et al., "Randomized Controlled Field Trials of Predictive Policing," *Journal of the American Statistical Association* 110, no. 512 (2015): 1399–1411, doi:10.1080/01621459.2015.1077710.

19. "Palantir to Seek at Least $26 Billion Valuation in Fundraising Push," CNBC, September 20, 2019, https://www.cnbc.com/2019/09/20/palantir-to-seek-at-least-26-billion-valuation-in-fundraising-push.html.

20. Patricia Ewick and Susan S. Silbey, *The Common Place of Law*, Chicago Series in Law and Society (Chicago: The University of Chicago Press, 1998); See Angela S. Garcia, *Legal Passing: Navigating Undocumented Life and Local Immigration Law* (Oakland: University of California Press, 2019) for similar warrant for focusing on local agencies in the immigration context.

21. "SWORN & CIVILIAN PERSONNEL BY CSCLASS, SEX, AND DESCENT" (Los Angeles Police Department, June 9, 2019), http://assets.lapdonline.org/assets/pdf/PR91%20Jun2019.pdf.

22. Torin Monahan and Neal A. Palmer, "The Emerging Politics of DHS Fusion Centers," *Security Dialogue* 40, no. 6 (2009): 617–36, doi:10.1177/0967010609350314.

23. "Special Order No. 11: Reporting Incidents Potentially Related to Foreign or Domestic Terrorism," Office of the Chief of Police, Los Angeles Police Department (2008). SARs, also referred to as tips or leads, rely on a reasonable indication standard for intelligence gathering, rather than reasonable suspicion (i.e., there is a lower threshold for reporting and storage). Officers may come across activity that is not indicative of a crime but is still suspicious, and these data can be recorded and shared with fusion centers. In LA, SARs are used to "document any reported or observed activity, or any criminal act or attempted criminal act, which an officer believes may reveal a nexus to foreign or domestic terrorism."

24. Michèle Lamont and Ann Swidler, "Methodological Pluralism and the Possibilities and Limits of Interviewing," *Qualitative Sociology* 37, no. 2 (2014): 153–71 (see p. 157), doi:10.1007/s11133-014-9274-z; see also Allison J. Pugh, "What Good Are Interviews for Thinking about Culture? Demystifying Interpretive Analysis," *American Journal of Cultural Sociology* 1, no. 1 (2013): 42–68, doi:10.1057/ajcs.2012.4.

25. Colin Jerolmack and Shamus Khan, "Talk Is Cheap: Ethnography and the Attitudinal Fallacy," *Sociological Methods & Research* 43, no. 2 (2014): 178–209, doi:10.1177/0049124114523396. Mitchell Duneier, "How Not to Lie with Ethnography," *Sociological Methodology* 41, no. 1 (2011): 1–11, doi:10.1111/j.1467-9531.2011.01249.x.

26. Stuart, *Down, Out, and Under Arrest*; Joshua Page, *The Toughest Beat: Politics, Punishment, and the Prison Officers Union in California*, reprint edition (New York: Oxford University Press, 2013); Peter Moskos, *Cop in the Hood: My Year Policing Baltimore's Eastern District* (Princeton, NJ: Princeton University Press, 2008).

27. E.g., Egon Bittner, *Aspects of Police Work* (Boston: Northeastern University Press, 1990); Manning and Van Maanen, *Policing*; James Q. Wilson, *Varieties of Police Behavior: The Management of Law and Order in Eight Communities, with a New Preface by the Author* (Cambridge, MA: Harvard University Press, 1968).

28. For early exceptions, see Ericson and Haggerty, *Policing the Risk Society*; Manning and Van Maanen, *Policing*; Moskos, *Cop in the Hood*; Wesley G. Skogan, *Police and Community in Chicago: A Tale of Three Cities*, Studies in Crime and Public Policy (New York: Oxford University Press, 2006); James J. Willis, Stephen D. Mastrofski, and David Weisburd, "Making Sense of COMPSTAT: A Theory-Based Analysis of Organizational Change in Three Police Departments," *Law & Society Review* 41, no. 1 (2007): 147–88.

29. Most existing work on algorithms in the criminal justice system implicitly assumes—usually without empirical data—that police officers, judges, and prosecutors rely uncritically on what algorithmic technologies direct them to do in their daily

routines. (e.g., see Mara Hvistendahl, "Can 'Predictive Policing' Prevent Crime before It Happens?," *Science*, September 27, 2016, https://www.sciencemag.org/news/2016/09/can-predictive-policing-prevent-crime-it-happens; Lennard, "Predictive Policing"; Jack Smith IV, "'Minority Report' Is Real—And It's Really Reporting Minorities," *Mic*, November 9, 2015, https://www.mic.com/articles/127739/minority-reports-predictive-policing-technology-is-really-reporting-minorities; Mohler et al., "Randomized Controlled Field Trials of Predictive Policing"; Craig D. Uchida and Marc L. Swatt, "Operation LASER and the Effectiveness of Hotspot Patrol: A Panel Analysis," *Police Quarterly* 16, no. 3 (2013): 287–304, doi:10.1177/1098611113497044; . For notable exceptions, see Kelly Hannah-Moffat, "Actuarial Sentencing: An 'Unsettled' Proposition," *Justice Quarterly* 30, no. 2 (2012): 270–96, doi:10.1080/07418825.2012.682603; Carrie B. Sanders, Crystal Weston, and Nicole Schott, "Police Innovations, 'Secret Squirrels' and Accountability: Empirically Studying Intelligence-Led Policing in Canada," *British Journal of Criminology* 55, no. 4 (2015): 711–29; Lyria Bennett Moses and Janet Chan, "Algorithmic Prediction in Policing: Assumptions, Evaluation, and Accountability," *Policing and Society* 28, no. 7 (2018): 806–22; Sarah Brayne and Angèle Christin, "Technologies of Crime Prediction: The Reception of Algorithms in Policing and Criminal Courts." *Social Problems*, March 5, 2020 (Online First), doi:10.1093/socpro/spz006.

30. Brian A. Reaves, "Local Police Departments, 2013: Personnel, Policies, and Practices" (Washington, DC: Bureau of Justice Statistics, 2015), https://bjs.gov/content/pub/pdf/lpd13ppp.pdf.

31. Robert Zussman, "People in Places," *Qualitative Sociology* 27, no. 4 (2004): 351–63 (see p. 362). See also Ermakoff (2014), who suggests exceptional cases offer an epistemic contribution of exemplifying the characteristics of new classes of objects with clarity. Ivan Ermakoff, "Exceptional Cases: Epistemic Contributions and Normative Expectations," *European Journal of Sociology/Archives Européennes de Sociologie* 55, no. 2 (August 2014): 223–43, doi:10.1017/S0003975614000101.

32. Herman Goldstein, "Police Discretion: The Ideal versus the Real," *Public Administration Review* 23, no. 3 (1963): 140–48; Albert J. Reiss, *The Police and the Public* (New Haven, CT: Yale University Press, 1971); Black, *Manners and Customs*; Bittner, *Police on Skid Row*; Van Maanen, "The Asshole."

33. Michael Lipsky, *Street-Level Bureaucracy: Dilemmas of the Individual in Public Services* (New York: Russell Sage Foundation, 1980).

34. Goldstein, "Police Discretion," 140.

35. Black, *Manners and Customs*.

36. Sarah Brayne, "Surveillance and System Avoidance: Criminal Justice Contact and Institutional Attachment," *American Sociological Review* 79, no. 3 (2014): 367–91.

37. David Lehr and Paul Ohm, "Playing with the Data: What Legal Scholars Should Learn about Machine Learning," *UC Davis Law Review* 51 (2017): 653–717.

Chapter 2

1. Malcolm M. Feeley and Jonathan Simon, "The New Penology: Notes on the Emerging Strategy of Corrections and Its Implications," *Criminology* 30, no. 4

(1992): 449–74, doi:10.1111/j.1745-9125.1992.tb01112.x; Bernard E. Harcourt, *Against Prediction: Profiling, Policing, and Punishing in an Actuarial Age* (Chicago: University of Chicago Press, 2006); Wendy Nelson Espeland and Berit Irene Vannebo, "Accountability, Quantification, and Law," *Annual Review of Law and Social Science* 3, no. 1 (2007): 21–43, doi:10.1146/annurev.lawsocsci.2.081805.105908; David Weisburd et al., "Reforming to Preserve: COMPSTAT and Strategic Problem Solving in American Policing," *Criminology & Public Policy* 2, no. 3 (2003): 421–56, doi:10.1111/j.1745-9133.2003.tb00006.x; James J. Willis, Stephen D. Mastrofski, and David Weisburd, "Making Sense of COMPSTAT: A Theory-Based Analysis of Organizational Change in Three Police Departments," *Law & Society Review* 41, no. 1 (2007): 147–88, doi:10.1111/j.1540-5893.2007.00294.x; Peter K. Manning, *The Technology of Policing: Crime Mapping, Information Technology, and the Rationality of Crime Control* (New York: NYU Press, 2008); Richard V. Ericson and Kevin D. Haggerty, *Policing the Risk Society* (Toronto: University of Toronto Press, 1997); David Lyon, ed., *Surveillance as Social Sorting* (New York: Routledge, 2003); Gary T. Marx, *Windows into the Soul: Surveillance and Society in an Age of High Technology* (Chicago: University of Chicago Press, 2016); Kelly Hannah-Moffat, "Algorithmic Risk Governance: Big Data Analytics, Race and Information Activism in Criminal Justice Debates," *Theoretical Criminology* 23, no. 4 (2019): 453–70, doi:10.1177/1362480618763582; Danielle Leah Kehl, Priscillia Guo, and Samuel Kessler, "Algorithms in the Criminal Justice System: Assessing the Use of Risk Assessments in Sentencing" (Responsive Communities Initiative, Berkman Klein Center for Internet & Society, Harvard Law School, 2017), http://nrs.harvard.edu/urn-3:HUL.InstRepos:33746041; Yoav Mehozay and Eran Fisher, "The Epistemology of Algorithmic Risk Assessment and the Path towards a Non-Penology Penology," *Punishment & Society* 21, no. 5 (2019): 523–41, doi:10.1177/1462474518802336; Gil Rothschild-Elyassi, Johann Koehler, and Jonathan Simon, "Actuarial Justice," in *The Handbook of Social Control*, ed. Mathieu Deflem (Hoboken, NJ: John Wiley & Sons, 2019), 194–206.

2. George L. Kelling and Mark H. Moore, "The Evolving Strategy of Policing" (Washington, DC: National Institute of Justice, 1988); David Weisburd and Anthony A. Braga, *Police Innovation: Contrasting Perspectives* (Cambridge, UK: Cambridge University Press, 2006); David Alan Sklansky, "The Persistent Pull of Police Professionalism" (New Perspectives in Policing: UC Berkeley Public Law Research Paper No. 1788463, March 23, 2011), https://ssrn.com/abstract=1788463.

3. Charles R. Epp, Steven Maynard-Moody, and Donald P. Haider-Markel, *Pulled Over: How Police Stops Define Race and Citizenship*, Chicago Series in Law and Society (Chicago: University of Chicago Press, 2014), 28.

4. Sklansky, "The Persistent Pull."

5. Seth Flaxman et al., "Scalable High-Resolution Forecasting of Sparse Spatiotemporal Events with Kernel Methods: A Winning Solution to the NIJ 'Real-Time Crime Forecasting Challenge,'" *Annals of Applied Statistics* 13, no. 4 (2019): 2564–85, citing H. G. Schutt, "Advanced Police Methods in Berkeley," *National Municipal Review* 11 (1922): 80–85 and William Bratton and Peter Knobler, *The Turnaround: How America's Top Cop Reversed the Crime Epidemic* (New York: Random House, 1998).

6. Julian Go, "The Imperial Origins of American Policing: Militarization and Imperial Feedback in the Early 20th Century," *American Journal of Sociology*, in press.

7. Julilly Kohler-Hausmann, "Militarizing the Police: Officer Jon Burge, Torture, and War in the 'Urban Jungle,'" in *Challenging the Prison-Industrial Complex: Activism, Arts, and Educational Alternatives,* ed. Stephen John Hartnett (Urbana: University of Illinois Press, 2011), 48.

8. Radley Balko, *Rise of the Warrior Cop: The Militarization of America's Police Forces* (Philadelphia: PublicAffairs, 2013); Jonathan Mummolo, "Militarization Fails to Enhance Police Safety or Reduce Crime but May Harm Police Reputation," *Proceedings of the National Academy of Sciences* 115, no. 37 (2018): 9181–86.

9. David Weisburd et al., "What Works in Crime Prevention and Rehabilitation: An Assessment of Systematic Reviews," *Criminology and Public Policy* 16, no. 2 (2017): 415–49, doi:10.1111/1745-9133.12298.

10. Anthony Allan Braga and David Weisburd, *Policing Problem Places: Crime Hot Spots and Effective Prevention* (Oxford: Oxford University Press, 2010); Lawrence W. Sherman, Patrick R. Gartin, and Michael E. Buerger, "Hot Spots of Predatory Crime: Routine Activities and the Criminology of Place," *Criminology* 27, no. 1 (1989): 27–56, doi:10.1111/j.1745-9125.1989.tb00862.x.

11. "Fusion Center Locations and Contact Information," US Department of Homeland Security (last modified December 27, 2019), https://www.dhs.gov/fusion-center-locations-and-contact-information.

12. Barry Friedman, *Unwarranted: Policing without Permission* (New York: Farrar, Straus and Giroux, 2017), 267.

13. Ibid.

14. Pasquale, Frank. 2015. *The Black Box Society: The Secret Algorithms That Control Money and Information.* Cambridge, MA: Harvard University Press, 45–46.

15. Craig Roush, "Quis Custodiet Ipsos Custodes—Limits on Widespread Surveillance and Intelligence Gathering by Local Law Enforcement after 9/11," *Marquette Law Review* 96 (2012): 315–75.

16. Walter L. Perry et al., *Predictive Policing: The Role of Crime Forecasting in Law Enforcement Operations* (Santa Monica, CA: Rand Corporation, 2013); David Thacher, "The Local Role in Homeland Security," *Law & Society Review* 39, no. 3 (2005): 635–76, doi:10.1111/j.1540-5893.2005.00236.x; Matthew C. Waxman, "Police and National Security: American Local Law Enforcement and Counter-Terrorism after 9/11," *Journal of National Security Law & Policy* 3 (2009): 377.

17. Although the term "predictive policing" was first used in 2008 (Bratton and Malinowski, "Police Performance"), algorithms were actually first used in policing in the 1960s (see the Police Beat Algorithm in Phillip Mitchell, "Optimal Selection of Police Patrol Beats," *Journal of Criminal Law and Criminology* 63, no. 4 (January 1, 1973): 577 and Charlton D. McIlwain, *Black Software: The Internet and Racial Justice, from the AfroNet to Black Lives Matter* (Oxford: Oxford University Press, 2019).

18. Brantingham's parents, Paul and Patricia Brantingham, were foundational scholars of environmental criminology, or, the study of how contextual factors influence crime. See Patricia L. Brantingham and Paul J. Brantingham, "Theoretical Model of Crime Site Selection," in *Crime, Law, and Sanctions: Theoretical Perspectives,* ed. Marvin D. Krohn and Ronald Akers (Thousand Oaks, CA: SAGE, 1978) and Paul J. Brantingham and Patricia L. Brantingham, eds., *Environmental Criminology* (Beverly Hills, CA: SAGE, 1981).

19. Perry et al. *Predictive Policing;* George O. Mohler et al., "Randomized Controlled Field Trials of Predictive Policing," *Journal of the American Statistical Association* 110, no. 512 (2015): 1399–1411, doi:10.1080/01621459.2015.1077710.

20. City of Chicago, "Strategic Subject List," Chicago Data Portal (last updated December 7, 2017), https://data.cityofchicago.org/Public-Safety/Strategic-Subject-List/4aki-r3np.

21. Consent Decree, U.S. v. City Of Los Angeles, No. 2:00-cv-11769- GAF-RC (C.D. Cal.) (U.S. District Court June 19, 2001), document available at https://www.justice.gov/crt/file/826956/download.

22. Paul J. DiMaggio and Walter W. Powell, "The Iron Cage Revisited: Institutional Isomorphism and Collective Rationality in Organizational Fields," *American Sociological Review* 48, no. 2 (1983): 147–60, doi:10.2307/2095101; John W. Meyer and Brian Rowan, "Institutionalized Organizations: Formal Structure as Myth and Ceremony," *American Journal of Sociology* 83, no. 2 (1977): 340–63; W. Richard Scott, "Reflections on a Half-Century of Organizational Sociology," *Annual Review of Sociology* 30, no. 1 (2004): 1–21, doi:10.1146/annurev.soc.30.012703.110644; Willis, Mastrofski, and Weisburd, "Making Sense of COMPSTAT"; see also Rob Kling, "Computerization and Social Transformations," *Science, Technology, & Human Values* 16, no. 3 (1991): 342–67, doi:10.1177/016224399101600304, on computerization.

23. "White House Police Data Initiative" (Police Data Initiative, US Department of Justice, 2015), https://www.policedatainitiative.org/.

24. Martin Innes, "Control Creep," *Sociological Research Online* 6, no. 3 (2001): 1–6, doi:10.5153/sro.634.

25. Mark Andrejevic and Kelly Gates, "Big Data Surveillance: Introduction," *Surveillance & Society* 12, no. 2 (2014): 185–96, doi:10.24908/ss.v12i2.5242,189.

26. Ericson and Haggerty, *Policing the Risk Society.*

27. Bernard Marr, "Who Are the Biggest Consumer Data Brokers and Where Can You Buy Big Data?," *HuffPost,* October 10, 2017, https://www.huffpost.com/entry/where-can-you-buy-big-data-here-are-the-biggest-consumer_b_59ca19dee4b0b7022a646d83.

28. Gil Press, "6 Predictions for the $203 Billion Big Data Analytics Market," *Forbes,* January 20, 2017, https://www.forbes.com/sites/gilpress/2017/01/20/6-predictions-for-the-203-billion-big-data-analytics-market/#523d37f22083.

29. "Data Brokers Opt Out List," *World Privacy Forum,* December 18, 2013, https://www.worldprivacyforum.org/2013/12/data-brokers-opt-out/.

30. Pasquale, *Black Box Society;* Chris Hoofnagle, "Big Brother's Little Helpers: How ChoicePoint and Other Commercial Data Brokers Collect and Package Your Data for Law Enforcement," *North Carolina Journal of International Law and Commercial Regulation* 29 (2003): 595–638.

31. Frank Pasquale, "The Dark Market for Personal Data," *New York Times,* October 16, 2014, sec. Opinion, https://www.nytimes.com/2014/10/17/opinion/the-dark-market-for-personal-data.html.

32. Hoofnagle, "Big Brother's Little Helpers."

33. Letter from James Milford, vice president, Database Technologies, Inc., to the USMS (May, 29, 1998), as cited in Hoofnagle, "Big Brother's Little Helpers."

34. Pasquale, *Black Box Society.*

35. Hoofnagle, "Big Brother's Little Helpers."

36. Soss, Fording, and Schram, *Disciplining the Poor*; Wacquant, *Punishing the Poor*.

37. Kling, "Computerization."

38. Race is considered here a socially constructed form of classification that is both a social structure and cultural frame that shapes social relations in real ways; Michael Omi and Howard Winant, *Racial Formation in the United States: From the 1960s to the 1980s* (London: Routledge & Kegan Paul, 1986); Eduardo Bonilla-Silva, "Rethinking Racism: Toward a Structural Interpretation," *American Sociological Review* 62, no. 3 (1997): 465–80, doi:10.2307/2657316; Soss, Fording, and Schram, *Disciplining the Poor*).

39. Sandra Bass, "Policing Space, Policing Race: Social Control Imperatives and Police Discretionary Decisions," *Social Justice* 28, no. 1 (83) (2001): 156–76.

40. Andrew Guthrie Ferguson, *The Rise of Big Data Policing: Surveillance, Race, and the Future of Law Enforcement* (New York: NYU Press, 2017).

41. Bennett Capers, "Policing, Place, and Race," *Harvard Civil Rights—Civil Liberties Law Review* 44 (2009): 43–78; Katherine Beckett and Steve Herbert, *Banished: The New Social Control in Urban America* (New York: Oxford University Press, 2010).

42. Michelle Alexander, *The New Jim Crow* (New York: New Press, 2012).

43. Weisburd and Braga, *Police Innovation*, 4.

44. George L. Kelling and James Q. Wilson, "Broken Windows: The Police and Neighborhood Safety," *The Atlantic*, March 1, 1982, https://www.theatlantic.com/magazine/archive/1982/03/broken-windows/304465/; Katherine Beckett, *Making Crime Pay: Law and Order in Contemporary American Politics* (New York: Oxford University Press, 1997); Jonathan Simon, *Governing through Crime: How the War on Crime Transformed American Democracy and Created a Culture of Fear* (New York: Oxford University Press, 2007); Forrest Stuart, *Down, Out, and Under Arrest: Policing and Everyday Life in Skid Row* (Chicago: University of Chicago Press, 2016); Epp, Maynard-Moody, and Haider-Markel, *Pulled Over*; Amy E. Lerman and Vesla M. Weaver, *Arresting Citizenship: The Democratic Consequences of American Crime Control* (Chicago: University of Chicago Press, 2014).

45. United States Code, "Violent Crime Control and Law Enforcement Act of 1994," Pub. L. No. 103–322, 136 42 (1994).

46. Abigail Gepner and Daniel Prendergast, "Bratton Blasts Stop-and-Frisk Critics," *New York Post*, September 12, 2016, https://nypost.com/2016/09/12/bratton-blasts-stop-and-frisk-critics/.

47. Elijah Anderson, *A Place on the Corner* (Chicago: University of Chicago Press, 1978).

48. Terry Tempest Williams, *Crackhouse: Notes from the End of the Line* (Reading, MA: Addison-Wesley, 1992).

49. John Van Maanen, "The Fact of Fiction in Organizational Ethnography," *Administrative Science Quarterly* 24, no. 4 (1979): 539–50, doi:10.2307/2392360; Manning, *Technology of Policing*; Alice Goffman, *On the Run: Fugitive Life in an American City* (Chicago: University of Chicago Press, 2014); Stuart, *Down, Out, and Under Arrest*; Epp, Maynard-Moody, and Haider-Markel, *Pulled Over*; Victor M. Rios, *Punished: Policing the Lives of Black and Latino Boys* (New York: NYU Press, 2011).

50. Andrew Gelman, Jeffrey Fagan, and Alex Kiss, "An Analysis of the New York City Police Department's 'Stop-and-Frisk' Policy in the Context of Claims of Racial Bias," *Journal of the American Statistical Association* 102, no. 479 (2007): 813–23, doi:10.1198/016214506000001040; Epp, Maynard-Moody, and Haider-Markel, *Pulled Over*.

51. Gelman, Fagan, and Kiss, "Stop-and-Frisk"; Robert D. Crutchfield et al., "Racial Disparity in Police Contacts," *Race and Justice* 2, no. 3 (2012): 179–202, doi:10.1177/2153368712448063; Epp, Maynard-Moody, and Haider-Markel, *Pulled Over*.

52. Gelman, Fagan, and Kiss, "Stop-and-Frisk."

53. Tom R. Tyler, "Procedural Justice, Legitimacy, and the Effective Rule of Law," *Crime and Justice* 30 (2003): 283–357, doi:10.1086/652233; David S. Kirk and Mauri Matsuda, "Legal Cynicism, Collective Efficacy, and the Ecology of Arrest," *Criminology: An Interdisciplinary Journal* 49, no. 2 (2011): 443–72, doi:10.1111/j.1745-9125.2011.00226.x; Robert J. Sampson and Dawn Jeglum Bartusch, "Legal Cynicism and (Subcultural?) Tolerance of Deviance: The Neighborhood Context of Racial Differences," *Law & Society Review* 32, no. 4 (1998): 777–804; Joscha Legewie, "Racial Profiling and Use of Force in Police Stops: How Local Events Trigger Periods of Increased Discrimination," *American Journal of Sociology* 122, no. 2 (September 2016): 379–424, doi:10.1086/687518; Monica C. Bell, "Police Reform and the Dismantling of Legal Estrangement," *Yale Law Journal* 126 (2017): 2054–2150.

54. Epp, Maynard-Moody, and Haider-Markel, *Pulled Over*, 27.

55. Anthony L. Bui, Matthew M. Coates, and Ellicott C. Matthay, "Years of Life Lost Due to Encounters with Law Enforcement in the USA, 2015–2016," *Journal of Epidemiology and Community Health* 72, no. 8 (2018): 715–18, doi:10.1136/jech-2017-210059; Radley Balko, "There's Overwhelming Evidence That the Criminal-Justice System Is Racist. Here's the Proof," *Washington Post*, September 18, 2018, sec. Opinion, https://www.washingtonpost.com/news/opinions/wp/2018/09/18/theres-overwhelming-evidence-that-the-criminal-justice-system-is-racist-heres-the-proof/.

56. Joan Donovan, n.d., "The Ferguson Effect: Public Sociology and the Making of an American Statistic."

57. Bruno Latour, "Visualisation and Cognition: Drawing Things Together," in *Knowledge and Society: Studies in the Sociology of Culture Past and Present*, vol. 6, ed. H. Kulick (Greenwich, CT: JAI Press, 1986), 21.

58. Lorraine Daston and Peter Galison, *Objectivity* (New York: Zone Books, 2007).

59. President's Task Force on 21st Century Policing, *Final Report of the President's Task Force on 21st Century Policing* (Washington, DC: Office of Community Oriented Policing Services, 2015). Note: The Initiative and Task Force were discontinued under the Trump administration.

60. "Before the Bullet Hits the Body: Dismantling Predictive Policing in Los Angeles" (California: Stop LAPD Spying Coalition, May 8, 2018), https://stoplapdspying.org/wp-content/uploads/2018/05/Before-the-Bullet-Hits-the-Body-May-8-2018.pdf.

61. Letter from Hamid Khan of the Stop LAPD Spying Coalition to Los Angeles Police Department Inspector General Mark Smith, May 8, 2018, https://stoplapdspying.org/wp-content/uploads/2018/05/Ltr-to-OIG-May-8-2018-min.pdf.

62. Two of the officers involved were later found guilty in federal court and sentenced to 30 months in prison.

63. The Decree was formally terminated in 2009, but the LAPD remained in a Transition Agreement until 2013.

64. Los Angeles Police Department, "Consent Decree Overview," 2000, http://www.lapdonline.org/search_results/content_basic_view/928.

65. Kling, "Computerization"; Stephen R. Barley, "Technology as an Occasion for Structuring: Evidence from Observations of CT Scanners and the Social Order of Radiology Departments," *Administrative Science Quarterly* 31, no. 1 (1986): 78–108, doi:10.2307/2392767; Wanda J. Orlikowski, "The Duality of Technology: Rethinking the Concept of Technology in Organizations," *Organization Science* 3, no. 3 (1992): 398–427.

66. Arpaio refers to himself as "America's Toughest Sheriff" and is the subject of several federal civil rights lawsuits.

67. Kling, "Computerization."

68. Deputy Attorney General Rod J. Rosenstein, "Remarks Prepared for Project Safe Neighborhoods National Meeting" (Project Safe Neighborhoods National Conference, Kansas City, MO, December 5, 2018), https://www.justice.gov/opa/speech/deputy-attorney-general-rod-j-rosenstein-delivers-remarks-project-safe-neighborhoods.

Chapter 3

1. Christopher Slobogin, "Policing as Administration," *University of Pennsylvania Law Review* 165, no. 1 (2016): 91–152; Daphne Renan, "The Fourth Amendment as Administrative Governance," *Stanford Law Review* 68, no. 5 (2016): 1039–1129; Gary T. Marx, "What's New about the 'New Surveillance'? Classifying for Change and Continuity," *Surveillance & Society* 1, no. 1 (2002): 9–29, doi:10.24908/ss.viii.3391; Gary T. Marx, *Windows into the Soul: Surveillance and Society in an Age of High Technology* (Chicago: University of Chicago Press, 2016).

2. As of 2018, foreclosure data was no longer integrated.

3. "Search over 82 Billion Public Records—LexisNexis® Public Records," LexisNexis (accessed August 26, 2019), https://www.lexisnexis.com/en-us/products/public-records/powerful-public-records-search.page.

4. Michael Sierra-Arévalo, "American Policing and the Danger Imperative," SSRN Scholarly Paper (Rochester, NY: Social Science Research Network, November 1, 2016), https://papers.ssrn.com/abstract=2864104.

5. Gelman, Fagan, and Kiss, "Stop-and-Frisk."

6. Vesla M. Weaver, Andrew Papachristos, and Michael Zanger-Tishler, "The Great Decoupling: The Disconnection between Criminal Offending and Experience of Arrest across Two Cohorts," *RSF: The Russell Sage Foundation Journal of the Social Sciences* 5, no. 1 (2019): 89–123.

7. Paul E. Tracy and Valerie Morgan, "Big Brother and His Science Kit: DNA Databases for 21st Century Crime Control?," *Journal of Criminal Law & Criminology* 90, no. 2 (2000): 635–90, doi:10.2307/1144232.

8. Brayne, "Surveillance and System Avoidance."

9. Fourcade and Healy, "Seeing Like a Market."

10. Pasquale, *Black Box Society*.

11. Mark Poster, *The Mode of Information: Poststructuralism and Social Context* (Chicago: University Of Chicago Press, 1990).

Chapter 4

1. William J. Bratton and Sean W. Malinowski, "Police Performance Management in Practice: Taking COMPSTAT to the Next Level," *Policing: A Journal of Policy and Practice* 2, no. 3 (2008): 259–65, doi:10.1093/police/pano36.

2. Police Executive Research Forum, "Future Trends in Policing" (Washington, DC: Office of Community Oriented Policing Services, 2014), https://www.policeforum.org/assets/docs/Free_Online_Documents/Leadership/future%20trends%20in%20policing%202014.pdf.

3. E.g., Loughrey, "Minority Report"; Lennard, "Predictive Policing"; Roston, "Chilling Tech."

4. Robert J. Sampson, Stephen W. Raudenbush, and Felton Earls, "Neighborhoods and Violent Crime: A Multilevel Study of Collective Efficacy," *Science* 277, no. 5328 (1997): 918–24, doi:10.1126/science.277.5328.918; Jerry H. Ratcliffe et al., "The Philadelphia Foot Patrol Experiment: A Randomized Controlled Trial of Police Patrol Effectiveness in Violent Crime Hotspots," *Criminology* 49, no. 3 (2011): 795–831, doi:10.1111/j.1745-9125.2011.00240.x; Brantingham and Brantingham, *Environmental Criminology*.

5. Ross L. Matsueda, Derek A. Kreager, and David Huizinga, "Deterring Delinquents: A Rational Choice Model of Theft and Violence," *American Sociological Review* 71 (2006): 95–122; Kees Keizer, Siegwart Lindenberg, and Linda Steg, "The Spreading of Disorder," *Science* 322, no. 5908 (2008): 1681–85, doi:10.1126/science.1161405.

6. Anthony A. Braga, David M. Kennedy, Elin J. Waring, and Anne Morrison Piehl, "Problem-Oriented Policing, Deterrence, and Youth Violence: An Evaluation of Boston's Operation Ceasefire," *Journal of Research in Crime and Delinquency* 38, no. 3 (2001): 195–225; Craig Uchida and Marc L. Swatt, "Operation LASER and the Effectiveness of Hotspot Patrol: A Panel Analysis," *Police Quarterly* 16, no. 3 (2013): 287–304.

7. Andrew V. Papachristos et al., "The Company You Keep? The Spillover Effects of Gang Membership on Individual Gunshot Victimization in a Co-offending Network," *Criminology* 53, no. 4 (2015): 624–49, doi:10.1111/1745-9125.12091.

8. Walter L. Perry et al., *Predictive Policing: The Role of Crime Forecasting in Law Enforcement Operations* (Santa Monica, CA: Rand Corporation, 2013).

9. Sarah Brayne, Alex Rosenblat, and danah boyd, "Predictive Policing" (workshop primer from Data & Civil Rights: A New Era of Policing and Justice, 2015), http://www.datacivilrights.org/pubs/2015-1027/Predictive_Policing.pdf.

10. Pamela Wilcox and Francis T. Cullen, "Situational Opportunity Theories of Crime," *Annual Review of Criminology* 1, no. 1 (2018): 123–48; Lawrence E. Cohen and Marcus Felson, "Social Change and Crime Rate Trends: A Routine Activities Approach," *American Sociological Review* 44 (1979): 588–608.

11. Lorraine Daston and Peter Galison, *Objectivity* (Cambridge, MA: Zone Books, 2007).

12. Lawrence W. Sherman, "The Rise of Evidence-Based Policing: Targeting, Testing, and Tracking," *Crime and Justice* 42, no. 1 (2013): 377–451.

13. David Weisburd et al., "Can Hot Spots Policing Reduce Crime in Urban Areas? An Agent-Based Simulation," *Criminology* 55, no. 1 (2017): 137–73, doi:10.1111/1745-9125.12131.

14. Bratton and Malinowski, "Police Performance."

15. Ibid.

16. Mark Smith, "Review of Selected Los Angeles Police Department Data-Driven Policing Strategies" (Los Angeles: Office of the Inspector General, Los Angeles Police Department, March 12, 2019), https://www.documentcloud.org/documents/5766472-BPC-19-0072.html.

17. Uchida and Swatt, "Operation LASER."

18. Part I crimes include both violent and property crimes, including aggravated assault, assault, forcible rape, murder, robbery, arson, burglary, larceny-theft, and motor vehicle theft. Part II crimes include simple assault, curfew offenses and loitering, embezzlement, forgery and counterfeiting, disorderly conduct, driving under the influence, drug offenses, fraud, gambling, liquor offenses, offenses against the family, prostitution, public drunkenness, runaways, sex offenses, stolen property, vandalism, vagrancy, and weapons offenses.

19. The point system changed slightly over time. In 2017, two criteria changed: instead of giving 5 points total if an individual had any violent crime arrests, in the new system they received 5 points for each violent crime arrest in the last two years and 5 points for each time they had "used a gun in the course of his/her activities." What constitutes "using a gun" is somewhat unclear.

20. Harry Hoijer, *Language in Culture: Conference on the Interrelations of Language and Other Aspects of Culture* (Chicago: University of Chicago Press, 1954).

21. Consensual stops may be conducted when the police lack the "specific and articulable facts" (*Terry v. Ohio*, 392 U.S. 1 [1968]) that justify detention or arrest. Individuals who are stopped are not required to give their identity or answer questions, nor are officers required to tell individuals they are not legally obligated to answer their questions.

22. Lauren B. Edelman, "Legal Ambiguity and Symbolic Structures: Organizational Mediation of Civil Rights Law," *American Journal of Sociology* 97, no. 6 (1992): 1531–76; Frank Dobbin et al., "Equal Opportunity Law and the Construction of Internal Labor Markets," *American Journal of Sociology* 99, no. 2 (September 1993): 396–427, doi:10.1086/230269.

23. Smith, "Review of Selected Los Angeles Police Department Data-Driven Policing Strategies."

24. LAPD areas where LASER was implemented include Newton, 77th Street, Southwest, Southeast, Rampart, Hollenbeck, Northeast, Harbor, Foothill, Hollywood, Mission, Olympic, Pacific, Wilshire, West Los Angeles, and Central.

25. Smith, "Review of Selected Los Angeles Police Department Data-Driven Policing Strategies."

26. See Appendix B of Smith for an example of Chronic Offender Letter.

27. Bernard E. Harcourt, *Against Prediction: Profiling, Policing, and Punishing in an Actuarial Age* (Chicago: University of Chicago Press, 2006).

28. The algorithm was published in a 2015 paper: George O. Mohler et al., "Randomized Controlled Field Trials of Predictive Policing," *Journal of*

the American Statistical Association 110, no. 512 (2015): 1399–1411, doi:10.1080/01621459.2015.1077710. It is now available on PredPol's website, at http://www.predpol.com/technology/.

29. Mohler et al., "Randomized Controlled Field Trials." The near-repeat model is but one type of location-based predictive policing models. There are different kinds of location-based policing models. Risk terrain modeling, in contrast to the near-repeat model, focuses less on past events and more on the interaction of a wide range of social, behavioral, and physical risk factors (Andrew Guthrie Ferguson, "Predictive Policing and Reasonable Suspicion," *Emory Law Journal* 62, no. 2 (2012): 259–325.). Near-repeat theory tends to be used to predict property crime, whereas risk terrain modeling is used for both property and violent crime. Critics of risk terrain modeling argue it factors in a problematically wide range of variables, such as the sociodemographic composition of an area, weather, and the number of bars in an area. Instead, PredPol includes no environmental or personal information, only historical crime data. Limiting modeling to using historical crime data, Brantingham and colleagues suggest, reduces the potential for misallocation of police resources and discrimination (see P. Jeffrey Brantingham, Matthew Valasik, and George O. Mohler, "Does Predictive Policing Lead to Biased Arrests? Results from a Randomized Controlled Trial," *Statistics and Public Policy* 5, no. 1 (2018): 1–6, doi:10.1080/2330443X.2018.1438940.). For an example of a platform that uses risk terrain modeling, see HunchLab by Azavea, currently being employed in Philadelphia. HunchLab uses risk terrain modeling to account for the interaction of social, behavioral, and physical risk factors. In contrast to PredPol's parsimonious model, HunchLab's models include a much wider range of variables (Brayne et al., "Predictive Policing"), such as population density, location of bars, churches, and transportation hubs, and census data. As of 2017, HunchLab is used in the Philadelphia Police Department, Miami Police Department, and New York Police Department, among others.

30. As of March 2015, Southwest, Northeast, Van Nuys, North Hollywood, Pacific, Olympic, Foothill, Devonshire, Topanga, and Newton Divisions use predictive policing methods. A 2019 audit indicated PredPol was available "Department-wide" (page 26) of https://www.documentcloud.org/documents/5766472-BPC-19-0072.html#document/p32/a486274.

31. Mark Puente, "LAPD Official behind Controversial Data Programs to Retire after Winning Lucrative Contract," *Los Angeles Times*, May 9, 2019, https://www.latimes.com/local/lanow/la-me-sean-malinowski-predictive-policing-20190508-story.html.

Chapter 5

1. Loughrey, "Minority Report"; Lennard, "Predictive Policing"; Roston, "Chilling Tech"; Matt McFarland, "'Minority Report' Warned about Predicting Crime. 15 Years Later, the Lesson Has Been Ignored," CNN Business, June 23, 2017, https://money.cnn.com/2017/06/23/technology/future/minority-report-15-years/index.html.

2. Rios, *Punished*; Goffman, *On the Run*; Mitchell Duneier, *Sidewalk* (New York: Macmillan, 2001). For exceptions, see Stuart, *Down, Out, and Under Arrest*; Peter Moskos, *Cop in the Hood: My Year Policing Baltimore's Eastern District* (Princeton, NJ: Princeton University Press, 2008); Bittner, "The Police on Skid Row"; Van Maanen, "The Asshole"; Manning, *Technology of Policing*.

3. Shoshana Zuboff, *In the Age of the Smart Machine: The Future of Work and Power* (New York: Basic Books, 1988); Kirstie Ball, "Workplace Surveillance: An Overview," *Labor History* 51, no. 1 (2010): 87–106, doi:10.1080/00236561003654776; Karen Levy, *Data Driven: Truckers and the New Workplace Surveillance* (Princeton, NJ: Princeton University Press, n.d.).

4. Zuboff, *Age of the Smart Machine*.

5. Stephen R. Barley, "Technicians in the Workplace: Ethnographic Evidence for Bringing Work into Organizational Studies," *Administrative Science Quarterly* 41, no. 3 (1996): 404–41, doi:10.2307/2393937; Wendy Nelson Espeland and Berit Irene Vannebo, "Accountability, Quantification, and Law," *Annual Review of Law and Social Science* 3, no. 1 (2007): 21–43, doi:10.1146/annurev.lawsocsci.2.081805.105908.

6. Wanda J. Orlikowski and Stephen R. Barley, "Technology and Institutions: What Can Research on Information Technology and Research on Organizations Learn from Each Other?," *MIS Quarterly* 25, no. 2 (2001): 145–65; see also Orlikowski and Scott, "Exploring Material-Discursive Practices"; Lucy A. Suchman, *Human-Machine Reconfigurations: Plans and Situated Actions*, 2nd ed. (New York: Cambridge University Press, 2007); and Wanda J. Orlikowski and Susan V. Scott, "Sociomateriality: Challenging the Separation of Technology, Work and Organization," *Academy of Management Annals* 2, no. 1 (2008): 433–74, doi:10.5465/19416520802211644.

7. Braverman, *Labor and Monopoly Capital;* Frederick W. Taylor, *Shop Management* (New York: Harper & Brothers, 1911); Paul Willis, *Learning to Labor: How Working Class Kids Get Working Class Jobs* (New York: Columbia University Press, 1981); Alvin W. Gouldner, *Patterns of Industrial Bureaucracy* (New York: Free Press of Glencoe, 1964); Gary T. Marx, "A Tack in the Shoe: Neutralizing and Resisting the New Surveillance," *Journal of Social Issues* 59, no. 2 (2003): 369–90; Finn Brunton and Helen Nissenbaum, "Vernacular Resistance to Data Collection and Analysis: A Political Theory of Obfuscation," *First Monday* 16, no. 5 (2011), doi:10.5210/fm.v16i5.3493; Randy Hodson, "Worker Resistance: An Underdeveloped Concept in the Sociology of Work," *Economic and Industrial Democracy* 16, no. 1 (1995): 79–110, doi:10.1177/0143831X9501600104.

8. Andrew J. Nelson and Jennifer Irwin, "'Defining What We Do—All Over Again': Occupational Identity, Technological Change, and the Librarian/Internet-Search Relationship," *Academy of Management Journal* 57, no. 3 (2013): 892–928, doi:10.5465/amj.2012.0201.

9. Levy, *Data Driven*.

10. Helen Wells and David Wills, "Individualism and Identity: Resistance to Speed Cameras in the UK," *Surveillance & Society* 6, no. 3 (2009): 259–74, doi:10.24908/ss.v6i3.3284.

11. Van Maanen and Barley define an occupational community as a group of people who consider themselves to be engaged in the same sort of work; whose identity is drawn from their work; who share with one another a set of values, norms, and perspectives that apply but extend beyond work related matters; and whose social relationships meld work and leisure. John Van Maanen and Stephen R. Barley, *Occupational Communities: Culture and Control in Organizations* (Cambridge, MA: Defense Technical Information Center, 1982), 287.

12. After initial resistance from union representatives and subsequent protracted negotiations, AVLs were finally turned on in Central Bureau in March 2015. The automatic vehicle locators are now functional, and automatically feed Palantir data about how many minutes a given squad car spends in specific LASER zones. Management enabled this after they reached an agreement with the union that the location data would not be used for disciplinary purposes.

13. Gary T. Marx, "A Tack in the Shoe"; Brunton and Nissenbaum, "Vernacular Resistance to Data Collection and Analysis."

14. Wells and Wills, "Individualism and Identity."

15. Max Weber, "Objectivity in Social Science and Social Policy," in *Methodology of Social Sciences*, ed. Henry A. Finch and Edward A. Shils (New York: Free Press of Glencoe, 1949).

16. Pasquale, *Black Box Society*.

17. The algorithm was published in a 2015 paper: George O. Mohler et al., "Randomized Controlled Field Trials of Predictive Policing," *Journal of the American Statistical Association* 110, no. 512 (2015): 1399–1411, doi:10.1080/01621459.2015.1077710. It is now available on PredPol's website, at http://www.predpol.com/technology/.

18. Pasquale, *Black Box Society*, 9.

19. See Zetka, "Occupational Divisions," on the relationship between occupational divisions of labor, cultural scripts, and technological innovation.

20. Ronald J. Ostrow, "Interagency Rivalries Said to Hinder Drug Fight : FBI, DEA Don't Trade Data, Ex-Trafficker Tells Senate Hearing," *Los Angeles Times*, August 18, 1989, https://www.latimes.com/archives/la-xpm-1989-08-18-mn-584-story.html.

21. Department of Homeland Security, "Information Sharing," last modified August 14, 2018, https://www.dhs.gov/information-sharing.

22. The Dorner case refers to a series of incidents in 2013 in which an involuntarily terminated LAPD officer, Christopher Dorner, shot and killed four people and wounded three others. The victims were law enforcement officers, their family members, and civilians Dorner mistook for LAPD officers. The rampage eventually ended in Dorner's suicide during a standoff with the police in the San Bernardino Mountains. The Dorner case came up many times during my fieldwork because the Palantir platform was used during the investigation.

23. Eric Holder was the US Attorney General from 2009 to 2015.

24. Van Maanen, "Police Socialization."

25. Barley, "Technicians in the Workplace."

26. Ibid., 437.

27. James Scott, *Weapons of the Weak: Everyday Forms of Peasant Resistance* (New Haven, CT: Yale University Press, 1987); Braverman, *Labor and Monopoly Capital*; Marx, "A Tack in the Shoe"; Brunton and Nissenbaum, "Vernacular Resistance."

28. See Barley, "Technology as an Occasion."

29. Kling, "Computerization," 359.

Chapter 6

1. Barley, "Technology as an Occasion"; Barley, "Technicians in the Workplace"; Kling, "Computerization."

2. danah boyd and Kate Crawford, "Critical Questions for Big Data," *Information, Communication & Society* 15, no. 5 (2012): 662–79, doi:10.1080/1369118X.2012.678878; Lisa Gitelman, ed., *"Raw Data" Is an Oxymoron* (Cambridge, MA: MIT Press, 2013); Rob Kitchin, "Big Data, New Epistemologies and Paradigm Shifts," *Big Data & Society* 1, no. 1 (2014), doi:10.1177/2053951714528481.

3. Jon Swaine, "Eric Holder Calls Failure to Collect Reliable Data on Police Killings Unacceptable," *The Guardian*, January 15, 2015, sec. US News, https://www.theguardian.com/us-news/2015/jan/15/eric-holder-no-reliable-fbi-data-police-related-killings.

4. Center for Policing Equity, "National Justice Database," published March 28, 2019, https://www.policingequity.org/what-we-do/national-justice-database.

5. Marie Ouellet et al., "Network Exposure and Excessive Use of Force: Investigating the Social Transmission of Police Misconduct," *Criminology and Public Policy* 18, no. 3 (2019): 675–704, doi:10.1111/1745-9133.12459.

6. Gelman, Fagan, and Kiss, "Stop-and-Frisk."

7. Sharad Goel et al., "Combatting Police Discrimination in the Age of Big Data," *New Criminal Law Review: An International and Interdisciplinary Journal* 20, no. 2 (2017): 181–232, doi:10.1525/nclr.2017.20.2.181.

8. Sharad Goel, Justin M. Rao, and Ravi Shroff, "Precinct or Prejudice? Understanding Racial Disparities in New York City's Stop-and-Frisk Policy," *Annals of Applied Statistics* 10, no. 1 (2016): 365–94, doi:10.1214/15-AOAS897.

9. Jennifer L. Eberhardt, "Strategies for Change: Research Initiatives and Recommendations to Improve Police-Community Relations in Oakland, Calif." (Stanford University, SPARQ: Social Psychological Answers to Real-world Questions, June 20, 2016).

10. Susan T. Fiske and Shelley E. Taylor, *Social Cognition*, 2nd ed. (New York: McGraw-Hill, 1991).

11. Lincoln Quillian and Devah Pager, "Black Neighbors, Higher Crime? The Role of Racial Stereotypes in Evaluations of Neighborhood Crime," *American Journal of Sociology* 107, no. 3 (2001): 717–67, doi:10.1086/338938; Jennifer L. Eberhardt et al., "Seeing Black: Race, Crime, and Visual Processing," *Journal of Personality and Social Psychology* 87, no. 6 (2004): 876–93, doi:10.1037/0022-3514.87.6.876.

12. Sampson and Bartusch, "Legal Cynicism"; Amy E. Lerman and Vesla Weaver, "Staying out of Sight? Concentrated Policing and Local Political Action," *ANNALS of the American Academy of Political and Social Science* 651, no. 1 (2014): 202–19, doi:10.1177/0002716213503085.

13. Lyon, *Surveillance as Social Sorting*.

14. Sandra G. Mayson, "Bias In, Bias Out," *Yale Law Journal* 128, no. 8 (2019): 2218–2300.

15. Solon Barocas and Andrew D. Selbst, "Big Data's Disparate Impact," *California Law Review* 104 (2016): 671–732, doi:10.15779/Z38BG31.

16. Pasquale, *Black Box Society*, 41–42.

17. Los Angeles Police Commission, Office of the Inspector General, "Review of Selected Los Angeles Police Department Data-Driven Policing Strategies," March 12, 2019, https://a27e0481-a3d0-44b8-8142-1376cfbb6e32.filesusr.com/ugd/b2dd23_21f6fe20fib84c179abf440d4c049219.pdf.

18. Gitelman, *"Raw Data."*

19. Los Angeles Police Commission, Office of the Inspector General, "Review."

20. Lynn Langton et al., "Victimizations Not Reported to the Police, 2006–2010," US Department of Justice, Bureau of Justice Statistics, 2012, 18.

21. Troy Duster, "Pattern, Purpose, and Race in the Drug War: The Crisis of Credibility in Criminal Justice," in *Crack in America: Demon Drugs and Social Justice*, ed. Craig Reinarman and Harry Levine (Berkeley: University of California Press, 1997), 260–87.

22. Sampson and Bartusch, "Legal Cynicism."

23. Katherine Beckett et al., "Drug Use, Drug Possession Arrests, and the Question of Race: Lessons from Seattle," *Social Problems* 52, no. 3 (2005): 419–41, doi:10.1525/sp.2005.52.3.419.

24. Pasquale, *Black Box Society*.

25. Robert K. Merton, "The Self-Fulfilling Prophecy," *Antioch Review* 8, no. 2 (1948): 193–210, doi:10.2307/4609267.

26. P. Jeffrey Brantingham, Matthew Valasik, and George O. Mohler, "Does Predictive Policing Lead to Biased Arrests? Results from a Randomized Controlled Trial," *Statistics and Public Policy* 5, no. 1 (2018): 1–6, doi:10.1080/2330443X.2018.1438940.

27. Tom R. Tyler, *Why People Obey the Law* (New Haven, CT: Yale University Press, 1990); Tracey Meares, "The Path Forward: Improving the Dynamics of Community-Police Relationships to Achieve Effective Law Enforcement Policies," *Columbia Law Review* 17, no. 5 (2017): 1355; Sampson and Bartusch, "Legal Cynicism"; Kirk and Matsuda, "Legal Cynicism, Collective Efficacy"; Harcourt, *Against Prediction*.

28. Tracy and Morgan, "Big Brother."

29. Stanley Cohen, *Visions of Social Control: Crime, Punishment and Classification* (Malden, MA: Polity Press, 1991).

30. Renan, "Fourth Amendment."

31. Poster, *Mode of Information*.

32. Epp, Maynard-Moody, and Haider-Markel, *Pulled Over*.

33. Ibid.

34. Troy Duster, "Race and Reification in Science," *Science* 307, no. 5712 (2005): 1050–51, doi:10.1126/science.1110303; Richard Hindmarsh and Barbara Prainsack, eds., *Genetic Suspects: Global Governance of Forensic DNA Profiling and Databasing* (Cambridge, UK: Cambridge University Press, 2010), doi:10.1017/CBO9780511778193; Michael Lynch et al., *Truth Machine: The Contentious History of DNA Fingerprinting* (Chicago: University of Chicago Press, 2008).

35. Albert Fox Cahn, "Manhattan DA Made Google Give Up Information on Everyone in Area as They Hunted for Antifa," *Daily Beast*, August 13, 2019, https://www.thedailybeast.com/manhattan-da-cy-vance-made-google-give-up-info-on-everyone-in-area-in-hunt-for-antifa-after-proud-boys-fight.

36. Samuel Gross, Maurice Possley, and Klara Stephens, "Race and Wrongful Convictions in the United States" (Irvine, CA: National Registry of Exonerations, Newkirk Center for Science and Society, March 7, 2017), https://repository.law.umich.edu/other/122.

37. Kevin D. Haggerty and Richard V. Ericson, "The Surveillant Assemblage," *British Journal of Sociology* 51, no. 4 (2000): 605–22, doi:10.1080/00071310020015280, 611.

38. Alexes Harris, Heather Evans, and Katherine Beckett, "Courtesy Stigma and Monetary Sanctions: Toward a Socio-Cultural Theory of Punishment," *American Sociological Review* 76, no. 2 (2011): 234–64, doi:10.1177/0003122411400054.

39. Brayne, "Surveillance and System Avoidance."

40. For a more detailed discussion, see methods section of Brayne, "Surveillance and System Avoidance."

41. Haggerty and Ericson, "Surveillant Assemblage," 619.

42. Sarah E. Lageson, *Digital Punishment* (New York: Oxford University Press, forthcoming); Lageson and Shadd Maruna, "Digital Degradation: Stigma Management in the Internet Age," *Punishment & Society* 20, no. 1 (2018): 113–33, doi:10.1177/1462474517737050; Lageson, "Found Out and Opting Out: The Consequences of Online Criminal Records for Families," *ANNALS of the American Academy of Political and Social Science* 665, no. 1 (2016): 127–41, doi:10.1177/0002716215625053.

43. "Americans with Criminal Records" (Washington, DC: The Sentencing Project, 2015), https://www.sentencingproject.org/wp-content/uploads/2015/11/Americans-with-Criminal-Records-Poverty-and-Opportunity-Profile.pdf; Robert Brame et al., "Cumulative Prevalence of Arrest from Ages 8 to 23 in a National Sample," *Pediatrics* 129, no. 1 (2012): 21–27, doi:10.1542/peds.2010-3710.

44. Devah Pager, *Marked: Race, Crime, and Finding Work in an Era of Mass Incarceration* (Chicago: University Of Chicago Press, 2007).

45. Pasquale, *Black Box Society*, 218; Oscar H. Gandy, *The Panoptic Sort: A Political Economy of Personal Information* (Boulder, CO: Westview Press, 1993).

46. Fourcade and Healy, "Seeing Like a Market," 24.

47. Fourcade and Healy, "Classification Situations."

48. Geoffrey C. Bowker and Susan Leigh Star, *Sorting Things Out: Classification and Its Consequences* (Cambridge, MA: MIT Press, 2000).

49. Elizabeth E. Joh, "The New Surveillance Discretion: Automated Suspicion, Big Data, and Policing," *Harvard Law and Policy Review* 10, no. 1 (2015): 15–42.

50. Kate Crawford, "Artificial Intelligence's White Guy Problem," *New York Times*, June 25, 2016, sec. Opinion, https://www.nytimes.com/2016/06/26/opinion/sunday/artificial-intelligences-white-guy-problem.html.

Chapter 7

1. For an exception, see Kathryne M. Young and Christin Munsch, "Fact and Fiction in Constitutional Criminal Procedure," *South Carolina Law Review* 66, no. 445 (2014), https://papers.ssrn.com/abstract=2583472.

2. Terry v. Ohio, 392 U.S. 1 (1968).

3. Elizabeth E. Joh, "Policing by Numbers: Big Data and the Fourth Amendment," *Washington Law Review* 89, no. 35 (2014): 56, https://papers.ssrn.com/abstract=2403028; Ferguson, *Rise of Big Data Policing*.

4. E.g. Joh, "Policing by Numbers"; Ferguson, *Rise of Big Data Policing*.

5. Ferguson, *Rise of Big Data Policing*, 77.

6. Andrew Guthrie Ferguson, "Big Data and Predictive Reasonable Suspicion," *University of Pennsylvania Law Review* 163, no. 2 (2015): 336.

7. Ferguson, "Predictive Policing and Reasonable Suspicion."

8. Meyer and Rowan, "Institutionalized Organizations."

9. L. Song Richardson, "Police Efficiency and the Fourth Amendment," *Indiana Law Journal* 87, no. 3 (2012): 1143.

10. Jennifer L. Eberhardt, *Biased: Uncovering the Hidden Prejudice That Shapes What We See, Think, and Do* (New York: Penguin, 2019); Fiske and Taylor, *Social Cognition*; Quillian and Pager, "Black Neighbors, Higher Crime?"

11. Renée Bolinger, "The Rational Impermissibility of Accepting (Some) Racial Generalizations," *Synthese*, 2018, doi:10.1007/s11229-018-1809-5.

12. Barry Lam, "S3, Episode 1: The Precrime Unit," *Hi-Phi Nation* (podcast), January 31, 2019, https://hiphination.org/season-3-episodes/s3-episode-1-the-precrime-unit/.

13. Issa Kohler-Hausmann, *Misdemeanorland: Criminal Courts and Social Control in an Age of Broken Windows Policing* (Princeton, NJ: Princeton University Press, 2018).

14. Friedman, *Unwarranted*, 161.

15. Kohler-Hausmann, *Misdemeanorland*.

16. Karen E. C. Levy, "Relational Big Data," *Stanford Law Review* 66 (September 2013), https://www.stanfordlawreview.org/online/privacy-and-big-data-relational-big-data/.

17. Viviana A. Zelizer, "How I Became a Relational Economic Sociologist and What Does That Mean?," *Politics & Society* 40, no. 2 (2012): 145–74, doi:10.1177/0032329212441591; Viviana A. Zelizer, "Pasts and Futures of Economic Sociology," *American Behavioral Scientist* 50, no. 8 (2007): 1056–69, doi:10.1177/0002764207299353.

18. U.S. Const. amend. IV.

19. United States v. Jones, 565 U.S. 400 (2012) (Alito, S., concurring). Opinions available online at https://www.supremecourt.gov/opinions/11pdf/10-1259.pdf. See also Justice Sotomayor's concurring opinion.

20. Orin Kerr, "The Mosaic Theory of the Fourth Amendment," *Michigan Law Review* 111, no. 3 (2012): 311–54.

21. Joh, "Policing by Numbers," 60 (emphasis added).

22. David C. Gray and Danielle Keats Citron, "The Right to Quantitative Privacy," *Minnesota Law Review* 98 (2013), https://papers.ssrn.com/abstract=2228919.

23. Terry v. Ohio, 392 U.S. 1 (1968).

24. Orin Kerr, "An Equilibrium-Adjustment Theory of the Fourth Amendment," *Harvard Law Review* 125, no. 2 (2011), https://harvardlawreview.org/2011/12/an-equilibrium-adjustment-theory-of-the-fourth-amendment/, 479.

25. Riley v. California, 573 U.S. (2014).

26. California v. Ciraolo, 476 U.S. 207, 215 (1986); Kyllo v. United States, 533 U.S. 27, 34–35 (2001); United States v. Karo, 468 U.S. 705, 714 (1984); United States v. Jones, 565 U.S. 400 (2012); Carpenter v. United States, 585 U.S. ___ (2018).

27. Taylor v. City of Saginaw, No. 17-cv-11067 (E.D. Mich. Aug. 27, 2019).

28. Kerr, "Equilibrium-Adjustment Theory," 480.

29. The Foreign Intelligence Surveillance Court may be an instructive case for considering programmatic, as opposed to transactional, surveillance. The court has cases interpreting the Fourth Amendment in ways that are not transactional and is executing programmatic warrants.

30. Renan, "Fourth Amendment," 1053.

31. Ibid., 1058.

32. Christopher Slobogin, "Policing and the Cloud," White Paper Series: A Twenty-First Century Framework for Digital Privacy (Philadelphia: National Constitution Center, 2017), https://constitutioncenter.org/digital-privacy/policing-and-the-cloud. Slobogin divides the various ways police access data into four categories: programmatic, suspect-driven, profile-driven, and event-driven. When police want to set up a data collection *program*, such as the ALPR system described throughout this book, Slobogin argues they can only do so if the legislature has authorized it and the police have promulgated implementing regulations, after some type of public comment period. If they use the ALPR system to track a particular *suspect* over several days, they would need some type of justification proportionate to the privacy intrusion—perhaps what courts call *reasonable suspicion*—before they could do so. If, instead, they construct a drug dealer *profile*—perhaps using a combination of ALPR data and knowledge about the type of cars and locations involved in drug sales to identify individuals they want to subject to investigative stops—they would need to demonstrate the profile has a hit rate that would justify such an action (Slobogin suggests 30 percent), and they would also have to apply the profile even-handedly (that is, to everyone who fit it) and allow courts to ensure that the profile does not use invidious risk factors. If police are trying to discover who may have been at the scene of a particular *event* (most commonly a crime), they might use ALPR to identify cars in the vicinity of the event at the time it occurred, which Slobogin would allow as long as their net was not cast too widely. Each category of data-based surveillance, he argues, should be subject to a specific regulatory regime, in addition to the minimal restrictions imposed by the Fourth Amendment.

33. Hoofnagle, "Big Brother's Little Helpers."

34. Joh, "Policing by Numbers," 64.

35. Harold J. Krent, "Of Diaries and Data Banks: Use Restrictions under the Fourth Amendment," *Texas Law Review* 74, no. 1995–1996 (1995), 80.

36. Ric Simmons, "The Mirage of Use Restrictions," *North Carolina Law Review* 96, no. 1 (2017): 133.

37. For a detailed discussion, see Erin Murphy, "The Politics of Privacy in the Criminal Justice System: Information Disclosure, the Fourth Amendment, and Statutory Law Enforcement Exemptions," *Michigan Law Review* 111, no. 4 (2013): 485–546.

38. "Big Data: Seizing Opportunities, Preserving Values" (Executive Office of the President, May 2014), https://obamawhitehouse.archives.gov/sites/default/files/docs/big_data_privacy_report_may_1_2014.pdf, 33. *Smith v. Maryland* allowed the police access to any information a suspect shares with a third party, such as a phone company.

39. Friedman, *Unwarranted*, 234.

40. Ibid.

41. I thank Katie Young for offering this example and helping me think through this chapter.

42. I thank Katie Young for her insight on this point.

43. Carpenter v. United States, 585 U.S. ____ (2018).

44. See also Riley v. California, 573 U.S. (2014), which required a search warrant for smartphones.

45. The defendant, Timothy Carpenter, was suspected of being involved in a series of robberies of cell phone stores. The police wanted to obtain Carpenter's CSLI, because they thought it would tell them whether or not he was near the crimes when they were committed. They applied for a court order under the Stored Communications Act, but Carpenter's lawyers argued the Fourth Amendment required they get a full probable cause judicial warrant to obtain private location data.

46. Brief for Data & Society Research Institute et al. as Amici Curiae Supporting Petitioner, Carpenter v. United States, 585 U.S. ____ (2018). Available online at https://datasociety.net/pubs/fatml/DataAndSociety_CarpentervUS_Amicus_Brief.pdf.

47. For example, in Maryland v. King, 569 U.S. 435 (2013), the US Supreme Court decided that states could compel DNA from arrestees (i.e., without their consent) and permanently store it in the CODIS database.

48. Viviana A. Zelizer, *The Social Meaning of Money: Pin Money, Paychecks, Poor Relief, and Other Currencies* (New York: Basic Books, 1995).

49. John Shiffman and Kristina Cooke, "Exclusive: U.S. Directs Agents to Cover Up Program Used to Investigate Americans," Reuters, August 5, 2013, https://www.reuters.com/article/us-dea-sod/exclusive-u-s-directs-agents-to-cover-up-program-used-to-investigate-americans-idUSBRE97409R20130805.

50. Joe Kloc, "DEA Investigated for Using NSA Data for Drug Busts," *Daily Dot*, August 7, 2013, sec. Layer 8, https://www.dailydot.com/layer8/dea-sod-nsa-snowden-investigation/.

51. Shiffman and Cooke, "U.S. Directs Agents."

52. Human Rights Watch, "Dark Side: Secret Origins of Evidence in US Criminal Cases" (New York: Human Rights Watch, January 9, 2018), https://www.hrw.org/report/2018/01/09/dark-side/secret-origins-evidence-us-criminal-cases.

53. Brady v. Maryland 373 U.S. 83 (1963).

54. It is worthwhile to note that there are a number of exceptions to the exclusionary rule. For example, if the tainted evidence would have been inevitably discovered without the tainted source, then it can be admitted. Likewise, otherwise tainted evidence can be deemed admissible if the police discovered it through a source independent from the illegal activity, if the link between the illegal action and the tainted evidence is attenuated, or if the police conducted the search in good faith, *thinking* it was legal.

55. Human Rights Watch, "Dark Side."

56. Edelman, "Legal Ambiguity."

57. Black, *Manners and Customs*.

58. Rebecca Wexler, "Life, Liberty, and Trade Secrets: Intellectual Property in the Criminal Justice System," *Stanford Law Review* 70 (2018): 1343.

59. Ibid.

Chapter 8

1. Smith, "Data-Driven Policing Strategies."

2. Chief of Police Michel Moore to Board of Police Commissioners, "Department's Response to the Board of Police Commissioner's Request to Review Selected Los Angeles Police Department Data-Driven Policing Strategies," Intradepartmental Correspondence, April 5, 2019.

3. Eva Ruth Moravec, "Do Algorithms Have a Place in Policing?," *The Atlantic*, September 5, 2019, https://www.theatlantic.com/politics/archive/2019/09/do-algorithms-have-place-policing/596851/.

4. City News Service, "LAPD Chief Will End Controversial Data Program," *LA Daily News*, April 9, 2019, https://www.dailynews.com/2019/04/09/lapd-chief-to-outline-new-data-policies/.

5. Moore to Board of Police Commissioners, "Department's Response," 4.

6. Ibid.

7. William J. Bratton, "Cops Count, Police Matter: Preventing Crime and Disorder in the 21st Century" (Heritage Foundation, September 21, 2017), https://www.heritage.org/crime-and-justice/report/cops-count-police-matter-preventing-crime-and-disorder-the-21st-century.

8. Wacquant, *Punishing the Poor*.

9. United States Office of the Press Secretary, "Fact Sheet: White House Police Data Initiative Highlights New Commitments" (White House, April 21, 2016), https://obamawhitehouse.archives.gov/the-press-office/2016/04/22/fact-sheet-white-house-police-data-initiative-highlights-new-commitments.

10. Pierre Bourdieu, *Distinction: A Social Critique of the Judgement of Taste* (Cambridge, MA: Harvard University Press, 1984).

11. DiMaggio and Powell, "Iron Cage Revisited"; Meyer and Rowan, "Institutionalized Organizations"; Willis, Mastrofski, and Weisburd, "Making Sense of COMPSTAT."

12. Nick Seaver, "What Should an Anthropology of Algorithms Do?," *Cultural Anthropology* 33, no. 3 (2018): 375–85, doi:10.14506/ca33.3.04.

13. Scott, *Seeing Like a State*.

14. Gilles Deleuze and Felix Guattari, *A Thousand Plateaus: Capitalism and Schizophrenia*, trans. Brian Massumi, 2nd ed. (Minneapolis: University of Minnesota Press, 1987); Haggerty and Ericson, "Surveillant Assemblage"; Marx, *Windows into the Soul*.

15. Poster, *Mode of Information*, 97.

16. Soss, Fording, and Schram, *Disciplining the Poor*; Stuart, *Down, Out, and Under Arrest*; Miller, "Devolving the Carceral State."

17. Barman, *Caring Capitalism*.

18. Wacquant, *Punishing the Poor*; Alexander, "Newest Jim Crow"; Miller, "Race, Hyper-Incarceration"; Ericson and Haggerty, *Policing the Risk Society*; Ronald Kramer, Valli Rajah, and Hung-En Sung, "Neoliberal Prisons and Cognitive Treatment: Calibrating the Subjectivity of Incarcerated Young Men to Economic Inequalities," *Theoretical Criminology* 17, no. 4 (2013): 535–56, doi:10.1177/1362480613497780.

19. Ari Ezra Waldman, "Power, Process, and Automated Decision-Making," *Fordham Law Review* 88 (2019), https://papers.ssrn.com/abstract=3461238.

20. Brayne, "Big Data Policing."

21. Brayne, "System Avoidance."

22. Ruha Benjamin, *Race after Technology: Abolitionist Tools for the New Jim Code* (Wiley, 2019).

23. Howard S. Becker, *Outsiders: Studies in the Sociology of Deviance* (New York: Free Press, 1963); Brayne, "System Avoidance"; Kohler-Hausmann, *Misdemeanorland*; Pager, *Marked*; Rios, *Punished*.

24. Pager, *Marked*; Lageson, *Digital Punishment*; Stuart, *Down, Out, and Under Arrest*; Rios, *Punished*.

25. See Wacquant, *Punishing the Poor*, on the "insatiable craving" for "technological gadgets" like computerized mapping of offenses, data-sharing across service agencies, and criminal profiling.

26. Mohler et al., "Randomized Controlled Field Trials."

27. Uchida and Swatt, "Operation LASER."

28. Mayson, *Bias In, Bias Out*.

29. Brayne and Christin, "Technologies of Crime Prediction."

30. Mark H. Moore, ed., *Recognizing Value in Policing: The Challenge of Measuring Police Performance* (Washington, DC: Police Executive Research Forum, 2002), 114.

31. Rachel A. Harmon, "Federal Programs and the Real Cost of Policing," *New York University Law Review* 90 (2015): 870–960; David G. Robinson, "The Challenges of Prediction: Lessons from Criminal Justice," *I/S: A Journal of Law and Policy for the Information Society* 14, no. 2 (2018): 151–86.

32. Goel et al., "Combatting Police Discrimination"; Goel, Rao, and Shroff, "Precinct or Prejudice?"

33. Berk Ustun, Alexander Spangher, and Yang Liu, "Actionable Recourse in Linear Classification," in *Proceedings of the Conference on Fairness, Accountability, and Transparency* (Atlanta, GA: ACM Press, 2019), 10–19, doi:10.1145/3287560.3287566.

34. Lageson, *Digital Punishment*.

35. This is a particularly (although not uniquely) American problem. For example, see EU "Right to Be Forgotten" legislation and the German Federal Constitutional Court's 1983 decision on "informal self-determination": Alessandro Mantelero, "The EU Proposal for a General Data Protection Regulation and the Roots of the 'Right to Be Forgotten,'" *Computer Law & Society Review* 29, no. 3 (2013): 229–35.

36. Stuart, *Down, Out, and Under Arrest*; Kohler-Hausmann, *Misdemeanorland*.

37. Haggerty and Ericson, "Surveillant Assemblage," 611.

38. Sarah Brayne, "Big Data Surveillance: The Case of Policing," *American Sociological Review* 82, no. 5 (2017): 977–1008, doi:10.1177/0003122417725865.

39. Chief of Police Charlie Beck, "Homicide Report 2017" (Los Angeles: Los Angeles Police Department, 2017), http://assets.lapdonline.org/assets/pdf/2017-homi-report-final.pdf.

40. Uchida and Swatt, "Operation LASER"; Mohler et al., "Randomized Controlled Field Trials."

41. For example, in their study of a risk assessment tool designed by COMPAS, the authors concluded that it was biased against Black defendants because they were more likely to be incorrectly labeled as higher risk, while white defendants were more likely to be incorrectly labeled as lower risk. Julia Angwin et al., "Machine Bias," ProPublica, May 23, 2016, https://www.propublica.org/article/machine-bias-risk-assessments-in-criminal-sentencing.

42. Jon Kleinberg, Sendhil Mullainathan, and Manish Raghavan, "Inherent Trade-Offs in the Fair Determination of Risk Scores," in *Proceedings of Innovations in Theoretical Computer Science*, 2016, http://arxiv.org/abs/1609.05807.

43. Wacquant, *Punishing the Poor*; Soss, Fording, and Schram, *Disciplining the Poor*.

44. Goel, Rao, and Shroff, "Precinct or Prejudice?"

45. Andrew D. Selbst, "Disparate Impact in Big Data Policing," *Georgia Law Review* 52 (2017), doi:10.2139/ssrn.2819182.

46. In California, there is legislation creating a 60-day retention limit, unless the data is being used as evidence in a felony case. However, this legislation only applies to one law enforcement agency in the state—the California Highway Patrol.

47. Virginia Eubanks, *Automating Inequality: How High-Tech Tools Profile, Police, and Punish the Poor* (New York: St. Martin's Press, 2018), 5.

48. Max Weber, *Economy and Society: An Outline of Interpretive Sociology* (Berkeley: University of California Press, 1978); Bowker and Starr, *Sorting Things Out*.

49. Fourcade and Healy, "Seeing Like a Market," 24; Fourcade and Healy, "Classification Situations"; Christin, "Counting Clicks"; Espeland and Vannebo, "Accountability"; Kiviat, "Deciding with Data"; Espeland and Stevens, "Sociology of Quantification"; Hacking, "Biopower"; Porter, *Trust in Numbers*.

50. John Fiske, "Surveilling the City: Whiteness, the Black Man and Democratic Totalitarianism," *Theory, Culture & Society* 15, no. 2 (1998): 67–88, doi:10.1177/026327698015002003.

51. Lyon, *Surveillance as Social Sorting*.

52. John Gilliom, *Overseers of the Poor: Surveillance, Resistance, and the Limits of Privacy* (Chicago: University of Chicago Press, 2001); Kaaryn S. Gustafson, *Cheating Welfare: Public Assistance and the Criminalization of Poverty* (New York: NYU Press, 2012); Soss, Fording, and Scram, *Disciplining the Poor*.

53. Kevin D. Haggerty and Richard V. Ericson, "The Surveillant Assemblage," *British Journal of Sociology* 51, no. 4 (2000): 605–22, doi:10.1080/00071310020015280.

54. Lyon, *Surveillance as Social Sorting*. See also Gandy, *Panoptic Sort*.

55. Fourcade and Healy, "Seeing Like a Market."

56. Ibid.

SELECTED BIBLIOGRAPHY

Alexander, Michelle. *The New Jim Crow*. New York: New Press, 2012.

Anderson, Elijah. *A Place on the Corner*. Chicago: University of Chicago Press, 1978.

Andrejevic, Mark, and Kelly Gates. "Big Data Surveillance: Introduction." *Surveillance & Society* 12, no. 2 (2014): 185–96. doi:10.24908/ss.v12i2.5242.

Angwin, Julia. *Dragnet Nation: A Quest for Privacy, Security, and Freedom in a World of Relentless Surveillance*. New York: St. Martin's Griffin, 2014.

Angwin, Julia, Jeff Larson, Surya Mattu, Lauren Kirchner, and ProPublica. "Machine Bias." Text/html. ProPublica, May 23, 2016. https://www.propublica.org/article/machine-bias-risk-assessments-in-criminal-sentencing.

Balko, Radley. *Rise of the Warrior Cop: The Militarization of America's Police Forces*. Philadelphia: PublicAffairs, 2013.

Ball, Kirstie. "Workplace Surveillance: An Overview." *Labor History* 51, no. 1 (2010): 87–106. doi:10.1080/00236561003654776.

Ball, Kirstie, and Frank Webster, eds. *The Intensification of Surveillance: Crime, Terrorism and Warfare in the Information Age*. London: Pluto Press, 2003.

Barley, Stephen R. "Technicians in the Workplace: Ethnographic Evidence for Bringing Work into Organizational Studies." *Administrative Science Quarterly* 41, no. 3 (1996): 404–41. doi:10.2307/2393937.

———. "Technology as an Occasion for Structuring: Evidence from Observations of CT Scanners and the Social Order of Radiology Departments." *Administrative Science Quarterly* 31, no. 1 (1986): 78–108. doi:10.2307/2392767.

Barman, Emily. *Caring Capitalism: The Meaning and Measure of Social Value*. New York: Cambridge University Press, 2016.

Barocas, Solon, Alex Rosenblat, danah boyd, Seeta Peea Gangadharan, and Corrine Yu. "Data & Civil Rights: Technology Primer." *SSRN Electronic Journal*, 2014. doi:10.2139/ssrn.2536579.

Barocas, Solon, and Andrew D. Selbst. "Big Data's Disparate Impact." *California Law Review* 104 (2016): 671–732. doi:10.15779/Z38BG31.

Bass, Sandra. "Policing Space, Policing Race: Social Control Imperatives and Police Discretionary Decisions." *Social Justice* 28, no. 1 (2001): 156–76.

Becker, Howard S. *Outsiders: Studies in the Sociology of Deviance.* New York: Free Press, 1963.

Beckett, Katherine, and Alexes Harris. "On Cash and Conviction." *Criminology & Public Policy* 10, no. 3 (2011): 509–37. doi:10.1111/j.1745-9133.2011.00726.x.

Beckett, Katherine, and Steve Herbert. *Banished: The New Social Control in Urban America.* New York: Oxford University Press, 2010.

Beckett, Katherine, Kris Nyrop, Lori Pfingst, and Melissa Bowen. "Drug Use, Drug Possession Arrests, and the Question of Race: Lessons from Seattle." *Social Problems* 52, no. 3 (2005): 419–41. doi:10.1525/sp.2005.52.3.419.

Bell, Monica C. "Police Reform and the Dismantling of Legal Estrangement." *Yale Law Journal* 126 (2017): 2054–2150.

Benjamin, Ruha. *Race after Technology: Abolitionist Tools for the New Jim Code.* Cambridge, UK: Polity Press, 2019.

Bijker, Wiebe E., Thomas Hughes, and Trevor Pinch, eds. *The Social Construction of Technological Systems.* Cambridge, MA: MIT Press, 1987.

Bittner, Egon. *Aspects of Police Work.* Boston: Northeastern, 1990.

———. "The Police on Skid-Row: A Study of Peace Keeping." *American Sociological Review* 32, no. 5 (1967): 699–715. doi:10.2307/2092019.

Black, Donald J. *The Manners and Customs of the Police.* New York: Academic Press, 1980.

Blank, Rebecca M., and Michael S. Barr. *Insufficient Funds: Savings, Assets, Credit, and Banking among Low-Income Households.* New York: Russell Sage Foundation, 2009.

Bolinger, Renee. "The Rational Impermissibility of Accepting (Some) Racial Generalizations." *Synthese*, May 23, 2018. doi:10.1007/s11229-018-1809-5.

Bourdieu, Pierre. *Distinction: A Social Critique of the Judgement of Taste.* Cambridge, MA: Harvard University Press, 1984.

Bowker, Geoffrey C., and Susan Leigh Star. *Sorting Things Out: Classification and Its Consequences.* Cambridge, MA: MIT Press, 2000.

boyd, danah, and Kate Crawford. "Critical Questions for Big Data." *Information, Communication & Society* 15, no. 5 (2012): 662–79. doi:10.1080/1369118X.2012.678878.

Braga, Anthony, David M. Kennedy, Elin J. Waring, and Anne Morrison Piehl. "Problem-Oriented Policing, Deterrence, and Youth Violence: An Evaluation of Boston's Operation Ceasefire." *Journal of Research in Crime and Delinquency* 38, no. 3 (2001): 195–225. doi:10.1177/0022427801038003001.

Brame, Robert, Michael G. Turner, Raymond Paternoster, and Shawn D. Bushway. "Cumulative Prevalence of Arrest from Ages 8 to 23 in a National Sample." *Pediatrics* 129, no. 1 (2012): 21–27. doi:10.1542/peds.2010-3710.

Brantingham, Paul J., and Patricia L. Brantingham, eds. *Environmental Criminology.* Beverly Hills, CA: SAGE, 1981.

———. "Theoretical Model of Crime Site Selection." In *Crime, Law, and Sanctions: Theoretical Perspectives*, edited by Marvin D. Krohn and Ronald Akers. Thousand Oaks, CA: SAGE, 1978.

Brantingham, P. Jeffrey, Matthew Valasik, and George O. Mohler. "Does Predictive Policing Lead to Biased Arrests? Results from a Randomized Controlled Trial." *Statistics and Public Policy* 5, no. 1 (2018): 1–6. doi:10.1080/2330443X.2018.1438940.

Bratton, William J., and Peter Knobler. *The Turnaround: How America's Top Cop Reversed the Crime Epidemic.* New York: Random House, 1998.

Bratton, William J., and Sean W. Malinowski. "Police Performance Management in Practice: Taking COMPSTAT to the Next Level." *Policing: A Journal of Policy and Practice* 2, no. 3 (2008): 259–65. doi:10.1093/police/pan036.

Braverman, Harry. *Labor and Monopoly Capital: The Degradation of Work in the Twentieth Century.* New York: Monthly Review Press, 1998.

Brayne, Sarah. "Big Data Surveillance: The Case of Policing." *American Sociological Review* 82, no. 5 (2017): 977–1008. doi:10.1177/0003122417725865.

———. "Surveillance and System Avoidance: Criminal Justice Contact and Institutional Attachment." *American Sociological Review* 79, no. 3 (2014): 367–91. doi:10.1177/0003122414530398.

Brayne, Sarah, Alex Rosenblat, and danah boyd. "Predictive Policing." Workshop primer. Data & Civil Rights: A New Era of Policing and Justice, 2015.

Brayne, Sarah and Angèle Christin. 2020. "Technologies of Crime Prediction: The Reception of Algorithms in Policing and Criminal Courts." *Social Problems,* March 5 (Online First). doi:10.1093/socpro/spaa004.

Brunton, Finn, and Helen Nissenbaum. "Vernacular Resistance to Data Collection and Analysis: A Political Theory of Obfuscation." *First Monday* 16, no. 5 (2011). doi:10.5210/fm.v16i5.3493.

Brynjolfsson, Erik, and Andrew McAfee. *The Second Machine Age: Work, Progress, and Prosperity in a Time of Brilliant Technologies.* New York: W. W. Norton, 2014.

Bui, Anthony L., Matthew M. Coates, and Ellicott C. Matthay. "Years of Life Lost Due to Encounters with Law Enforcement in the USA, 2015–2016." *Journal of Epidemiology and Community Health* 72, no. 8 (2018): 715–18. doi:10.1136/jech-2017-210059.

Capers, Bennett. "Policing, Place, and Race." *Harvard Civil Rights-Civil Liberties Law Review* 44 (2009): 43–78.

Christin, Angèle. "Counting Clicks: Quantification and Variation in Web Journalism in the United States and France." *American Journal of Sociology* 123, no. 5 (2018): 1382–1415. doi:10.1086/696137.

Cohen, Lawrence E., and Marcus Felson. "Social Change and Crime Rate Trends: A Routine Activities Approach." *American Sociological Review* 44 (1979): 588–608.

Cohen, Stanley. *Visions of Social Control: Crime, Punishment, and Classification.* Malden, MA: Polity Press, 1991.

Cottom, Tressie McMillan. *Lower Ed.* New York: The New Press, 2018.

Crutchfield, Robert D., Martie L. Skinner, Kevin P. Haggerty, Anne McGlynn, and Richard F. Catalano. "Racial Disparity in Police Contacts." *Race and Justice* 2, no. 3 (2012): 179–202. doi:10.1177/2153368712448063.

Daston, Lorraine, and Peter Galison. "The Image of Objectivity." *Representations,* no. 40 (1992): 81–128. doi:10.2307/2928741.

———. *Objectivity.* Cambridge, MA: Zone Books, 2007.

Davis, Fred D. "Perceived Usefulness, Perceived Ease of Use, and User Acceptance of Information Technology." *MIS Quarterly* 13, no. 3 (1989): 319–40. doi:10.2307/249008.

Deleuze, Gilles, and Felix Guattari. *A Thousand Plateaus: Capitalism and Schizophrenia.* Translated by Brian Massumi. 2nd ed. Minneapolis: University of Minnesota Press, 1987.

Desmond, Matthew. "Relational Ethnography." *Theory and Society* 43, no. 5 (2014): 547–79. doi:10.1007/s11186-014-9232-5.

DiMaggio, Paul J., and Walter W. Powell. "The Iron Cage Revisited: Institutional Isomorphism and Collective Rationality in Organizational Fields." *American Sociological Review* 48, no. 2 (1983): 147–60. doi:10.2307/2095101.

Dobbin, Frank, John R. Sutton, John W. Meyer, and Richard Scott. "Equal Opportunity Law and the Construction of Internal Labor Markets." *American Journal of Sociology* 99, no. 2 (September 1993): 396–427. doi:10.1086/230269.

Duneier, Mitchell. "How Not to Lie with Ethnography." *Sociological Methodology* 41, no. 1 (2011): 1–11. doi:10.1111/j.1467-9531.2011.01249.x.

———. *Sidewalk.* New York: Macmillan, 2001.

Duster, Troy. "Pattern, Purpose and Race in the Drug War: The Crisis of Credibility in Criminal Justice." In *Crack in America: Demon Drugs and Social Justice*, edited by Craig Reinarman and Harry Levine, 260–87. Berkeley: University of California Press, 1997.

———. "Race and Reification in Science." *Science* 307, no. 5712 (2005): 1050–51. doi:10.1126/science.1110303.

Eberhardt, Jennifer L. *Biased: Uncovering the Hidden Prejudice That Shapes What We See, Think, and Do.* New York: Penguin, 2019.

———. "Strategies for Change: Research Initiatives and Recommendations to Improve Police-Community Relations in Oakland, Calif." Stanford University, SPARQ: Social Psychological Answers to Real-World Questions, June 20, 2016.

Eberhardt, Jennifer L., Phillip Atiba Goff, Valerie J. Purdie, and Paul G. Davies. "Seeing Black: Race, Crime, and Visual Processing." *Journal of Personality and Social Psychology* 87, no. 6 (2004): 876–93. doi:10.1037/0022-3514.87.6.876.

Edelman, Lauren B. "Legal Ambiguity and Symbolic Structures: Organizational Mediation of Civil Rights Law." *American Journal of Sociology* 97, no. 6 (1992): 1531–76.

Edelman, Lauren B., and Mark C. Suchman. "The Legal Environments of Organizations." *Annual Review of Sociology* 23, no. 1 (1997): 479–515. doi:10.1146/annurev.soc.23.1.479.

Epp, Charles R., Steven Maynard-Moody, and Donald P. Haider-Markel. *Pulled Over: How Police Stops Define Race and Citizenship.* Chicago Series in Law and Society. Chicago: University of Chicago Press, 2014. https://www.press.uchicago.edu/ucp/books/book/chicago/P/bo17322831.html.

Ericson, Richard V., and Kevin D. Haggerty. *Policing the Risk Society.* Toronto: University of Toronto Press, 1997.

Ermakoff, Ivan. "Exceptional Cases: Epistemic Contributions and Normative Expectations." *European Journal of Sociology/Archives Européennes de Sociologie* 55, no. 2 (2014): 223–43. doi:10.1017/S0003975614000101.

Espeland, Wendy Nelson, and Mitchell L. Stevens. "A Sociology of Quantification." *European Journal of Sociology* 49, no. 3 (2008): 401–36. doi:10.1017/S0003975609000150.

Espeland, Wendy Nelson, and Berit Irene Vannebo. "Accountability, Quantification, and Law." *Annual Review of Law and Social Science* 3, no. 1 (2007): 21–43. doi:10.1146/annurev.lawsocsci.2.081805.105908.

Eubanks, Virginia. *Automating Inequality: How High-Tech Tools Profile, Police, and Punish the Poor*. New York: St. Martin's Press, 2018.

Ewick, Patricia, and Susan S. Silbey. *The Common Place of Law*. Chicago Series in Law and Society. Chicago: The University of Chicago Press, 1998. https://www.press.uchicago.edu/ucp/books/book/chicago/C/bo3615912.html.

Feeley, Malcolm M., and Jonathan Simon. "The New Penology: Notes on the Emerging Strategy of Corrections and its Implications." *Criminology* 30, no. 4 (1992): 449–74. doi:10.1111/j.1745-9125.1992.tbo1112.x.

Feldman, Martha S., and James G March. "Information in Organizations as Signal and Symbol." *Administrative Science Quarterly* 26, no. 2 (1981): 171–86.

Ferguson, Andrew Guthrie. "Big Data and Predictive Reasonable Suspicion." *University of Pennsylvania Law Review* 163, no. 2 (2015): 327–410.

———. "Future-Proofing the Fourth Amendment." *Harvard Law Review Blog*, June 25, 2018. https://blog.harvardlawreview.org/future-proofing-the-fourth-amendment/.

———. "Policing Predictive Policing." *Washington University Law Review* 94, no. 5 (2017): 1109–89.

———. "Predictive Policing and Reasonable Suspicion." *Emory University School of Law* 62, no. 2 (2012): 259–325.

———. *The Rise of Big Data Policing: Surveillance, Race, and the Future of Law Enforcement*. New York: NYU Press, 2017.

Fiske, John. "Surveilling the City: Whiteness, the Black Man and Democratic Totalitarianism." *Theory, Culture & Society* 15, no. 2 (1998): 67–88. doi:10.1177/026327698015002003.

Fiske, Susan T., and Shelley E. Taylor. *Social Cognition*. 2nd ed. New York: McGraw-Hill, 1991.

Flaxman, Seth, Michael Chirico, Pau Pereira, and Charles Loeffler. "Scalable High-Resolution Forecasting of Sparse Spatiotemporal Events with Kernel Methods: A Winning Solution to the NIJ 'Real-Time Crime Forecasting Challenge.'" *Annals of Applied Statistics* 13, no. 4 (2019): 2564–85.

Fourcade, Marion, and Kieran Healy. "Classification Situations: Life-Chances in the Neoliberal Era." *Accounting, Organizations and Society* 38, no. 8 (2013): 559–72. doi:10.1016/j.aos.2013.11.002.

———. "Seeing Like a Market." *Socio-Economic Review* 15, no. 1 (2017): 9–29. doi:10.1093/ser/mww033.

Friedman, Barry. *Unwarranted: Policing without Permission*. New York: Farrar, Straus and Giroux, 2017.

Gandy, Oscar H. *The Panoptic Sort: A Political Economy of Personal Information*. Boulder, CO: Westview Press, 1993.

Garcia, Angela S. *Legal Passing: Navigating Undocumented Life and Local Immigration Law*. Oakland: University of California Press, 2019. https://www.ucpress.edu/book/9780520296756/legal-passing.

Garland, David. *The Culture of Control: Crime and Social Order in Contemporary Society*. Chicago: University of Chicago Press, 2002.

Gelman, Andrew, Jeffrey Fagan, and Alex Kiss. "An Analysis of the New York City Police Department's 'Stop-and-Frisk' Policy in the Context of Claims of Racial

Bias." *Journal of the American Statistical Association* 102, no. 479 (2007): 813–23. doi:10.1198/016214506000001040.

Gilliom, John. *Overseers of the Poor: Surveillance, Resistance, and the Limits of Privacy.* Chicago: University of Chicago Press, 2001.

Gitelman, Lisa, ed. *"Raw Data" Is an Oxymoron.* Cambridge, MA: MIT Press, 2013.

Goel, Sharad, Maya Perelman, Ravi Shroff, and David Alan Sklansky. "Combatting Police Discrimination in the Age of Big Data." *New Criminal Law Review: An International and Interdisciplinary Journal* 20, no. 2 (2017): 181–232. doi:10.1525/nclr.2017.20.2.181.

Goel, Sharad, Justin M. Rao, and Ravi Shroff. "Precinct or Prejudice? Understanding Racial Disparities in New York City's Stop-and-Frisk Policy." *Annals of Applied Statistics* 10, no. 1 (2016): 365–94. doi:10.1214/15-AOAS897.

Goffman, Alice. *On the Run: Fugitive Life in an American City.* Chicago: University of Chicago Press, 2014.

———. "On the Run: Wanted Men in a Philadelphia Ghetto." *American Sociological Review* 74, no. 3 (2009): 339–57. doi:10.1177/000312240907400301.

Goldstein, Herman. "Police Discretion: The Ideal versus the Real." *Public Administration Review* 23, no. 3 (1963): 140–48.

Gouldner, Alvin W. *Patterns of Industrial Bureaucracy.* New York: Free Press of Glencoe, 1964.

Gray, David C., and Danielle Keats Citron. "The Right to Quantitative Privacy." *Minnesota Law Review* 98 (2013). https://papers.ssrn.com/abstract=2228919.

Gustafson, Kaaryn S. *Cheating Welfare: Public Assistance and the Criminalization of Poverty.* New York: NYU Press, 2012.

Guzik, Keith. "Discrimination by Design: Predictive Data Mining as Security Practice in the United States' 'War on Terrorism.'" *Surveillance & Society* 7, no. 1 (2009): 3–20. doi:10.24908/ss.v7i1.3304.

Hacking, Ian. "Biopower and the Avalanche of Printed Numbers." *Humanities in Society* 5 (1982): 279–95.

Haggerty, Kevin D., and Richard V. Ericson. "The Surveillant Assemblage." *British Journal of Sociology* 51, no. 4 (2000): 605–22. doi:10.1080/00071310020015280.

Hannah-Moffat, Kelly. "Actuarial Sentencing: An 'Unsettled' Proposition." *Justice Quarterly* 30, no. 2 (2012): 270–96. doi:10.1080/07418825.2012.682603.

———. "Algorithmic Risk Governance: Big Data Analytics, Race and Information Activism in Criminal Justice Debates." *Theoretical Criminology* 23, no. 4 (2019): 453–70. doi:10.1177/1362480618763582.

Harcourt, Bernard E. *Against Prediction: Profiling, Policing, and Punishing in an Actuarial Age.* Chicago: University of Chicago Press, 2006.

Harcourt, Bernard E., and Jens Ludwig. "Reefer Madness: Broken Windows Policing and Misdemeanor Marijuana Arrests in New York City, 1989–2000." *Criminology & Public Policy* 6, no. 1 (2007): 165–81. doi:10.1111/j.1745-9133.2007.00427.x.

Harmon, Rachel A. "Federal Programs and the Real Cost of Policing." *New York University Law Review* 90 (2015): 870–960.

Harris, Alexes, Heather Evans, and Katherine Beckett. "Courtesy Stigma and Monetary Sanctions: Toward a Socio-Cultural Theory of Punishment." *American Sociological Review* 76, no. 2 (2011): 234–64. doi:10.1177/0003122411400054.

Hindmarsh, Richard, and Barbara Prainsack, eds. *Genetic Suspects: Global Governance of Forensic DNA Profiling and Databasing.* Cambridge, UK: Cambridge University Press, 2010.

Hodson, Randy. "Worker Resistance: An Underdeveloped Concept in the Sociology of Work." *Economic and Industrial Democracy* 16, no. 1 (1995): 79–110. doi:10.1177/0143831X9501600104.

Hoijer, Harry. *Language in Culture: Conference on the Interrelations of Language and Other Aspects of Culture.* Chicago: University of Chicago Press, 1954.

Hoofnagle, Chris. "Big Brother's Little Helpers: How ChoicePoint and Other Commercial Data Brokers Collect and Package Your Data for Law Enforcement." *North Carolina Journal of International Law and Commercial Regulation* 29 (2003): 595–638.

Innes, Martin. "Control Creep." *Sociological Research Online* 6, no. 3 (2001): 1–6. doi:10.5153/sro.634.

Jerolmack, Colin, and Shamus Khan. "Talk Is Cheap: Ethnography and the Attitudinal Fallacy." *Sociological Methods & Research* 43, no. 2 (2014): 178–209. doi:10.1177/0049124114523396.

Joh, Elizabeth E. "The New Surveillance Discretion: Automated Suspicion, Big Data, and Policing." *Harvard Law and Policy Review* 10, no. 1 (2015): 15–42.

———. "Policing by Numbers: Big Data and the Fourth Amendment." *Washington Law Review* 89, no. 35 (2014). https://papers.ssrn.com/abstract=2403028.

Kehl, Danielle Leah, Priscillia Guo, and Samuel Kessler. "Algorithms in the Criminal Justice System: Assessing the Use of Risk Assessments in Sentencing." Responsive Communities Initiative, Berkman Klein Center for Internet & Society, Harvard Law School, 2017. http://nrs.harvard.edu/urn-3:HUL.InstRepos:33746041.

Keizer, Kees, Siegwart Lindenberg, and Linda Steg. "The Spreading of Disorder." *Science* 322, no. 5908 (2008): 1681–85. doi:10.1126/science.1161405.

Kerr, Orin. "An Equilibrium-Adjustment Theory of the Fourth Amendment." *Harvard Law Review* 125, no. 2 (2011). https://harvardlawreview.org/2011/12/an-equilibrium-adjustment-theory-of-the-fourth-amendment/.

———. "The Mosaic Theory of the Fourth Amendment." *Michigan Law Review* 111, no. 3 (2012): 311–54.

Kirk, David S., and Mauri Matsuda. "Legal Cynicism, Collective Efficacy, and the Ecology of Arrest." *Criminology* 49, no. 2 (2011): 443–72. doi:10.1111/j.1745-9125.2011.00226.x.

Kitchin, Rob. "Big Data, New Epistemologies and Paradigm Shifts." *Big Data & Society* 1, no. 1 (2014). doi:10.1177/2053951714528481.

Kiviat, Barbara. "The Art of Deciding with Data: Evidence from How Employers Translate Credit Reports into Hiring Decisions." *Socio-Economic Review* 17, no. 2 (2019): 283–309. doi:10.1093/ser/mwx030.

Kleinberg, Jon, Sendhil Mullainathan, and Manish Raghavan. "Inherent Trade-Offs in the Fair Determination of Risk Scores." *Proceedings of Innovations in Theoretical Computer Science*, 2016. http://arxiv.org/abs/1609.05807.

Kling, Rob. "Computerization and Social Transformations." *Science, Technology, & Human Values* 16, no. 3 (1991): 342–67. doi:10.1177/016224399101600304.

Kohler-Hausmann, Issa. "Misdemeanor Justice: Control without Conviction." *American Journal of Sociology* 119, no. 2 (2013): 351–93. doi:10.1086/674743.

———. *Misdemeanorland: Criminal Courts and Social Control in an Age of Broken Windows Policing*. Princeton, NJ: Princeton University Press, 2018.

Kohler-Hausmann, Julilly. "Militarizing the Police: Officer Jon Burge, Torture, and War in the 'Urban Jungle.'" In *Challenging the Prison-Industrial Complex: Activism, Arts, and Educational Alternatives*, edited by Stephen John Hartnett, 43–71. Urbana: University of Illinois Press, 2011.

Kramer, Ronald, Valli Rajah, and Hung-En Sung. "Neoliberal Prisons and Cognitive Treatment: Calibrating the Subjectivity of Incarcerated Young Men to Economic Inequalities." *Theoretical Criminology* 17, no. 4 (2013): 535–56. doi:10.1177/1362480613497780.

Krent, Harold J. "Of Diaries and Data Banks: Use Restrictions under the Fourth Amendment." *Texas Law Review* 74, no. 1995–1996 (1995): 49–100.

Lageson, Sarah E. "Crime Data, the Internet, and Free Speech: An Evolving Legal Consciousness." *Law & Society Review* 51, no. 1 (2017): 8–41. doi:10.1111/lasr.12253.

———. *Digital Punishment: Privacy, Stigma, and the Harms of Data-Driven Criminal Justice*. New York: Oxford University Press, 2020.

———. "Found Out and Opting Out: The Consequences of Online Criminal Records for Families." *ANNALS of the American Academy of Political and Social Science* 665, no. 1 (2016): 127–41. doi:10.1177/0002716215625053.

Lageson, Sarah E., and Shadd Maruna. "Digital Degradation: Stigma Management in the Internet Age." *Punishment & Society* 20, no. 1 (2018): 113–33. doi:10.1177/1462474517737050.

Lam, Barry. "S3, Episode 1: The Precrime Unit." *Hi-Phi Nation* (podcast). January 31, 2019. https://hiphination.org/season-3-episodes/s3-episode-1-the-precrime-unit/.

Lamont, Michèle, and Ann Swidler. "Methodological Pluralism and the Possibilities and Limits of Interviewing." *Qualitative Sociology* 37, no. 2 (2014): 153–71. doi:10.1007/s11133-014-9274-z.

Latour, Bruno. "Visualisation and Cognition: Drawing Things Together." In *Knowledge and Society: Studies in the Sociology of Culture Past and Present*, vol. 6, edited by H. Kulick, 1–40. Greenwich, CT: JAI Press, 1986.

Lazer, David, and Jason Radford. "Data Ex Machina: Introduction to Big Data." *Annual Review of Sociology* 43, no. 1 (2017): 19–39. doi:10.1146/annurev-soc-060116-053457.

Legewie, Joscha. "Racial Profiling and Use of Force in Police Stops: How Local Events Trigger Periods of Increased Discrimination." *American Journal of Sociology* 122, no. 2 (2016): 379–424. doi:10.1086/687518.

Lehr, David, and Paul Ohm. "Playing with the Data: What Legal Scholars Should Learn about Machine Learning." *UC Davis Law Review* 51 (2017): 653–717.

Lerman, Amy E., and Vesla Weaver. *Arresting Citizenship: The Democratic Consequences of American Crime Control*. Chicago: University of Chicago Press, 2014.

———. "Staying out of Sight? Concentrated Policing and Local Political Action." *ANNALS of the American Academy of Political and Social Science* 651, no. 1 (2014): 202–19. doi:10.1177/0002716213503085.

Levy, Karen. *Data Driven: Truckers and the New Workplace Surveillance*. Princeton, NJ: Princeton University Press, n.d.

———. "Relational Big Data." *Stanford Law Review* 66, no. 73 (September 2013). https://www.stanfordlawreview.org/online/privacy-and-big-data-relational-big-data/.

Lipsky, Michael. *Street-Level Bureaucracy: Dilemmas of the Individual in Public Services.* New York: Russell Sage Foundation, 1980.

Loewen, James W. *Sundown Towns: A Hidden Dimension of American Racism.* New York: New Press, 2005.

Los Angeles Police Commission, Office of the Inspector General. "Review of Selected Los Angeles Police Department Data-Driven Policing Strategies." March 12, 2019. https://a27e0481-a3d0-44b8-8142-1376cfbb6e32.filesusr.com/ugd/b2dd23_21f6f e20fib84c179abf440d4c049219.pdf.

Lynch, Michael, Simon Cole, Ruth McNally, and Kathleen Jordan. *Truth Machine: The Contentious History of DNA Fingerprinting.* Chicago: University of Chicago Press, 2008.

Lyon, David. *Surveillance as Social Sorting.* New York: Routledge, 2003.

Manning, Peter K. *The Technology of Policing: Crime Mapping, Information Technology, and the Rationality of Crime Control.* New York: NYU Press, 2008.

Manning, Peter K., and John Van Maanen, eds. *Policing: A View from the Street.* Santa Monica, CA: Goodyear, 1978.

Mantelero, Alessandro. "The EU Proposal for a General Data Protection Regulation and the Roots of the 'Right to Be Forgotten.'" *Computer Law & Society Review* 29, no. 3 (2013): 229–235.

Marr, Bernard. "Who Are The Biggest Consumer Data Brokers And Where Can You Buy Big Data?" *HuffPost*, October 10, 2017. https://www.huffpost. com/entry/where-can-you-buy-big-data-here-are-the-biggest-consumer_b_ 59ca19dee4b0b7022a646d83.

Marx, Gary T. "Some Information Age Techno-Fallacies." *Journal of Contingencies and Crisis Management* 11, no. 1 (2003): 25–31. doi:10.1111/1468-5973.1101005.

———. "A Tack in the Shoe: Neutralizing and Resisting the New Surveillance." *Journal of Social Issues* 59, no. 2 (2003): 369–90. doi:10.1111/1540-4560.00069.

———. "What's New about the 'New Surveillance'? Classifying for Change and Continuity." *Surveillance & Society* 1, no. 1 (2002): 9–29. doi:10.24908/ss.v1i1.3391.

———. *Windows into the Soul: Surveillance and Society in an Age of High Technology.* Chicago: University of Chicago Press, 2016.

Matsueda, Ross L., Derek A. Kreager, and David Huizinga. "Deterring Delinquents: A Rational Choice Model of Theft and Violence." *American Sociological Review* 71 (2006): 95–122.

Mayer-Schönberger, Viktor, and Kenneth Cukier. *Big Data: A Revolution That Will Transform How We Live, Work, and Think.* Boston: Houghton Mifflin Harcourt, 2013.

Mayson, Sandra G. "Bias In, Bias Out." *Yale Law Journal* 128, no. 8 (2019): 2218–2300.

Meares, Tracey. "The Path Forward: Improving the Dynamics of Community-Police Relationships to Achieve Effective Law Enforcement Policies." *Columbia Law Review* 17, no. 5 (2017): 1355.

Mehozay, Yoav, and Eran Fisher. "The Epistemology of Algorithmic Risk Assessment and the Path towards a Non-penology Penology." *Punishment & Society* 21, no. 5 (2019): 523–41. doi:10.1177/1462474518802336.

Merton, Robert K. "The Self-Fulfilling Prophecy." *Antioch Review* 8, no. 2 (1948): 193–210. doi:10.2307/4609267.

Meyer, John W., and Brian Rowan. "Institutionalized Organizations: Formal Structure as Myth and Ceremony." *American Journal of Sociology* 83, no. 2 (1977): 340–63.

Miller, Reuben Jonathan. "Devolving the Carceral State: Race, Prisoner Reentry, and the Micro-Politics of Urban Poverty Management." *Punishment & Society* 16, no. 3 (2014): 305–35. doi:10.1177/1462474514527487.

———. "Race, Hyper-Incarceration, and US Poverty Policy in Historic Perspective." *Sociology Compass* 7 (2013): 573–89. doi:10.1111/soc4.12049.

Mohler, George O., Martin B. Short, Sean Malinowski, Mark Johnson, G. E. Tita, Andrea L. Bertozzi, and P. J. Brantingham. "Randomized Controlled Field Trials of Predictive Policing." *Journal of the American Statistical Association* 110, no. 512 (2015): 1399–1411. doi:10.1080/01621459.2015.1077710.

Monahan, Torin, and Neal A. Palmer. "The Emerging Politics of DHS Fusion Centers." *Security Dialogue* 40, no. 6 (2009): 617–36. doi:10.1177/0967010609350314.

Moravec, Eva Ruth. "Do Algorithms Have a Place in Policing?" *The Atlantic*, September 5, 2019. https://www.theatlantic.com/politics/archive/2019/09/do-algorithms-have-place-policing/596851/.

Moses, Lyria Bennett, and Janet Chan. "Algorithmic Prediction in Policing: Assumptions, Evaluation, and Accountability." *Policing and Society* 28, no. 7 (2018): 806–22. doi:10.1080/10439463.2016.1253695.

Moskos, Peter. *Cop in the Hood: My Year Policing Baltimore's Eastern District*. Princeton, NJ: Princeton University Press, 2008.

Mummolo, Jonathan. "Militarization Fails to Enhance Police Safety or Reduce Crime but May Harm Police Reputation." *Proceedings of the National Academy of Sciences* 115, no. 37 (2018): 9181–86.

Murphy, Erin. "The Politics of Privacy in the Criminal Justice System: Information Disclosure, the Fourth Amendment, and Statutory Law Enforcement Exemptions." *Michigan Law Review* 111, no. 4 (2013): 485–546.

National Research Council. *The Growth of Incarceration in the United States: Exploring Causes and Consequences*. Washington, DC: National Academies Press, 2014. doi:10.17226/18613.

Nelson, Andrew J., and Jennifer Irwin. "'Defining What We Do—All Over Again': Occupational Identity, Technological Change, and the Librarian/Internet-Search Relationship." *Academy of Management Journal* 57, no. 3 (2013): 892–928. doi:10.5465/amj.2012.0201.

Orlikowski, Wanda J., and Stephen R. Barley. "Technology and Institutions: What Can Research on Information Technology and Research on Organizations Learn from Each Other?" *MIS Quarterly* 25, no. 2 (2001): 145–65. doi:10.2307/3250927.

Orlikowski, Wanda J., and Susan V. Scott. "Exploring Material-Discursive Practices." *Journal of Management Studies* 52, no. 5 (2015): 697–705. doi:10.1111/joms.12114.

———. "Sociomateriality: Challenging the Separation of Technology, Work and Organization." *Academy of Management Annals* 2, no. 1 (2008): 433–74. doi:10.5465/19416520802211644.

Ouellet, Marie, Sadaf Hashimi, Jason Gravel, and Andrew V. Papachristos. "Network Exposure and Excessive Use of Force: Investigating the Social Transmission of Police Misconduct." *Criminology and Public Policy* 18, no. 3 (2019): 675–704. doi:10.1111/1745-9133.12459.

Page, Joshua. *The Toughest Beat: Politics, Punishment, and the Prison Officers Union in California.* Reprint edition. Oxford: Oxford University Press, 2013.

Pager, Devah. *Marked: Race, Crime, and Finding Work in an Era of Mass Incarceration.* Chicago: University of Chicago Press, 2007.

Papachristos, Andrew V., Anthony A. Braga, Eric Piza, and Leigh S. Grossman. "The Company You Keep? The Spillover Effects of Gang Membership on Individual Gunshot Victimization in a Co-offending Network." *Criminology* 53, no. 4 (2015): 624–49. doi:10.1111/1745-9125.12091.

Pasquale, Frank. *The Black Box Society: The Secret Algorithms That Control Money and Information.* Cambridge, MA: Harvard University Press, 2015.

Perry, Walter L., Brian McInnis, Carter C. Price, Susan C. Smith, and John S. Hollywood. *Predictive Policing: The Role of Crime Forecasting in Law Enforcement Operations.* Santa Monica, CA: Rand Corporation, 2013.

Pinch, Trevor J., and Wiebe E. Bijker. "The Social Construction of Facts and Artefacts: Or How the Sociology of Science and the Sociology of Technology Might Benefit Each Other." *Social Studies of Science* 14, no. 3 (1984): 399–441.

Porter, Theodore M. *Trust in Numbers: The Pursuit of Objectivity in Science and Public Life.* Princeton, NJ: Princeton University Press, 1995.

Poster, Mark. *The Mode of Information: Poststructuralism and Social Context.* Chicago: University of Chicago Press, 1990.

Pugh, Allison J. "What Good Are Interviews for Thinking about Culture? Demystifying Interpretive Analysis." *American Journal of Cultural Sociology* 1, no. 1 (2013): 42–68. doi:10.1057/ajcs.2012.4.

Quillian, Lincoln, and Devah Pager. "Black Neighbors, Higher Crime? The Role of Racial Stereotypes in Evaluations of Neighborhood Crime." *American Journal of Sociology* 107, no. 3 (2001): 717–67. doi:10.1086/338938.

Ratcliffe, Jerry H., Travis Taniguchi, Elizabeth R. Groff, and Jennifer D. Wood. "The Philadelphia Foot Patrol Experiment: A Randomized Controlled Trial of Police Patrol Effectiveness in Violent Crime Hotspots." *Criminology* 49, no. 3 (2011): 795–831. doi:10.1111/j.1745-9125.2011.00240.x.

Reiss, Albert J. *The Police and the Public.* New Haven, CT: Yale University Press, 1971.

Renan, Daphne. "The Fourth Amendment as Administrative Governance." *Stanford Law Review* 68, no. 5 (2016): 1039–1129.

Richardson, L. Song. "Police Efficiency and the Fourth Amendment." *Indiana Law Journal* 87, no. 3 (2012): 1143.

Rios, Victor M. *Punished: Policing the Lives of Black and Latino Boys.* New York: NYU Press, 2011.

Robinson, David G. "The Challenges of Prediction: Lessons from Criminal Justice." *I/S: A Journal of Law and Policy for the Information Society* 14, no. 2 (2018): 151–86.

Rothschild-Elyassi, Gil, Johann Koehler, and Jonathan Simon. "Actuarial Justice." In *The Handbook of Social Control,* edited by Mathieu Deflem, 194–206. Hoboken, NJ: John Wiley & Sons, 2019.

Roush, Craig. "Quis Custodiet Ipsos Custodes—Limits on Widespread Surveillance and Intelligence Gathering by Local Law Enforcement after 9/11." *Marquette Law Review* 96 (2012): 315–75.

Sampson, Robert J., and Dawn Jeglum Bartusch. "Legal Cynicism and (Subcultural) Tolerance of Deviance: The Neighborhood Context of Racial Difference." *Law & Society Review* 32 (1998): 777–804.

Sampson, Robert J., and Charles Loeffler. "Punishment's Place: The Local Concentration of Mass Incarceration." *Daedalus* 139, no. 3 (2010): 20–31. doi:10.1162/DAED_a_00020.

Sampson, Robert J., Stephen W. Raudenbush, and Felton Earls. "Neighborhoods and Violent Crime: A Multilevel Study of Collective Efficacy." *Science* 277, no. 5328 (1997): 918–24. doi:10.1126/science.277.5328.918.

Sanders, Carrie B., Crystal Weston, and Nicole Schott. "Police Innovations, 'Secret Squirrels' and Accountability: Empirically Studying Intelligence-Led Policing in Canada." *British Journal of Criminology* 55, no. 4 (2015): 711–29. doi:10.1093/bjc/azv008.

Schutt, H. G. "Advanced Police Methods in Berkeley." *National Municipal Review* 11 (1922): 80–85.

Scott, James C. *Seeing Like a State: How Certain Schemes to Improve the Human Condition Have Failed*. New Haven, CT: Yale University Press, 1999.

———. *Weapons of the Weak: Everyday Forms of Peasant Resistance*. New Haven, CT: Yale University Press, 1987.

Scott, W. Richard. "Reflections on a Half-Century of Organizational Sociology." *Annual Review of Sociology* 30, no. 1 (2004): 1–21. doi:10.1146/annurev.soc.30.012703.110644.

Seaver, Nick. "What Should an Anthropology of Algorithms Do?" *Cultural Anthropology* 33, no. 3 (2018): 375–85. doi:10.14506/ca33.3.04.

Selbst, Andrew D. "Disparate Impact in Big Data Policing." *Georgia Law Review* 52 (2017). doi:10.2139/ssrn.2819182.

Sherman, Lawrence W. "The Rise of Evidence-Based Policing: Targeting, Testing, and Tracking." *Crime and Justice* 42, no. 1 (2013): 377–451.

Sherman, Lawrence W., Patrick R. Gartin, and Michael E. Buerger. "Hot Spots of Predatory Crime: Routine Activities and the Criminology of Place." *Criminology* 27, no. 1 (1989): 27–56. doi:10.1111/j.1745-9125.1989.tb00862.x.

Simmons, Ric. "The Mirage of Use Restrictions." *North Carolina Law Review* 96, no. 1 (2017): 133–199.

Simon, Jonathan. *Governing through Crime: How the War on Crime Transformed American Democracy and Created a Culture of Fear*. New York: Oxford University Press, 2007.

Sklansky, David Alan. "The Persistent Pull of Police Professionalism." New Perspectives in Policing: UC Berkeley Public Law Research Paper No. 1788463, March 23, 2011. https://ssrn.com/abstract=1788463.

Skogan, Wesley G. *Police and Community in Chicago: A Tale of Three Cities*. Studies in Crime and Public Policy. New York: Oxford University Press, 2006.

Slobogin, Christopher. "Policing and the Cloud." White Paper Series: A Twenty-First Century Framework for Digital Privacy. Philadelphia: National Constitution Center, 2017. https://constitutioncenter.org/digital-privacy/policing-and-the-cloud.

———. "Policing as Administration." *University of Pennsylvania Law Review* 165, no. 1 (2016): 91–152.

Soss, Joe. "Lessons of Welfare: Policy Design, Political Learning, and Political Action." *American Political Science Review* 93, no. 2 (1999): 363–80.

Soss, Joe, Richard C. Fording, and Sanford F. Schram. *Disciplining the Poor: Neoliberal Paternalism and the Persistent Power of Race.* Chicago: University of Chicago Press, 2011.

Stuart, Forrest. *Down, Out, and Under Arrest: Policing and Everyday Life in Skid Row.* Chicago: University of Chicago Press, 2016.

Suchman, Lucy A. *Human-Machine Reconfigurations: Plans and Situated Actions.* 2nd ed. New York: Cambridge University Press, 2007.

Taylor, Frederick W. *Shop Management.* New York: Harper & Brothers, 1911.

Thacher, David. "The Local Role in Homeland Security." *Law & Society Review* 39, no. 3 (2005): 635–76. doi:10.1111/j.1540-5893.2005.00236.x.

Thompson, Anthony. "Stopping the Usual Suspects: Race and the Fourth Amendment." *NYU Review of Law and Social Change* 74 (1999): 956.

Tracy, Paul E., and Valerie Morgan. "Big Brother and His Science Kit: DNA Databases for 21st Century Crime Control?" *Journal of Criminal Law & Criminology* 90, no. 2 (2000): 635–90. doi:10.2307/1144232.

Travis, Jeremy. "Invisible Punishment: An Instrument of Social Exclusion." In *Invisible Punishment: The Collateral Consequences of Mass Imprisonment,* edited by Marc Mauer and Meda Chesney-Lind, 15–36. New York: New Press, 2002.

Tyler, Tom R. "Procedural Justice, Legitimacy, and the Effective Rule of Law." *Crime and Justice* 30 (2003): 283–357. doi:10.1086/652233.

———. *Why People Obey the Law.* New Haven, CT: Yale University Press, 1990.

Uchida, Craig D., and Marc L. Swatt. "Operation LASER and the Effectiveness of Hotspot Patrol: A Panel Analysis." *Police Quarterly* 16, no. 3 (2013): 287–304. doi:10.1177/1098611113497044.

Van Maanen, John. "The Asshole." In *Policing: A View from the Street,* edited by Peter K. Manning and John Van Maanen, 221–37. Santa Monica, CA: Goodyear Pub. Co., 1978.

———. "The Fact of Fiction in Organizational Ethnography." *Administrative Science Quarterly* 24, no. 4 (1979): 539–50. doi:10.2307/2392360.

———. "Police Socialization: A Longitudinal Examination of Job Attitudes in an Urban Police Department." *Administrative Science Quarterly* 20, no. 2 (1975): 207–28. doi:10.2307/2391695.

Van Maanen, John, and Stephen R. Barley. *Occupational Communities: Culture and Control in Organizations.* Cambridge, MA: Defense Technical Information Center, 1982.

Wacquant, Loïc. *Punishing the Poor: The Neoliberal Government of Social Insecurity.* Durham, NC: Duke University Press, 2009.

Wakefield, Sara, and Christopher Uggen. "Incarceration and Stratification." *Annual Review of Sociology* 36, no. 1 (2010): 387–406. doi:10.1146/annurev.soc.012809.102551.

Waldman, Ari Ezra. "Power, Process, and Automated Decision-Making." *Fordham Law Review* 88 (2019). https://papers.ssrn.com/abstract=3461238.

Waxman, Matthew C. "Police and National Security: American Local Law Enforcement and Counter-Terrorism after 9/11." *Journal of National Security Law & Policy* 3 (2009): 377.

Weber, Max. *Economy and Society: An Outline of Interpretive Sociology.* Berkeley: University of California Press, 1978.

———. "Objectivity in Social Science and Social Policy." In *Methodology of Social Sciences,* edited by Henry A. Finch, and Edward A. Shils. New York: Free Press of Glencoe, 1949.

Weisburd, David. "Hot Spots of Crime and Place-Based Prevention." *Criminology & Public Policy* 17, no. 1 (2018): 5–25. doi:10.1111/1745-9133.12350.

Weisburd, David, and Anthony A. Braga. *Police Innovation: Contrasting Perspectives.* Cambridge, UK: Cambridge University Press, 2006.

Weisburd, David, Anthony A. Braga, Elizabeth R. Groff, and Alese Wooditch. "Can Hot Spots Policing Reduce Crime in Urban Areas? An Agent-Based Simulation." *Criminology* 55, no. 1 (2017): 137–73. doi:10.1111/1745-9125.12131.

Weisburd, David, David P. Farrington, Charlotte Gill, Mimi Ajzenstadt, Trevor Bennett, Kate Bowers, Michael S. Caudy, et al. "What Works in Crime Prevention and Rehabilitation: An Assessment of Systematic Reviews." *Criminology and Public Policy* 16, no. 2 (2017): 415–49. doi:10.1111/1745-9133.12298.

Weisburd, David, Stephen D. Mastrofski, Ann Marie McNally, Rosann Greenspan, and James J. Willis. "Reforming to Preserve: COMPSTAT and Strategic Problem Solving in American Policing." *Criminology & Public Policy* 2, no. 3 (2003): 421–56. doi:10.1111/j.1745-9133.2003.tb00006.x.

Wells, Helen, and David Wills. "Individualism and Identity: Resistance to Speed Cameras in the UK." *Surveillance & Society* 6, no. 3 (2009): 259–74. doi:10.24908/ss.v6i3.3284.

Wexler, Rebecca. "Life, Liberty, and Trade Secrets: Intellectual Property in the Criminal Justice System." *Stanford Law Review* 70 (2018): 1343.

Wilcox, Pamela, and Francis T. Cullen. "Situational Opportunity Theories of Crime." *Annual Review of Criminology* 1, no. 1 (2018): 123–48.

Williams, Terry Tempest. *Crackhouse: Notes from the End of the Line.* Reading, MA: Addison-Wesley, 1992.

Willis, James J., Stephen D. Mastrofski, and David Weisburd. "Making Sense of COMPSTAT: A Theory-Based Analysis of Organizational Change in Three Police Departments." *Law & Society Review* 41, no. 1 (2007): 147–88. doi:10.1111/j.1540-5893.2007.00294.x.

Willis, Paul. *Learning to Labor: How Working Class Kids Get Working Class Jobs.* New York: Columbia University Press, 1981.

Wilson, James Q. *Varieties of Police Behavior: The Management of Law and Order in Eight Communities, with a New Preface by the Author.* Cambridge, MA: Harvard University Press, 1968.

Young, Kathryne M., and Christin Munsch. "Fact and Fiction in Constitutional Criminal Procedure." *South Carolina Law Review* 66, no. 445 (2014). https://papers.ssrn.com/abstract=2583472.

Zelizer, Viviana A. "How I Became a Relational Economic Sociologist and What Does That Mean?" *Politics & Society* 40, no. 2 (2012): 145–74. doi:10.1177/0032329212441591.

———. "Pasts and Futures of Economic Sociology." *American Behavioral Scientist* 50, no. 8 (2007): 1056–69. doi:10.1177/0002764207299353.

————. *The Social Meaning of Money: Pin Money, Paychecks, Poor Relief, and Other Currencies*. New York: Basic Books, 1995.

Zetka, James R. "Occupational Divisions of Labor and Their Technology Politics: The Case of Surgical Scopes and Gastrointestinal Medicine." *Social Forces* 79, no. 4 (2001): 1495–1520. doi:10.1353/sof.2001.0056.

Zuboff, Shoshana. *In the Age of the Smart Machine: The Future of Work and Power*. New York: Basic Books, 1988.

Zussman, Robert. "People in Places." *Qualitative Sociology* 27, no. 4 (2004): 351–63. doi:10.1023/B:QUAS.0000049237.24163.e5.

INDEX

For the benefit of digital users, indexed terms that span two pages (e.g., 52–53) may, on occasion, appear on only one of those pages.

field interview cards (FIs) (*Cont.*)
  gang affiliations noted in, 65
  image of, 64*f*
  inequalities exacerbated by, 113
  location data captured in, 67, 90–91
  operational planning and,
    46–47, 64–65
  Palantir and, 41, 43–44, 45–47, 111
  "persons with suspect" data
    and, 111–12
  predictive policing and, 62, 64
  types of information contained on, 64
fingerprint data, 3*f*, 3, 111–12, 157
Foothill Division (Los Angeles Police
    Department), 70, 151*f*
Fording, Richard, 145–46
Foreign Intelligence Service Act
    (FISA), 130–31
Fourth Amendment (US Constitution)
  Carpenter v. United States and, 131–32
  data sharing practices and, 129–30
  exclusionary rule and, 120, 124–25, 133
  mosaic theory of, 127
  Nardone v. United States and, 133
  parallel construction and, 133
  police stops and, 104, 105, 125, 128, 135
  probable cause doctrine and, 126, 128
  quantitative privacy and, 127
  racial bias in policing and, 135
  reasonable suspicion doctrine and,
    120–21, 122
  Riley v. California and, 128
  sociological dimensions of, 119–20,
    125, 135
  Terry v. Ohio and, 128
  third-party doctrine and,
    119–20, 131–32
  tire chalking and, 128
  United States v. Jones and, 74, 126–27
Friedman, Barry, 131
"fruit of the poisonous tree"
    doctrine, 133
Fugitive Slave Act, 27–28
fusion centers, 8–9, 21–22. *See also*
    Joint Regional Intelligence
    Center (JRIC)

Gates, Kelly, 23–24
Gertner, Nancy, 132–33
Gettings, Nathan, 7
Gitelman, Lisa, 108
Goel, Sharad, 104–5
GPS (Global Positioning System) data
  automatic vehicle locators in police
    cars and, 78–79, 80, 103
  field interview cards (FIs) and, 64
  parolee tracking and, 44
  United States v. Jones and, 74, 126–27
Gray, David, 127

Haggerty, Kevin, 115
Health Insurance Portability
    and Accountability Act
    (HIPAA), 129–30
Hispanics. *See* Latinos
Holder, Eric, 92–93, 102
Holliday, George, 30
Homeland Security Act of 2002, 22
Hoofnagle, Christopher, 25
"hot spots policing," 21, 58, 86–87
HunchLab, 25, 110, 146

Immigration and Customs Enforcement
    (ICE), 7, 8–9, 26, 35–36, 130–31
individualized suspicion. *See under*
    reasonable suspicion doctrine
Information Sharing Environment (ISE)
    initiative, 21
Intelligence Reform and Terrorism
    Prevention Act of 2004, 21
Internal Revenue Service, 130–31

Joh, Elizabeth, 127
Joint Regional Intelligence Center
    (JRIC), 8–9, 32, 33, 40–41, 91–93
Justice and Security Strategies (JSS), 61,
    93–94, 141–42

Karp, Alex, 7
Kerr, Orin, 127, 128–29
King, Rodney, 30
Kling, Rob, 34–35, 99
Kohler-Hausmann, Issa, 124–25

Kohler-Hausmann, Julilly, 19–20
Krent, Harold, 130

Lageson, Sarah, 115–16, 143–44
Lamont, Michèle, 10
Latinos, 28–29, 48–49, 104–5, 107–8, 110
Latour, Bruno, 29
LexisNexis Accurint database, 24,
    41, 42, 54
Lonsdale, Joe, 7
Los Angeles County Sheriff's
    Department (LASD)
  big data policing and personnel
    decisions in, 99
  California Assembly Bill 109 on
    parole management and, 31–32
  Joint Regional Intelligence Center
    and, 91–92
  resource constraints at, 103
  size of, 8–9
Los Angeles Interagency Metropolitan
    Police Apprehension Crime Team
    (LA IMPACT), 31–32
Los Angeles Police Department (LAPD)
  Air Support Division, 72
  Board of Police Commissioners
    and, 136–37
  California Assembly Bill 109 on
    parole management and, 31–32
  COMPSTAT and, 59
  consent decree (2001-13) placed on, 31,
    103, 138
  data integration challenges at, 33–34
  Foothill Division in, 70, 151f
  Joint Regional Intelligence Center
    and, 91–93
  King case (1991) and, 30
  Newton Division in, 60–61, 69,
    72, 151f
  Operation LASER and, 35, 61, 62–64,
    68–69, 121, 125, 136–37, 145
  organizational structure of, 8, 11
  Rampart Division in, 30, 151f
  Real-Time Crime Analysis Center
    (RACR) and, 8, 9f, 33, 37, 83, 94
  research access to, 11–13

resource constraints at, 103
Risk Management Information
    System (RMIS) and, 95–97
size of, 8, 47
Smart Policing Initiative and, 23, 35
South Bureau in, 81–82
TEAMS II employee risk
    management system and, 31,
    95–97, 103
Lyon, David, 107

machine learning, 2–4, 86–87, 107, 142
Malinowski, Sean, 56, 59, 70, 72–73
militarization of police, 17–18, 19, 26,
    34–35, 57
Minority Report, 3–4, 26, 56–57, 76, 89
Mohler, George, 22, 60, 110
Moore, Mark Harrison, 143
Moore, Michel, 137

Nardone v. United States, 133
National Instant Criminal Background
    Check System (NICS), 55
National Justice Database, 102
National Security Agency (NSA), 7
neoliberalism, 5, 17–18, 26, 145–46
Newton Division (Los Angeles Police
    Department), 60–61, 69, 72, 151f
New York Police Department (NYPD),
    7–8, 59, 104–5
Nissenbaum, Helen, 129–30

Oakland (California), 105, 147
Obama, Barack, 102
Office of the Inspector General (Los
    Angeles Police Department),
    29–30, 136–37
Olmstead v. United States, 118
Operation LASER (Los Angeles'
    Strategic Extraction and
    Restoration Program)
  cancellation (2019) of, 137
  Chronic Offender Program and, 62–
    64, 69–70, 121, 125
  Crime Intelligence Detail unit (CID)
    and, 62